"Justin Irving is masterful at elaborating all the essentials necessary to cultivate leadership that creates environments where people can flourish. Providing practical tools, he empowers readers to discover where they are and offers a clear path to thriving. Grounded in biblical truth, wisdom from accomplished practitioners, and sound research, *Healthy Leadership for Thriving Organizations* is a vital guide for leaders at every level."

—**Tami Heim**, president and CEO, Christian Leadership Alliance

"In this excellent and needed book, Justin Irving engages widely with Scripture and draws on helpful insights from the field of leadership studies to equip Christian leaders to pursue faithfulness for the glory of God and the flourishing of the organizations they are called to steward. I look forward to assigning this book in my own classes on leadership. Highly recommended."

—**Nathan A. Finn**, executive director, Institute for Transformational Leadership, North Greenville University

"Many Christians who believe that God has called them into roles as organizational leaders have wrestled with worldly expectations to be charismatic and all-knowing, yet Scripture urges them to 'live a life worthy of the calling you have received' by being 'completely humble' (Eph. 4:1–2). Irving reconciles humility and organizational leadership throughout this practical and theologically grounded guide to the kind of leadership our society so sorely needs."

—**Katherine Leary Alsdorf**, founding director, Redeemer's Center for Faith & Work; former Silicon Valley CEO

"You can't have a healthy organization without healthy leadership. Does that sound simplistic or obvious? The reality is that failed leadership hinders organizations and harms real people. In this book, Justin Irving has done us all a great service by integrating Christian truth with current research, as well as collecting insights from a wide range of effective leaders. The result is a resource that has the potential to clear the fog of much that distracts us from the priority of healthy organizational leadership."

—**Matthew J. Hall**, provost, Biola University

"In *Healthy Leadership for Thriving Organizations*, Justin Irving provides a theological framework for individuals and organizations that desire to flourish. Utilizing astute sources, best practices, and qualitative research from current ministry and marketplace leadership, Irving offers invaluable wisdom on leadership. Whether you are training leaders or establishing a thriving organizational culture, this book is a must-have resource. I highly recommend it."

—**Jamaal E. Williams**, lead pastor, Sojourn Church Midtown; president, Harbor Network; coauthor of *In Church as It Is in Heaven: Cultivating a Multiethnic Kingdom Culture*

"*Healthy Leadership for Thriving Organizations* is a gift to anyone ready to lead or live in a healthier organization. A sage once said that people will take care of the mission if their leaders first take care of them. This timely book helps turn such wisdom into transformed teams one page at a time. Its practical blend of Scripture, research, and firsthand reports from the front lines provides a recipe for leadership effectiveness and organizational success that should be on every leader's menu."

—**Dondi E. Costin**, major general, US Air Force (retired)

HEALTHY LEADERSHIP *for* THRIVING ORGANIZATIONS

HEALTHY LEADERSHIP *for* THRIVING ORGANIZATIONS

Creating Contexts Where People Flourish

JUSTIN A. IRVING

Baker Academic
a division of Baker Publishing Group
Grand Rapids, Michigan

Published by Baker Academic
a division of Baker Publishing Group
Grand Rapids, Michigan
www.bakeracademic.com

Printed in the United States of America

Library of Congress Cataloging-in-Publication Data
Names: Irving, Justin A., author.
Title: Healthy leadership for thriving organizations : creating contexts where people flourish / Justin A. Irving.
Description: Grand Rapids, Michigan : Baker Academic, a division of Baker Publishing Group, [2023] | Includes bibliographical references and index.
Identifiers: LCCN 2023015036 | ISBN 9781540964809 (paperback) | ISBN 9781540966827 (casebound) | ISBN 9781493442829 (ebook) | ISBN 9781493442836 (pdf)
Subjects: LCSH: Leadership—Religious aspects—Christianity. | Leadership—Biblical teaching.
Classification: LCC BV4597.53.L43 I775 2023 | DDC 253—dc23/eng/20230526
LC record available at https://lccn.loc.gov/2023015036

Emphasis in Scripture quotations is the author's addition.

Survey responses attributed to specific individuals are shared with their permission.

Baker Publishing Group publications use paper produced from sustainable forestry practices and post-consumer waste whenever possible.

23 24 25 26 27 28 29 7 6 5 4 3 2 1

To Mark McCloskey:
who modeled for me a vision of leadership
scholarship deeply shaped by biblical wisdom

And to my children, Abigail, Hannah, Caleb, Kareena, and Nadia:
the group of people my wife, Tasha, and I care most about leading to a life
of Christ-centered flourishing—may you ground your lives
in the beauty of Christ and the treasure of the gospel

CONTENTS

ILLUSTRATIONS

Tables

Figures

ACKNOWLEDGMENTS

A project like this is carried along by the support of many people. I would like to offer my sincere gratitude to four groups in particular. First, I am very grateful to the over two hundred executive leaders who offered their perspectives and insights through the survey that informed and shaped this project. These are busy people with important responsibilities; I'm profoundly appreciative that they took the time to share their leadership insights.

Second, I'm grateful for the support of those in the institution where I serve: the Southern Baptist Theological Seminary. From the writing sabbatical granted by the board of trustees to the encouragement of the administration and colleagues, I am thankful for the consideration provided as I worked on this project.

Third, I'm grateful for the many colleagues, doctoral students, and friends who have provided feedback on the developing manuscript and prayed for me throughout the journey. This project is stronger on account of both the feedback provided and the prayers offered on behalf of me and this writing process.

Finally, I am profoundly grateful for the support of my family and church community during this focused season of research and writing. I appreciate your understanding and investment in this work together with me. Your support has carried me along in this journey. Thank you.

PART 1

Wisdom for Organizational Leaders

> Organizational cultures can be brutal, or they can be life-giving. Good and godly leadership contributes to human flourishing when it creates cultures and environments that are fair, just, and caring.
>
> —Richard Stearns, *Lead Like It Matters to God*

The complex challenges and demands faced by today's leaders will not be overcome by simply applying administrative techniques or business best practice. Today's leaders need something more—they need *wisdom* to lead their communities through complex times. This is especially true for organizational leaders. In contrast to those responsible for leading individuals, those responsible for leading an organization require a stewardship mindset that considers the needs of wider teams, divisions, or organizations as a whole. And, as the scope of leadership expands, so expands the complexity and demands associated with this leadership.

In our pursuit of wisdom for organizational leaders, the chapters in Part 1 will explore the nature of organizational leadership (chap. 1) and a vision for human and organizational flourishing (chap. 2). Organizational leaders have a unique and important responsibility to nurture thriving organizations within which humans may thrive and flourish. My aim in this book is to provide better insight and wisdom to inform the practice of organizational leadership. Let's begin our journey by considering how leaders may create contexts within which organizational members may develop and flourish in a manner consistent with their design as people created in God's image.

ONE

Defining Organizational Leadership

Who Is This Book For?

Many leadership books focus on how to work with and lead individuals. This level of reflection is vital, especially for direct supervisors and those seeking to effectively influence others in workplaces or ministry contexts. This book has another set of leaders in mind—*those with stewardship responsibilities for wider teams, divisions, or organizations.*

This is a book for those leading at what we might call the thirty-thousand-foot level of leadership. As you might imagine, leadership at this level does not mean setting aside best practices for leading individuals. People still matter. How we engage the individuals within organizations matters. But leadership at the organizational level also requires leaders to consider additional factors—it requires them to look at the big picture and to ponder what will set the conditions that allow the organization to thrive, enabling people to flourish and the organization's mission to be fulfilled.

In order to better understand the primary responsibilities and commitments of organizational leaders, I'll be sharing insights and perspectives I gained from a survey of over two hundred executive leaders. Table 1.1 provides an overview of the occupations represented by these executive leaders. I provide this overview to give you a sense of the type of leader who may benefit from the topics covered in this book. If you find yourself serving in one of these roles—or in a role similar to these—then this book is for you.

Table 1.1. Executive Leader Survey Participants—Categorized

Business	Church	Education	Nonprofit
• CEOs/presidents • senior partners • COOs • C-suite leaders • vice presidents	• lead pastors or senior pastors • executive ministers • department or area ministers	• presidents • provosts • vice presidents • deans • cabinet members • superintendents • heads of schools • principals	• executive directors • presidents/CEOs • vice presidents • regional executives • program directors

Note: Survey participants were largely drawn from the business, church, education, and nonprofit sectors. Organizational leadership is certainly relevant for other sectors, such as government or military; however, the study focused primarily on nongovernmental leaders. Quotations from the survey attributed to named individuals are shared with their permission.

Who Else May Benefit from This Book?

In addition to readers who occupy roles listed in table 1.1, there are a few other groups of readers who may benefit from the themes covered in this book: (1) board members, (2) students of leadership, (3) aspiring organizational leaders, and (4) support staff and team members of organizational leaders. Though this list is not exhaustive, people serving in these roles will particularly benefit from understanding the responsibilities and priorities associated with organizational leadership.

First, for *organizational board members*, one of their top responsibilities is to hire the executive leader of an organization and then hold this leader accountable to the organization's mission and primary purpose. Boards essentially have one employee. To execute their stewardship responsibility effectively, board members must understand the nature of organizational leadership and the priorities associated with faithfully and effectively leading an organization.

Next, for both *students of leadership* and *aspiring organizational leaders*, this book provides insight about how organizational leadership differs from dyadic leadership responsibilities involving a single leader and a single follower. Leadership, as a field of study, includes diverse levels of reflection and analysis. I conceptualize the levels of leadership in the following manner: (1) self-leadership, (2) dyadic leadership, (3) team leadership, (4) organizational leadership, and (5) societal leadership. While there are overlapping conversations across these levels, for students of leadership and aspiring organizational leaders, it is important to recognize how these levels differ as well as how they relate to the stewardship responsibilities of organizational leaders. The topics covered in this book will guide students and aspiring organizational leaders in their future leadership endeavors.

Finally, there is often a wide network of team members and support staff working with organizational leaders. In order for *support staff and team members of organizational leaders* to effectively partner with the organizational leader with whom they work, it is important to understand what is required of the role and what challenges organizational leaders face and navigate. Organizational leaders have diverse and complex responsibilities, and they cannot face these responsibilities alone. Those serving on the team of an organizational leader may be able to assist and partner with their leader more effectively by gaining insight into the priorities and themes of this book.

This Book's Aim: Wisdom for Organizational Leaders

Organizational leaders face unique and challenging demands. Some of these demands are perennial. Other demands are occasioned by unique events in history and the changing landscapes within which organizations exist. Though I will be going into the challenges reported by leaders in more depth throughout the book, some of the reoccurring challenges surround issues of mission focus; finding, developing, and retaining team members; societal change; and financial limitations. Consider the following examples. Perhaps you can identify with several of these challenges and concerns:

- "Remaining relentlessly focused on what is most essential to advance our vision while navigating the ongoing uncertainties that can distract us." (a president/CEO)
- "Keeping people together and pointed in the same direction in the midst of a divisive, intense social and cultural context." (a president)
- "Assuring clarity of vision, living our values, and putting people first. . . . Assuring I am listening and in tune with the mental health of other leaders in the organization. . . . Providing clarity of direction and assurance of hope during times of uncertainty, volatility, and turbulence." (a CEO)
- "The first [challenge I face daily] is talent acquisition and retention. We are in a talent war that is affecting all industries and sectors." (a vice president for human resources)
- "Maintaining unity among diverse and increasingly impassioned opinions." (a senior pastor)
- "Leading change through uncertain times (crisis)." (a president)

- "In today's world, extreme labor shortages and elevated rates of employee turnover are easily the most pressing issues." (a COO)
- "Higher employee turnover rates. Rising costs of living. Developing younger generations' (Gen Z, and some millennials) talent." (an executive pastor)
- "Addressing institutional needs that help advance our mission within a limited budget, and doing so while the future has many uncertainties." (a vice president of academic affairs)
- "Navigating shifting cultural values that run counter to historic Christian faith; changing demographics that result in a downward slope of potential traditional students in higher ed. . . . Financial models in higher ed that no longer work." (a president)
- "Where to begin: . . . financial sustainability; emotional and mental health; finding and developing high-quality leaders; challenge for people to be committed in the midst of busy lives; figuring out how to run healthy small group ministries (along with other ministries) when you don't have funds to hire the position; rebuilding after Covid, along with trying to lead people that have left or haven't come back for various reasons. Teaching people how to become disciples and actually practice following Jesus in our post-Christian, consumeristic, sexualized, me-centered culture." (a lead pastor)

The list of challenges and concerns that organizational leaders face today is long and complex. The issues noted by the leaders quoted above only begin to scratch the surface, illustrating the multifaceted nature of these challenges. Because of this reality, I aim to go beyond providing administrative descriptions of managerial tactics and effective business practice. I'm not arguing that understanding such subjects is unimportant. In fact, one of the reasons I pursued an MBA was to gain insight and perspective about practices such as marketing, accounting, finance, economics, organizational behavior, data analytics, operations management, and project management—all of which have a place in well-run organizations. Effective administrative practices *are* important for organizational leaders. But they are not sufficient.

Rather than just disseminating knowledge of managerial or business practices, this book is seeking to explore what healthy organizational leadership looks like; I am aiming at what we might better refer to as *wisdom for organizational leaders*. The complex challenges that face today's leaders will not be overcome simply by applying administrative or business best practice. Today's leaders need wisdom both in the face of challenges and in the way they navigate their communities through complex times. In other words, my hope is that this book will not be merely informational but rather infused with wisdom for organizational leaders.

An important qualification is needed at this point: if wisdom for organizational leaders is the aim, then my voice on the matter is insufficient. While I do have insights I'll want to share along the way, we need deeper roots than what I alone am able to offer. In fact, I think we need deeper roots than any one human leader is able to offer. We need to pursue better and deeper sources. Toward that end, throughout the book we'll be seeking to gain insight from at least three sources.

Today's leaders need wisdom both in the face of challenges and in the way they navigate their communities through complex times.

Biblical and Theological Perspective for Organizational Leadership

First, and most importantly, I will turn to *biblical and theological sources* in order to gain perspective for organizational leaders. While the Bible is not a leadership textbook, there is nevertheless vital perspective to be found within it for leaders. For instance, it is wise for leaders in general—and especially Christian leaders—to understand how a biblical view of creation, the fall, redemption, and restoration ought to shape the way they consider the people and mission of their communities. We will look to the Bible regularly throughout this book as we seek wisdom for leading organizations.

Theoretical and Research-Based Perspective for Organizational Leadership

Second, I will turn to *established books and research* within the leadership literature that can provide guidance for organizational leaders. While the leadership literature is broad in terms of the subjects and leadership variables covered, I am thankful that the field continues to grow along with research streams that explore the nature and effectiveness of various leadership approaches. As with any field of study, students and readers must engage leadership books and research-based articles wisely, particularly with an eye toward discerning what aligns with a biblical vision of people and leadership and what does not.

Organizational leaders exhibit wisdom when they recognize they are not all-knowing in their understanding of leadership practice. As many have affirmed, *leaders are learners*. This translates into reflective engagement (both critical and charitable reflection)[1] with others as we consider the practice of leadership in organizations. While insights from books and journal articles should never supplant the primary focus on gaining wisdom through Scripture, leadership researchers and authors do have helpful insights for organizational leaders navigating many of the complex challenges and concerns noted above.

Practical and Experiential Perspective for Organizational Leadership

Finally, we will turn to *established executive leaders* in order to enhance the perspective of organizational leaders. Because we have a specific focus in this book—*helping those with stewardship responsibilities for wider teams, divisions, or organizations to lead wisely*—it is prudent to turn to the voices of those serving in such roles. The book of Proverbs points to the pattern of considering the advice and guidance offered by others. Consider the following verses:

- "Where there is no guidance, a people falls, but in an abundance of counselors there is safety." (Prov. 11:14)
- "The way of a fool is right in his own eyes, but a wise man listens to advice." (Prov. 12:15)
- "Without counsel plans fail, but with many advisers they succeed." (Prov. 15:22)
- "Whoever trusts in his own mind is a fool, but he who walks in wisdom will be delivered." (Prov. 28:26)

While our primary source of wisdom is from above (James 3:17), wise people consider the advice and guidance of those who bring relevant experience to the conversation. In this book, you'll have the opportunity to reflect on the experience you bring to the table, some of the experience I bring to the table, and—more importantly—insights and wisdom from over two hundred executive leaders. These leaders—primarily Christians serving in diverse executive roles—bring to the table years of experience from their work serving as executive leaders in businesses, churches, schools, and nonprofits. This group includes more than sixty leaders who serve in the role of president, CEO, or executive director and more than sixty leaders who serve as either the lead or senior pastor of a church. Whether you are thinking about organizational leadership as an aspect of ministry or as a responsibility of Christians involved in executive leadership, there is wisdom to be gained from these leaders.

Describing the Practice of Organizational Leadership

As noted above, organizational leaders are those with stewardship responsibilities for wider teams, divisions, or organizations. Since this book focuses on these leaders and the practice of organizational leadership, I want to take time to describe what it is that organizational leaders do. Let's begin with a short description:

> *Faithful and effective organizational stewards are those who strategically align and deploy human and organizational resources in fulfillment of an organization's mission.*

At a basic level, organizational leaders make sure the organization's mission is clear, and then they align and deploy people and resources for the purpose of fulfilling this mission. This description is brief, but it is far from simple. Organizations are complex, and so is the work required to lead them well.

Other important dimensions to organizational leadership are implied and included in the conversation of mission, but I think it is helpful to call out the importance of purpose, beliefs, and values in particular. Toward that end, I offer this expanded description:

> *Faithful and effective organizational stewards, motivated by an abiding purpose, are those who strategically align and deploy human and organizational resources in fulfillment of an organization's mission, in a manner consistent with and shaped by the beliefs and values of the organization.*

Let's take some time to walk through the various dimensions of this description.

Faithful . . .

At a foundational level, faithful people hold to beliefs and convictions beyond themselves and beyond mere personal preferences for their lives. Christian leaders joyfully celebrate their need to be faithful. While most of this book will lean into practices for *effective* organizational leadership, we begin the discussion of faithful and effective leaders with the more meaningful and weightier theme of *faithfulness*. Christian leaders are not merely called to lead effectively; they are called, first and foremost, to lead faithfully. Faithfulness relates to both the small and the larger dimensions of our life and leadership: as Jesus said to his disciples, "One who is faithful in a very little is also faithful in much, and one who is dishonest in a very little is also dishonest in much" (Luke 16:10).

When we reflect on the priority of faithfulness in human leaders, it is important to look to the ultimate source of faithfulness—God himself. Consider how the faithful nature of God is described throughout the pages of the Bible: In Exodus 34:6, Moses describes God as "merciful and gracious, slow to anger, and *abounding in steadfast love and faithfulness*." In Deuteronomy 7:9, Moses describes God as "*the faithful God* who keeps covenant and steadfast love." In Lamentations 3:22–23 we read, "The steadfast love of the LORD never ceases; his mercies never come to an end; they are new every morning; *great is your faithfulness*."

We need to understand not only that the faithfulness of God is one of his core attributes but also that God's faithfulness is the ultimate source of human faithfulness. Consider Hebrews 10:23, where we see God's faithfulness as the primary source of our confidence, faith, and hope: "Let us hold fast the confession of our hope without wavering, *for he who promised is faithful*."

God is the source of our faithfulness, and our faithfulness as people finds its direction in the guidance of God's Word. The Bible provides a vision for the character and priorities of Christian leaders. The Bible provides an understanding and vision for humans in the biblical accounts of creation, the fall, redemption, and restoration. And the Bible provides wisdom for leaders as they seek to enact organizational ends and means in light of the core faith and belief to which they are committed. In other words, the word *faithful* in my description is a reminder that healthy Christian leadership is ultimately shaped by the faithful God and the truth "once for all delivered to the saints" (Jude 3) in the Bible. Shaped by a biblical worldview and a biblical vision of the faithfulness of God, organizational leaders first and foremost prioritize leading faithful endeavors. Richard Stearns, president emeritus of World Vision US, sums it up thus: "God calls us to be faithful, not successful."[2]

Effective . . .

Although faithfulness is God's primary call for leaders, faithfulness in organizational leadership also involves effectively stewarding the mission of the organization. Organizational leaders are charged with getting things done and with moving the organization forward in its mission. The best leaders do not pass the buck when it comes to seeing progress toward what the organization is called to accomplish. They take ownership as stewards of that over which they are called to be faithful.

Toward this end, executive leaders are often required to successfully occupy and fulfill multiple roles and responsibilities as they effectively lead organizations. Paul Maurer, president of Montreat College, shares his experience of this: "I have three essential identities in my role as CEO: minister, educator, businessman. This third is no less important than the first two. Indeed, if I don't successfully execute the third, the first two won't matter." Although the business function of a presidency may not always be the most animating part of an executive leader's responsibilities, it is nevertheless a central part of leading faithfully and effectively.

In keeping with the proverbial wisdom of management expert Peter Drucker, organizational leaders must not *confuse motion with progress* as they focus on stewarding an organization effectively.[3] Organizations do not need leaders who simply look busy. Rather, organizations need leaders who help their communities make progress toward vital organizational goals. Organizations need leaders who are being productive, making progress, and advancing what matters most in the communities they serve. As Max De Pree, a former CEO and the author of several books on effective leadership, puts it, "Leaders can delegate efficiency, but they must deal personally with effectiveness."[4] Healthy organizations prioritize both faithful and effective leadership.

Organizational Stewards (Leaders) . . .

The next step in our description of organizational leadership is the definition of organizational stewardship. Healthy organizational leadership begins with faithful and effective *organizational stewards (leaders)*. I put "leaders" in parentheses to make the point that organizational leaders at their core are primarily organizational stewards.

The first part of the phrase is the word *organizational*. The role of the organizational leader is not about personal self-service; it is not primarily about serving the needs of one's personal team or department; it is not about serving personal preference or personal agendas. Instead, organizational leaders must think organizationally—they must provide leadership on behalf of the entire organization or unit that is under their care. Just as a parent must consider the health of all the dimensions and members of a household, organizational stewards need to think about the health of all the dimensions and members of the organization. This demands that leaders consider the needs of the community holistically rather than maintain a myopic focus on their personal interests.

In addition to thinking organizationally, organizational leaders also understand that they are primarily *stewards* rather than owners. This distinction can get a bit complex in the business environment, where the leader may indeed be a partner or owner of the business. But in God's economy, Christian leaders must begin by recognizing that they are stewarding people and things that do not ultimately belong to them. Consider the declaration of Psalm 24:1: "The earth is the LORD's and the fullness thereof, the world and those who dwell therein." Or consider the way Abraham Kuyper, a theologian and prime minister of the Netherlands in the first part of the twentieth century, expressed this truth: "There is not a square inch in the whole domain of our human existence over which Christ, who is Sovereign over all, does not cry, 'Mine!'"[5]

Therefore, Christian leaders are primarily stewards in their organizations. They understand that they are stewarding something that is bigger than any one person or department, something that will likely outlast their leadership, something that ultimately belongs to another. Because of this stewardship mindset, Christian leaders understand that organizational leadership is not primarily about them as leaders. It is about building others up in a community for the betterment of others and the organization. Healthy organizational leadership begins with faithful and effective organizational stewardship.

Motivated by an Abiding Purpose . . .

We turn now to the role that *purpose* plays in animating the value and significance of the stewardship responsibilities named above. While my emphasis on stewardship is consistent with our nature as people created in the image of God, the other-centered nature of stewardship runs counter to the self-serving nature of sinful and fallen humans. A story from the first family illustrates this human tendency. Consider Cain's infamous question to the Lord after he was asked about the murder of Abel: "Am I my brother's keeper?" (Gen. 4:9). While our sinful nature likes to argue that we are keepers only of our own affairs, a biblical ethic answers Cain's question with a resounding *yes*—we are called to live in a manner that considers the good of those around us.

But this other-centered focus—a focus that is essential for a stewardship approach to leadership—does not come naturally. We need a reorientation of our direction and purpose. For Christian leaders, this is primarily accomplished by orienting our purpose around the glory of God (1 Cor. 10:31) and around the purposes of God revealed in the creation mandate and the Great Commission.[6] Leaders who are motivated beyond self-interest understand the power and importance of a transcendent purpose.

I have provided an academic argument for the importance of leader purposefulness elsewhere.[7] In that work, I argue that purpose is a priority at both the organizational and personal levels. I'll be placing an emphasis on the importance of organizational purpose later in this book. Here I want to emphasize the importance of a leader's own sense of purpose and how this contributes to faithful and effective leadership.

When leaders see clearly what motivates their leadership at a personal level, this clarity provides an interpretive lens for connecting with the purposes of others and with the larger purposes of organizations. Bill George, the former CEO of Medtronic, notes the importance of leaders understanding the purpose that motivates them: "You can study the purposes others pursue and you can work with them in common purposes, but in the end the purpose for your leadership must be uniquely yours."[8]

In my own research on the importance of purpose in the lives of leaders, higher levels of leader purposefulness served as a statistically significant predictor of higher levels of leadership effectiveness and followers' job satisfaction, organizational commitment, and sense of person-organization fit.[9] In other words, it is not just a good idea for leaders to have a transcendent purpose motivating their leadership, it also practically helps organizational leaders to be more effective in their practice.

Who Strategically Align and Deploy . . .

John Kotter, a distinguished authority on leadership, notes that interdependence is a central feature of modern organizations, "where no one has complete autonomy, where most employees are tied to many others by their work, technology, management systems, and hierarchy."[10] While managerial thinking tends to view organizing as the primary need in light of such organizational complexity, Kotter argues that, more than mere systemic organizing, the community needs leaders engaging in the work of alignment. This alignment activity is a communicative endeavor: it entails bringing anyone relevant to the implementation of the organization's vision and strategies into alignment and aiming them at the same target.

Though easy to articulate, this is vital and difficult organizational work. Kotter writes, "Trying to get people to comprehend a vision of an alternative future is . . . a communication challenge of a completely different magnitude from organizing them to fulfill a short-term plan."[11] But this work is essential. Not only does it reduce the number of potentially conflicting agendas that may emerge among organizational members, it also leads to a pathway where organizational members are empowered by means of the clarity provided to a community aligned around a common vision of the future.

Here it is important to note what might be obvious to some: a leadership vision cannot be carried out by an isolated individual. Leadership is done through a network of aligned people and resources within the organizational context. And if we are talking about the work of strategic alignment—rather than mere tactical organizing—then we need wisdom as leaders. While tactical decisions are often informed by best-practice knowledge, strategic decision making requires wisely applying knowledge in unique and complex circumstances.

Wise organizational leaders also recognize that their leadership is not about an individual's or a unit's success in isolation. Rather, the work of organizational leadership is about the alignment of multiple individuals, resources, and systems engaged in coordinated work toward a common goal. It is about coordinated effectiveness. It is about coordinated mission fulfillment.

A leadership vision cannot be carried out by an isolated individual. Leadership is done through a network of aligned people and resources within the organizational context.

The importance of alignment and coordination may be seen in many organizations and endeavors. One of my doctoral students recently provided me with a unique example. As I was eating lunch with him and several others on campus, Troy began to talk casually about an upcoming challenge that he and three of his brothers will confront together. They are working toward rowing across the Atlantic Ocean.

What unfolded at that lunch table was an amazing introduction for me into the world of ocean rowing. Through many battles—such as sleep deprivation, the harsh saltwater conditions, and changing weather patterns—these brothers will join in a race with other ocean-rowing vessels that takes them about forty days and over three thousand nautical miles, as they navigate from the La Gomera, Canary Islands, to Antigua in the West Indies.[12] To provide a sense of the magnitude of what they are undertaking, most teams engage in over 1.5 million oar strokes to make the journey. It's difficult to put into words what such a journey will require.

This daunting task is not something to be undertaken without extensive preparation and significant alignment of people and resources. In the case of Troy and his brothers, it involved finding the right people for their team, acquiring the right boat for the unique task, engaging in the right training and preparation, developing the right plan and strategy for their team rowing, ensuring the right physical conditioning of the team members, attending to the right safety training and precautions, preparing the right supplies for the journey, determining the right path for navigation, partnering with the right meteorologist who will offer weather updates throughout the journey—and the list goes on. For this four-man crew, the alignment of people, plans, and resources will be essential for effectively and safely completing their mission to cross the Atlantic Ocean.

So it is with organizations. As leaders align people and resources behind a common vision of a preferred future, these people and resources may be faithfully and effectively deployed in fulfillment of the organization's mission. Aligning the people and the resources of an organization to metaphorically row in the same direction is an essential requirement of faithful and effective organizational leadership.

Human Resources . . .

As leadership thinkers such as David Gergen and Peter Drucker have insisted, "The people in an organization are its No. 1 asset."[13] When faithful and effective leaders consider strategic alignment for their organizations, the alignment and deployment of the people within the organization is essential.

The human resource dimension of organizational leadership encompasses several priorities, including the recruitment, development, and deployment of organizational members. This engagement, equipping, and empowerment work is vital to effectively aligning and deploying people in service of the organization's mission. Human resource considerations also take into account how people and teams relate to and work with each other. Rather than normalizing individual work in isolation, organizational leaders insist on coordinated and aligned community members working in concert toward a coordinated mission.

Evidencing the importance of human resources for any leadership endeavor, the executive leaders surveyed for this project listed issues related to working with people at the top of the challenges they face as organizational leaders (see appendix A). Out of more than six hundred coded items in the research analysis process, more than one-third of them grouped around people-oriented themes associated with staff and volunteers. Top considerations in this area include hiring, equipping and developing people, motivating and caring for people, aligning people with the organizational mission, and team cohesion.

One of the research participants, Steve Wareham, has over twenty years of experience in his field, including nine years as the director of a major international airport. Wareham emphasized "having the right people in the right positions and giving them the proper amount of support and guidance to be successful" as his top leadership challenge and commitment. Other research participants emphasized similar concerns, noting as top priorities and considerations "finding, equipping, and retaining young staff" and the "alignment of people toward the direction of the organization as we pursue our vision."

While the pressing demands of acquiring talent and then developing and retaining people for sustained service can feel like isolated challenges or crises for an organization, all of these themes fall under the broader priority of strategically aligning and deploying human resources in fulfillment of the organization's mission. Throughout this book, I will argue that work in organizations is an opportunity to enact genuine flourishing in the lives of those volunteering or working for our communities. People matter to God, and they should matter to those who provide leadership for the organizations of which they are part. Just as our mission matters, so does pursuing our mission in a way that leads to the flourishing of the people with whom we partner in the fulfillment of the mission.

Organizational Resources . . .

Although, as was noted in the previous section, "the people in an organization are its No. 1 asset," working toward the fulfillment of organizational mission also necessitates the alignment of other organizational resources. The alignment and deployment of organizational resources also takes place in areas such as finances, facilities, fleets, technology, auxiliary services, and general infrastructure.

We will not be diving into too many specifics related to these topics.[14] However, I do want to briefly consider the areas of finances and facilities. Finding a financial equilibrium that sustains the mission is crucial to anyone charged with leading an entire organization, as is the consideration of space and place. The subject of organizational space and place has taken on new dimensions amid the work-from-home movement of the 2020s, but it is important to consider how the spaces where people connect physically or virtually align with the organization's mission—or don't align. Though some dimensions of stewarding the finances and facilities of an organization may be delegated, ultimate responsibility for charting a course toward financial equilibrium and appropriate space utilization belongs to the executive leader. As noted above, "Leaders can delegate efficiency, but they must deal personally with effectiveness."[15] Leading well in the areas of finances and facilities provides a basis for the strategic alignment and deployment of mission-focused resources.

Gordon Smith serves as the president of Ambrose University. I appreciate the attention he gives in his writing to both the financial and the facility discussions noted above. On the financial front, Smith argues in his book *Institutional Intelligence* that institutions need to make economic sustainability a top commitment. Although the strategic alignment and deployment of organizational resources involves more than just financial resources, finding a place of financial equilibrium within an organization is central to mission fulfillment. Smith writes, "Institutional intelligence requires an appreciation of the economic charter of institutions and a recognition of one's own role [as an executive leader], within the institution, of fostering financial equilibrium and sustainability."[16]

Smith argues that financial equilibrium and sustainability translate into a balanced budget: "Simply put, an effective institution operates with a balanced budget that delivers mission."[17] For Smith, this means that every president or executive of an organization must be attuned to the revenue and expense sides of the budget, because "long-term effectiveness is dependent on the fiscal health" of the organization.[18] The financial side of an organization is not ultimate, and in many ways it is right to argue for the priority of mission over the financial aspects of organizational leadership. However, the presence of financial equilibrium and organizational financial margin is vital to sustaining organizational mission. In both nonprofit and for-profit institutions, the mission of the organization is not sustainable over the long term without a balanced budget.

Leading as a steward of that which does not ultimately belong to us translates into an explicit dependence on God in these matters of financial leadership. Smith does not see intentional organizational planning in the financial arena as at odds with a dependent posture before God. He writes, "Wise leaders know that radical dependence on God is and can be matched with a keen insight into the economics of how organizations work: how revenue is secured and how funds are managed and accounted for. It is all, in the end, a matter of good stewardship."[19]

Smith also considers facilities and the broader category of creating built space. For Smith, organizational purpose should drive the creation and use of space, not the other way around. He notes, "Built space can also be thought of in light of institutional purpose: what is the mission of this particular agency?"[20] This idea of purpose prompts leaders to ask whether the mission of the institution is fostered by the space, facility, or building in question. Smith notes that an institution's purpose can be facilitated by its space, but the space can alternatively be something that the purpose subtly fights against because the space is not congruent with the identity or purpose of the institution.[21] Because thoughtfully built space—in both the physical and virtual organizational realms—often requires a significant investment of both human and financial capital, it is incumbent upon the organizational leader to make sure that this significant investment is well aligned with institutional purpose and mission.

In Fulfillment of an Organization's Mission . . .

In many ways, I have been explaining the phrase "in fulfillment of the organization's mission" throughout this description. Effective and faithful organizational stewards strategically align and deploy human and organizational resources to this end: *fulfillment of an organization's mission.*

Organizations exist to accomplish something. Even organizations like country clubs and social clubs often have a clear mission they are seeking to fulfill on behalf of the people associated with the social enterprise. Because organizations exist to accomplish something, the goal of an effective organization is not to facilitate random and disconnected activities and efforts but to ensure that the products, programs, or services provided by the organization are missionally aligned with what the organization intends to accomplish.

I see mission as essentially asking the "what" question of organizational identity and culture. If an organization's purpose provides an answer to the organizational "why" question, mission tells us what an organization does when it is motivated by its purpose. The reality is that organizations need good answers to both questions. We should understand what is motivating us as an organization, but we also need to understand what it is that we are primarily about (our mission) as we align ourselves with the reasons behind our organizational existence (our purpose). While the mission of an organization should be preserved—consider all the examples of mission drift in the past century—mission also orients a community to the future as organizational members work to advance the mission to which they are committed. This is why executive search experts such as Price Harding of CarterBaldwin emphasize mission advancement over simply focusing on mission preservation.[22]

I will provide a broader examination of purpose and mission in chapter 8, but for now it is important to see that organizational leaders must give close attention and effort to clearly and effectively communicating the mission of organizations and ensuring that both human and organizational resources are faithfully and effectively aligned and deployed in service of the mission. The work being accomplished by the organization—and the well-being and flourishing of those within the community—are closely related to the effective stewardship of organizational mission.

In a Manner Consistent with and Shaped by the Beliefs and Values of the Organization

I began my description of organizational leadership with the word *faithful.* We return to a similar theme at the end of the description as well—bookends that prioritize that which matters most. Faithful organizational leadership is most often defined by what the leader and the organization believe and value. Thomas Watson, CEO of IBM from 1956 to 1971, made the following statement about beliefs and core values: "I firmly believe that any organization, in order to survive and achieve success, must have a sound set of beliefs on which it premises all its policies and actions."[23]

This type of logic should resonate with Christians. Christians understand the importance of confessions and statements of faith because what we believe is core to our faith and practice. Beliefs and values point us to primary commitments, and these commitments not only shape and influence what we pursue for our organizational mission, they also shape and influence the way we go about our mission. We will spend more time on these themes in chapter 8, but I will say here that I see beliefs and values as the guardrails for organizations. These guardrails clarify our organizational identity, and they keep us on the road that honors both the desired *destination* and the desired *pathway* to this destination. Rather than imposing stifling limitations, lived and aspirational beliefs and values provide great freedom and clarity to those working within and with the organization.

Richard Stearns argues that "the values Christian leaders embrace are more important than the success they achieve."[24] Some ends, or results, are not worth the price of admission. When we pursue organizational goals in a manner that is at odds with organizational beliefs and values, this is a dangerous path. If, in their efforts to fulfill their mission, organizational leaders compromise on core values and beliefs, the journey is no longer worth it. Christian leaders value both the *ends* and the *means* when it comes to organizational leadership. Values and beliefs provide the guardrails along the way that ensure that we are both pursuing the right ends and doing so in the right ways.

Summing Up the Description

> *Faithful and effective organizational stewards, motivated by an abiding purpose, are those who strategically align and deploy human and organizational resources in fulfillment of an organization's mission, in a manner consistent with and shaped by the beliefs and values of the organization.*

While we will examine the multifaceted nature of organizational leadership throughout this book, walking through this description provides a helpful starting point as we seek to better understand the nature and practice of organizational leadership. In the remaining sections of this chapter, I will briefly highlight the pressing concerns identified by executive leaders and provide an overview of how the remainder of the book is organized.

Pressing Concerns for Executive Leaders

This book is designed to provide guidance for those with stewardship responsibilities for wider teams, divisions, or organizations. As we seek to better understand this vital work of strategically aligning and deploying human and organizational resources in fulfillment of an organization's mission, I want us to engage real questions and issues that leaders face. In this section, I provide a brief overview of the specific concerns and challenges reported by the leaders who participated in the survey.

This survey opened with the following question for executive leaders: "*What are the most pressing (or most significant) challenges/issues you face in your leadership responsibilities?*" As I noted above, the analysis of leadership challenges yielded over six hundred coded occurrences. These included ninety-five distinct codes grouped into twenty-five categories surrounding four levels of leadership (self-leadership, people and teams, organizational dynamics, external dynamics). I provide a more detailed overview of these codes and categories in appendix A.

As I analyzed the number of occurrences for each code and category, five primary areas of concern emerged. I note them here, along with the portion of the more than six hundred code occurrences associated with the area: (1) *people*, with 212 occurrences; (2) *self-leadership*, with 100 occurrences; (3) *mission and vision*, with 94 occurrences; (4) *changing landscape*, with 88 occurrences; and (5) *financial margin*, with 39 occurrences. There is a dominant story of shared challenges and issues of concern that group around these five areas.

Although the challenges and concerns expressed by these executive leaders are many and multifaceted, the five primary concerns noted in the previous

Table 1.2. Executive Leaders' Challenges Associated with Four Levels of Leadership

Self-Leadership	People and Teams	Organizational Dynamics	External Dynamics
• self-leadership • spiritual and emotional care • time management • decision making	• hiring, talent acquisition • equipping, developing • motivation, care • mission alignment • team cohesion • managing, evaluating • retaining, retention	• mission • financial margin • goal prioritization and strategic planning • leading change • constituency, stakeholder expectations • communication	• changing landscape • culture, societal • division, tension, factions • pandemic

paragraph group around four broad levels of leadership reflection: (1) self-leadership, (2) people and teams, (3) organizational dynamics, and (4) external dynamics. Table 1.2 provides an overview of major coded items drawn from appendix A. Each of the items noted in the table represents at least ten occurrences in participant responses.

How the Rest of This Book Is Organized

In chapter 2, I provide a vision for human and organizational flourishing. I argue that human flourishing really is central to the biblical view of life and that organizational leaders have a unique and important responsibility to nurture thriving organizations within which humans may thrive and flourish. The parts that follow then seek to address the leadership concerns raised by the executive leaders in the survey laid out in table 1.2. I will focus on self-leadership in Part 2, on people and teams in Part 3, and then go on to discuss organizational and external dynamics in Part 4. The following subsections provide a brief overview of the remaining three parts of the book.

Part 2: The Leader and Thriving Organizations

Although we might want to jump quickly to what organizational leaders do and the priorities that assist organizational leaders in their work, healthy organizational leadership begins with healthy leaders. Because of this, we turn to the importance of self-leadership near the beginning of our journey.

This is not because leaders are more important than other organizational members. Rather, it is because the people of our organizations need to be led by healthy leaders, leaders of character. This notion should be familiar to Christian leaders who are students of the Bible. The priority of the character and spiritual health of leaders is emphasized throughout the pages of Scripture. Consider Paul's instructions to Christian leaders in the Ephesian church: "Pay careful attention to yourselves and to all the flock, in which the Holy Spirit has made you overseers, to care for the church of God, which he obtained with his own blood" (Acts 20:28).

We cannot faithfully and effectively care for and pay attention to others without also caring for and paying attention to our own character and health as leaders.

Paul sees an intimate connection between paying "careful attention to yourselves" as leaders and paying "careful attention to . . . the flock, . . . the church of God." In fact, we cannot faithfully and effectively care for and pay attention to others without also caring for and paying attention to our own character and health as leaders. The two duties are necessarily connected in the minds of the biblical authors. Stewarding our own lives as leaders is part of stewarding organizations effectively and well.

In Part 2, we will focus on the characteristics of leaders who are able to practice this type of leadership well.

Part 3: The Role of People and Teams within Thriving Organizations

After we spend time reflecting on the characteristics of healthy leaders, in Part 3 of the book I emphasize the importance of the people and teams that compose organizations. Leadership is not an isolated activity. Organizational leaders recruit, develop, and deploy aligned leaders in the fulfillment of the organization's mission. Building on a commitment to cultivate others, this entails both a commitment to collaboration and ensuring that teams are contributing to the mission of the organization in an aligned manner.

A well-known African proverb asserts, "If you want to go fast, go alone. If you want to go far, go together." Organizational leadership is not just about speed and efficiency. It is about effectiveness and engaging the mission of the organization in a sustained manner—it is about *going far* together. The Bible often paints pictures of similar values, noting the necessity that all parts of the church work together.

Consider Paul's words in 1 Corinthians 12:21: "The eye cannot say to the hand, 'I have no need of you,' nor again the head to the feet, 'I have no need of you.'" The implication of this and the surrounding instructions by Paul is that we are interdependent within the organizational context of the church. We are not designed to do things in complete isolation. We are designed to work together. Stewarding people and teams well is an essential part of effectively stewarding organizations well.

In Part 3, we will focus on how to organize people so as to facilitate effective team and organizational practice.

Part 4: Leadership Priorities for Thriving Organizations

Finally, building on the foundational concept of healthy organizational leaders committed to nurturing their organizations' people and teams, in Part 4 I focus on four priorities for faithfully and effectively leading organizations. These priorities relate to both internal organizational dynamics and external dynamics (that is, conditions beyond the organization). The changing landscape surrounding organizations is a pressing issue in the minds of the surveyed executive leaders. The four priorities discussed in Part 4 will help organizational leaders to guide their communities through this complex and changing landscape.

The four priorities I have chosen to focus on are leadership communication, organizational culture, crisis leadership, and change leadership. While we could consider many priorities, these four hold special importance for leaders seeking to faithfully and effectively navigate the practice of organizational leadership. The changing landscape within which organizational leaders must lead today can feel daunting. But, as daunting as this reality may be, leaders also have the opportunity and privilege to nurture healthy and thriving organizational environments within which people may flourish and mission is fulfilled. Communicating well, nurturing organizational culture, leading effectively through crisis, and navigating change are four key priorities for organizational thriving in these unique and complex days.

Summary

In this first chapter we have explored a description of organizational leadership and identified key challenges and issues that executive leaders face. Before we move on to our exploration of these key concerns—self-leadership, people and teams, organizational dynamics, and external dynamics—I want to take some time to consider a vision for human and organizational flourishing. Human flourishing is central to the biblical view of life, though not all recognize it as such. In chapter 2, I will argue for the centrality of human flourishing and explain how and why thriving organizations contribute to it.

Organizational leadership matters. The nature of our leadership affects and shapes people's lives and their experience of flourishing. Doing the work of organizational leadership well provides a context within which organizational members may develop in a manner consistent with their design as those created in God's image.

With this in mind, we turn now to looking at the significance and meaning behind the work that organizational leaders do.

TWO

A Vision for Human and Organizational Flourishing

In the previous chapter I contended that our aim in this journey is *wisdom for organizational leaders*. Organizational leaders do not merely need additional information; what they need most is wisdom to guide their leadership and practice. While we will explore multiple sources in our pursuit of wisdom for leaders, the Bible clarifies that true wisdom is found in God himself by those who approach him in a right and humble posture (e.g., Job 28:28; Ps. 111:10).

If wisdom for organizational leaders is our aim, exploring the biblical vision for true human flourishing—the design God has for his people in redemptive history—is a helpful starting place for us. Before we dive into this exploration, it might help you to note that this chapter will have a slightly different tone and focus from the rest of this book. While most of the remaining chapters will pursue wisdom for the practice of organizational leadership, this chapter sets the stage for the importance of this work.

In this chapter, I will argue that human flourishing is central to the biblical view of life and that organizational leaders have a unique and important responsibility to nurture thriving organizations within which humans may flourish. Human flourishing is dependent on much more than organizations, but organizations—especially the contexts within which people worship and work—play a vital role in how people become all that God has designed them to be. Toward the end of better understanding the nature of human flourishing and the nature of thriving organizations, we will explore the biblical priority of human flourishing, how organizations create a context where people may flourish, and how leaders may steward their organizational responsibilities in a way that helps enact rather than undermine the flourishing that God intends for us.

Human Flourishing and Thriving Organizations

The language of human flourishing is drawing renewed attention from authors these days. But more than a contemporary curiosity, the language of human flourishing gets at deeply biblical concepts related to the way people are created and the ends for which they are designed.

Pastor and New Testament scholar Jonathan Pennington makes a case for the importance of flourishing in multiple books. For instance, in his book *Jesus the Great Philosopher*, Pennington provides the following observation: "I think we can confidently say—even though it sounds odd today and could be misunderstood—that at the very core of the Bible's message is the idea of true happiness and flourishing. 'Shalom' is how the Old Testament describes it. 'Flourishing' or 'entering the Kingdom' or 'being glorified' or 'entering life' is how the New Testament talks. It's all wrapped up together, no matter which words or metaphors we use. The Bible is all about true happiness."[1]

Pennington also argues that the term *makarios* (typically translated as "blessed" and related to the broader Greek idea of *eudaimonia*) in well-known passages like the Sermon on the Mount is more accurately a pronouncement of flourishing to a particular person or state.[2] In keeping with this, as we walk through God's work in creation, the fall, redemption, and restoration, I seek to demonstrate the centrality of human flourishing in God's work throughout redemptive history.

Other authors highlight the concept of *eudaimonia* and flourishing as interchangeable with "thriving," "the good life," "a good life well lived," or a "life worth living,"[3] noting that "to have a good life is to live in a way that one flourishes as a person."[4] Scholar Christian Smith builds on this argument by observing that flourishing in one sense is striving to be who we are. He writes that the flourishing life is experienced "by becoming as fully as possible in actual *experience* that which one *is* ontologically, namely, a human person." He adds, "People flourish, thrive, and are most genuinely happy when they develop and actualize what they by nature *are*."[5]

When language of "the good life" is used, images of power, wealth, and riches might come to mind. But flourishing gets at more basic and meaningful life issues. One source argues that flourishing, at its core, "means being in right relationship with God and neighbor. It means becoming the person God made you to be and achieving the fullest use of your potential to the glory of God by loving him, loving others, and making the world a better place."[6] This understanding is relevant for anyone, but it holds special importance for Christians leading at the organizational level. Christian leaders have an expanded level of responsibility and an expanded opportunity to influence and add value to the organizations they lead. It is important to steward this opportunity in a manner that contributes to the health and flourishing of those with whom these leaders work and serve.

Christian leaders have an expanded level of responsibility and an expanded opportunity to influence and add value to the organizations they lead.

As we consider human flourishing and why it is important for leaders as they guide people in the organizational context, we turn now to the following considerations: (1) human flourishing and redemptive history, (2) thriving organizations contribute to human flourishing, and (3) healthy leaders, thriving organizations, and human flourishing.

Human Flourishing and Redemptive History

Creation and Flourishing

The story of human flourishing begins in the first chapter of the Bible. Consider Genesis 1:26–28:

> Then God said, "Let us make man in our image, after our likeness. And let them have dominion over the fish of the sea and over the birds of the heavens and over the livestock and over all the earth and over every creeping thing that creeps on the earth."
>
> So God created man in his own image,
> in the image of God he created him;
> male and female he created them.
>
> And God blessed them. And God said to them, "Be fruitful and multiply and fill the earth and subdue it, and have dominion over the fish of the sea and over the birds of the heavens and over every living thing that moves on the earth."

In these short verses we find at least two key insights that inform a picture of human flourishing. First, humans were made in the *image of God*. As those formed and fashioned in the image of God, people have inherent worth, dignity, and value. This reality also points us to the trajectory of our flourishing.

While human beings are made *in* the image of God, the New Testament affirms that Jesus *is* the image of God (Col. 1:15). Part of the trajectory of our flourishing relates to the process of us being transformed in an ever-increasing manner into the image of the Son of God (Rom. 8:29; 2 Cor. 3:18). This is where we find the fullest expression of human flourishing in God's image.

Second, human beings were given *stewardship responsibility*. They are called to "be fruitful and multiply and fill the earth and subdue it, and have dominion . . . over every living thing" (Gen. 1:28). While some have misapplied or misunderstood this dominion mandate to mean simply using and subduing according to our own will and desires, rightly understood we see the mandate providing a case for flourishing that is aligned with God's created order. Consequently, this stewardship is not ultimate with humans; it is a delegated stewardship given by God to be used in a manner in keeping with his created design and purposes.

Rick Langer provides a helpful observation on this point: "These facts"—namely, that humans are made in God's image and charged with a dominion mandate—"entail a certain stewardship vision of human leadership. The world is populated with objects that have purposes of their own. . . . We have done well by the object of our stewardship when it blossoms into what it was meant to be."[7] For Christian leaders seeking to lean into this type of stewardship responsibility, the implications are weighty. Our dominion stewardship responsibility is not simply the responsibility of ruling; it is the responsibility of helping that which is under our care blossom and flourish in a manner consistent with God's design.

This type of stewardship work "evidences our dignity as human beings—because it reflects the image of God the Creator in us."[8] The creation mandate reminds us that—amazingly—we are working and leading in God's place as vice-regents. This weighty responsibility is not to be taken lightly or dismissed outright. As Tim Keller and Katherine Leary Alsdorf remind us, "The material creation was made by God to be developed, cultivated, and cared for in an endless number of ways through human labor. But even the simplest of these ways are important. Without them all, human life cannot flourish."[9]

In light of such realities, it is important to feel both the humility and dignity associated with such weighty work as God's vice-regents. This is especially true for leaders. Michael Wilder and Timothy Paul Jones observe, "The leadership to which we are called is never sovereignty above or separation from the rest of humanity but stewardship within the community for the glory of God."[10] Stewardship in leadership is about owning the responsibility entrusted to us by God and by the communities we lead. The work of leadership has *dignity* because it reflects the image of God in us; the work of leadership should also be infused with *humility* because ours is a delegated authority. When we recognize God as the source of this stewardship responsibility, we also recognize that we are ultimately accountable to him.

The Fall and Flourishing

While Genesis 1 and 2 paint a picture of God's design for human flourishing, it does not take long for us to read about a fall from flourishing in Genesis 3. The human labors given by God in the creation mandate were good and were part of God's created design before the fall. Now the human labors once experienced in a state of perfect flourishing are marred by sin. The joyful call to "be fruitful and multiply" (Gen. 1:28) is now accompanied by pain and relational division (3:16). The joyful call to have dominion and subdue the earth is now filled with "thorns and thistles" (3:18) and carried out through pain and by the sweat of our brow (3:17, 19).

Is this the end of the story for human flourishing? We might be tempted to throw up our hands and assume that the story of human flourishing is completely on pause until we see the new heavens and new earth that John describes (see Rev. 21). While the story of future flourishing is part of the Christian hope that sustains us, there is also a story of present hope for flourishing. Jonathan Pennington puts it this way: "The story of Israel from creation through the prophets casts a vision of the possibility of deep flourishing even in the midst of inevitable loss and suffering."[11] We have hope for flourishing when we push against the fall and lean into God's created design for our lives; we also have hope that flourishing is possible in the face of pain, affliction, hardship, and suffering.

This is the type of logic we see in Psalm 90. Note the proximity of flourishing gladness alongside affliction and evil in verses 14–15: "Satisfy us in the morning with your steadfast love, that we may rejoice and be glad all our days. Make us glad for as many days as you have afflicted us, and for as many years as we have seen evil." Although the Genesis 3 marring of flourishing is present in our lives through hardship, suffering, affliction, evil, and trouble, the story of hope and gladness is still available to those satisfied in the all-sufficient love of God.

In any work—and certainly in the work of leadership—the creational good of our labors is constantly at odds with the broken and fallen dimensions of our work and the world. For those with stewardship responsibilities at the organizational level, there is a persistent and steady need both to call a community to the aspirational vision of human flourishing aligned with the creation mandate and to push back human and organizational thorns and thistles that lead people and organizations away from flourishing and thriving realities. This side of eternity, the work remains; but in the midst of this work, we are called to satisfied gladness in the steadfast love of God as we push back the thorns and thistles in our realms.

Redemption and Flourishing

Andy Crouch argues that "no human being ever embodied flourishing more than Jesus of Nazareth."[12] While the story of Israel throughout the Old Testament points to the possibility of flourishing, only in Christ is this flourishing fully embodied and renewed. In contrast to humanity's fall from flourishing in Genesis 3, Jesus Christ inaugurates a new kingdom and a new story of flourishing in the gospel. Consider the following description of this reality: "The gospel unlocks this flourishing, shining the light of God's holiness and love into the darkness of the world. . . . We rediscover what it means to flourish and how to flourish in the presence and provision of God."[13]

Earlier I noted Christian Smith's comments that flourishing in one sense is striving to be who we are. In many ways, these observations parallel God's redemptive work in the life of the Christian. While Christians are justified by grace (see Rom. 3:21–25 and 5:1), we are also in a process of *becoming* (sanctification) what we already *are* (justification). In the gospel, we are called to experience that which Christ has already made true. Pennington puts it this way: "Humans who share in the Son's Spirit-filled resurrection life will begin to experience a transformation away from cursedness to flourishing."[14]

While Smith's discussion emphasizes the dimensions of striving and achieving, the gospel emphasizes that Christ is both the *model* of a flourishing life and the *means* by which the flourishing life is experienced. Jesus perfectly models the flourishing life for us; he also is the ultimate source and means by which a full and flourishing life of salvation is brought about in the life of the Christian (see Phil. 2:12–13). The beauty of the gospel is that through Jesus Christ, God produces in us that which we are not able to produce in and of ourselves (Heb. 13:20–21).

This side of the age to come, while the flourishing purchased for God's people in Christ has been inaugurated, it is not yet fully experienced. Anthony Hoekema puts it this way: "Believers . . . should see themselves and each other as persons who are *genuinely* new, though not yet *totally* new."[15] Here we live in what theologians often describe as the *already* and *not yet* paradox of life in the kingdom of God. While we will one day be flourishing with the Lord completely and fully (Rev. 21), this reality is nevertheless presently inaugurated and experienced genuinely (though not totally) by God's people. In fact, while

God's presence was once mediated by priests and a temple among the Israelites, in Christ, God's people are now presently—amazingly—his temple (1 Cor. 3:16; 2 Cor. 6:16; 1 Pet. 2:4–6) and his priests (1 Pet. 2:5, 9), mediating God's presence in this world as his ambassadors and agents of kingdom flourishing.

Restoration and Flourishing

While God's faithful work on behalf of creating and restoring human flourishing is seen throughout redemptive history, it is perhaps the bookends of creation and re-creation that capture this work most explicitly. Miroslav Volf observes:

> The two most potent images of human flourishing in the Western cultural traditions come from the Bible, from the opening chapters of its first book and from the final chapters of its last. One is an image of the verdant garden, beautiful and nourishing, a habitat for humans to "till and keep" and a temple in which to converse with their God (Gen. 2). The other is a universal city that has become a temple, "the new Jerusalem" on a "new earth," rich in the glory and honor of nations and utterly secure (Rev. 21).[16]

While redemption in Christ makes flourishing with gladness possible amid a broken world, the flourishing we see in Genesis 1 and 2 will fully be restored only when God establishes his rule and reign on earth.

Jonathan Pennington sees this future hope as central to what motivates a flourishing life today. A Christian approach to life emphasizes "an honest assessment of the brokenness of life that is always oriented toward a sure hope for God's restoration of true flourishing to our world."[17] In fact, that is what Pennington sees at work in the Sermon on the Mount. He sees the sermon as essentially "aretegenic": that is, the sermon functions with the purpose of forming character or virtue. There are significant implications of this logic for Christian leaders.

While some may argue that people can be "so heavenly minded that they are no earthly good," biblical wisdom pushes back on multiple parts of this critique. First, the vision of Revelation 21 is not only a heavenly vision but also an earthly vision—it paints a picture of a renewed and restored *earth* (vv. 1–4) where the labors of people and cultures will be on display (v. 26) and humans will be flourishing beyond the pain of sin's curse (v. 4).

Second, those who embrace the future hope depicted in Revelation 21 are of unspeakable value for the world they live in now. As people orient their lives around the virtues of the restored earth and coming age, this provides a shaping influence on their life and work today. Pennington argues that a

Christian approach to living in the world is shaped by a virtue ethic that is unique to the Bible in that it is both "from above" (based on divine revelation) and "from beyond" (based on the Christian hope of the age to come).[18]

As we consider the nature of restoration and flourishing, there is one additional theme to highlight in Revelation 21. A vision of a renewed earth is also—more importantly—a vision of the presence and accessibility of God: "Behold, the dwelling place of God is with man. He will dwell with them, and they will be his people, and God himself will be with them as their God" (Rev. 21:3). The great joy and treasure of the flourishing life is relationship with God himself—a relationship we may have in part now and that will be fully realized in the age to come. God is not simply a means to a flourishing life; the fullest expression of the flourishing life is found in relation to him. As Volf writes, "Attachment to God amplifies and deepens enjoyment of the world."[19] The hope of full enjoyment of God's presence in the future motivates us today both to enjoy God in our present and to nurture and enjoy the flourishing life envisioned for us throughout redemptive history.

God is not simply a means to a flourishing life; the fullest expression of the flourishing life is found in relation to him.

Thriving Organizations Contribute to Human Flourishing

Now that we have spent time looking at the priority of flourishing within redemptive history, let's turn to the role organizations play in the story of human flourishing.

Human Flourishing and Social Contexts

Although it might be easy to consider human flourishing primarily through an individualistic lens, people made in the image of the triune God are naturally wired for community and relationship. Amy Sherman writes that "true biblical flourishing involves the good of others as well as our own good. Flourishing is meant to be a shared experience. We are blessed *to be* a blessing (Gen. 12:2)."[20]

Christian Smith argues that, while persons are not dependent on the social for their ontological personal being, "all persons are radically dependent upon the social for their existential development and flourishing."[21] The implications of this are vital. While we do not depend on social or organizational contexts to make us any more human than we already are as people made in God's image, people and the social contexts of organizations do hold potential for our development and flourishing as humans. Miroslav Volf affirms such logic, noting that "social arrangements can both help life go well for people and plunge them into misery."[22] Both experientially and developmentally, the presence and absence of social and organizational influences—or the positive and negative dimensions of these influences—may have a profound and shaping effect on our growth and development.

All of this points to the reality that we live a majority of our lives in the context of families, churches, schools, workplaces, and communities. Human flourishing is not an isolated pursuit. Human potential flourishes within immediate and broader social contexts—including the organizational context. Noting the importance of individuals making prudent commitments and choices that promote rather than compromise their own flourishing, Smith also highlights the dangers and benefits associated with the absence or presence of a variety of institutional influences. He writes, "In the absence of these kinds of material, relational and institutional contexts, persons will likely not flourish. In their presence, however, persons enjoy environments that nourish, though not guarantee, their flourishing."[23]

Organizations and Productive Contribution

So organizations provide one of many social contexts within which human flourishing may occur. Part of this flourishing relates to our nature as those made in the image of a creative and working God. In keeping with what we addressed above, the creation mandate highlights the dignity of the work and stewardship responsibility given by God to humans. In this mandate, we are tasked with both procreativity and productivity. Addressing productivity, Tom Nelson asserts that "one of the primary ways we live into God's creation design is by living a flourishing life of God-honoring productivity."[24] Organizations provide the context where many live out this call to productivity through service and work.

Our work in organizations plays a basic role in promoting human flourishing. Volf notes, "We work in order to make a flourishing life possible."[25] Organizations provide a context where people are able to make a living, provide for themselves and their families, and develop resources that may be shared with their churches and given to other worthwhile causes. But the story of work in organizations is not valuable merely for its utilitarian purposes (what we get out of it). Organizations also provide a context for contribution that is valuable to others. The work itself has both utilitarian and intrinsic value.

Arguing for the importance of institutions and productive contribution, Gordon Smith writes, "Institutions give us an opportunity and a mechanism, a means, to invest in something much larger than ourselves and to make a contribution that we would never be able to make individually and on our own."[26] This logic can run contrary to our cultural value of individual autonomy, but it is an important reminder that our vocations or callings most often find a place within broader organizational contexts.

Although productive contribution to the lives of others can take many forms (paid or unpaid) and can take place in many contexts (inside or outside organizations), organizations and institutions often are part of the story of human flourishing—providing space, and a place, for us to lean into the God-honoring productivity to which we are called as divine image bearers.

Healthy and Thriving Organizations

Organizations—both healthy and unhealthy, effective and ineffective—can and do play a part in the story of human flourishing as work is carried out in the midst of "thorns and thistles." However, I would argue that the nature and health of organizations significantly affect the flourishing of those working within them. Said another way, while human flourishing can take place in various organizations, not all organizations promote human flourishing in an equally helpful or meaningful manner.

Richard Stearns puts it this way: "Organizational cultures can be brutal, or they can be life-giving. Good and godly leadership contributes to human flourishing when it creates cultures and environments that are fair, just, and caring."[27] The nature of the organizational culture—whether brutal or life-giving—will have a major effect on the people working and serving within the organization. In addition to environments that are fair, just, and caring, the nature of the organization as a productive context for work also matters. If it is a business, is the business not only fair, just, and caring but also productive and profitable in order to facilitate stable employment for its employees? If it is a nonprofit, is the organization both being faithful to its mission and operating from a place of financial stability and equilibrium?

While we have been speaking at length about human flourishing, it may not be entirely helpful to think of organizations as flourishing. Perhaps a better term is "thriving." *Thriving* organizations contribute to *flourishing* humans. This is true for leaders, for organizational members, and for the various constituents served by a thriving organization. Whether an organization thrives is not irrelevant to human flourishing. When people relate to one another within or between organizations, the extent to which these organizations are thriving has a profound impact on the overall flourishing of the people connected to these organizations.

Matthew Hall, provost of Biola University, puts it this way: "At the most profound human level, I believe human beings were actually created to flourish in places. Perpetual transience is not our original factory setting. Rather, as Heclo puts it, we are 'disposed toward rootedness.'"[28] Organizations provide a place and space for individuals to dig deep roots, not merely for flourishing in a personal sense but also for contributing to the flourishing of others in a communal sense. Healthy and thriving organizations provide a context for this part of our created nature to thrive.

Here is one noteworthy final point from Miroslav Volf on the importance of healthy and thriving organizations for human flourishing: "We work in order to make flourishing life possible, but things are at their best when we also flourish as we work, when working doesn't undermine flourishing but enacts it."[29] This comment raises vital questions for those thinking about the health and thriving nature of the organizations of which they are a part. Are we creating and sustaining organizations that are fit for human beings? Are we creating and sustaining organizations that help to enact human flourishing rather than undermining it? Are we creating and sustaining organizations that become part of God's kingdom work of promoting human flourishing throughout redemptive history, or are we focused on building our own kingdoms in a manner that disregards the flourishing of others?

Here it might be helpful to draw a distinction between ultimate human flourishing and temporal or subordinate human flourishing. While *ultimate* human flourishing is found in God himself, there is a story of *temporal* or *subordinate* human flourishing to which thriving organizations may contribute. The point is not to make organizational thriving a primary or ultimate aim, but rather to recognize that by God's grace he uses people, along with churches and organizations, to bring about great good in the lives of others. Thriving organizations tend to be used by God to bring about important aspects of human flourishing, and for this I am very grateful.

Healthy Leaders, Thriving Organizations, and Human Flourishing

If human flourishing matters as a theme woven throughout redemptive history and if organizations are an important context within which human flourishing may be enacted, helping people to develop, grow, and thrive, then the manner in which these organizations are led becomes a weighty and significant consideration for organizational leaders. Stewards entrusted with the responsibility of leading organizations have a unique responsibility—I would even argue that this is a moral responsibility—to lead these organizations well. Thriving organizations often translate into people thriving and flourishing as well.

As noted previously, human flourishing is meant to be a shared experience: *we are blessed to be a blessing* (Gen. 12:2). Christian Smith argues that "the happiness and flourishing of any given person is inextricably tied up with their promoting the happiness and flourishing of other persons."[30] Human flourishing is present in an organization when leaders and followers alike are part of a network that not only allows them to make a living but also helps them draw out the potential for flourishing in others.

Arguing for the importance of leaders driving results for their communities through a commitment to serving others, Cheryl Bachelder, former CEO of Popeyes Louisiana Kitchen, writes, "Your leadership actions will change lives for the better, leave them unchanged, or, regrettably, leave them worse off. Which will it be?"[31] Leaders might not always love to think through how their work can have such a weighty impact on others, but that's what leadership entails. The only question is what type of impact and impression you will leave as a leader.

Human flourishing is present in an organization when leaders and followers alike are part of a network that not only allows them to make a living but also helps them draw out the potential for flourishing in others.

At this point it is important to note a difference between organizational members and organizational leaders. Organizational members also have responsibility to steward their work and influence effectively; a growing focus on followership in the wider leadership literature highlights the characteristics of effective followership and celebrates the importance of organizational followers.[32] Followers bring value to others through their work. Followers have a responsibility to effectively perform their roles as stewards even in the midst of diverse organizational conditions—that is, whether the organization is healthy and thriving or unhealthy and dysfunctional. Having said this, there are limits to what followers are able to influence in terms of the overall culture and health of an organization.

Though organizational leaders may also face constraints related to organizational conditions, they are not positionally constrained in the same way that other organizational members may be. They have both the opportunity and the responsibility to do something when an organization needs change. In contrast to organizational members at large, leaders do in fact possess some positional power and influence through their stewardship role, and this power and influence may be used to enact change when change is needed. They have a stewardship responsibility—and a moral responsibility—to help improve the organization's capacity to contribute to the thriving and flourishing of the people working for the organization. It's true that some internal and external factors cannot be changed, but leaders must be committed to acting where they can to develop thriving churches and other kinds of organizations that contribute to the overall flourishing of the people in these communities.

Summary

As noted above, Richard Stearns argues that "good and godly leadership contributes to human flourishing when it creates cultures and environments that are fair, just, and caring."[33] Human flourishing matters. Thriving organizations matter to human flourishing. And healthy leaders who engage their own leadership in a faithful and effective manner have an outsized influence on the health and thriving of organizations and the people within these organizations.

Because leadership matters to human flourishing and the well-being of the people connected to our communities, the remainder of this book focuses on providing guidance for organizational leaders seeking to better understand how to effectively steward their leadership responsibilities. I hope this will be a meaningful journey for you as we reflect on the type of leaders that contribute to thriving organizations (Part 2), the role of followers and teams within thriving organizations (Part 3), and several core leadership responsibilities that support thriving organizations (Part 4).

PART 2

The Leader and Thriving Organizations

Pay careful attention to yourselves and to all the flock.

—Paul (Acts 20:28)

In Part 1, we explored a description of organizational leadership (chap. 1) and considered a vision for human flourishing and organizational thriving (chap. 2). As leaders do the work of organizational leadership well, this creates contexts within which organizational members may develop and flourish in a manner consistent with their design as people created in God's image.

In Part 2, we turn to the character and commitments of healthy organizational leaders. Though leaders are not more important than other organizational members, attending to the leader's character and commitments *is a sequential priority*. For better or worse, organizational leaders have a disproportionate effect on organizations and on the people they lead. The question is not whether they affect others but whether they bring health and effectiveness or dysfunction and ineffectiveness.

For instance, the biblical call for church leaders to "pay careful attention to yourselves" is intimately connected to the call to also "pay careful attention to . . . the flock, . . . the church of God" (Acts 20:28). Stewarding our own lives as leaders is part of effectively stewarding our teams and organizations well.

Because of this priority, in Part 2 we will focus on the character and commitments of leaders who are able to practice this type of healthy leadership for the sake of organizational thriving and human flourishing.

THREE

The Character of Healthy Organizational Leaders

One school administrator in the survey reflects, "Leading during this time of history is not easy."[1] I think this comment resonates with most organizational leaders—perhaps it even feels a bit understated. The work of organizational leadership is difficult. It is particularly difficult within the historical context of the present decade.

Today's leaders face unique demands: guiding their organizations through global pandemics, addressing the implications of rising costs and recession fears, responding to resignation trends and hiring wars, navigating complex and changing dynamics on both the political and industry landscapes, and building trust within a context of increasing distrust of both institutions and their leaders.

With the general demands of organizational leadership in view—and the unique demands of the present decade—it is important for leaders to take time to ensure that they are nurturing the character and health in their lives that can sustain them in this important work. As one former denomination president puts it, "The leader sets the tone in the organization." A leader is not the only important aspect of a thriving organization, but the leader's health and character do have significant consequences for an organization's ability to thrive in a healthy and effective way.

This chapter and the following one explore multiple dimensions related to the work of self-leadership, and together they paint a picture of what characterizes healthy leaders who serve and work on behalf of thriving organizations. In chapter 4, I highlight the spiritual, emotional, relational, physical, intellectual, and practical *commitments* of healthy organizational leaders. Here in chapter 3, I focus on the priority of *character* in the life of the leader. I also focus on how character that is shaped by the gospel provides a basis for courage, competence, trust, an effective bottom line, and humility. As we begin, let's consider why the focus on self-leadership in chapters 3 and 4 is so important.

Why Focus on Self-Leadership?

Some readers might be asking, "Why begin the conversation about organizational leadership with a chapter on self-leadership?" That's a fair question. This section presents four responses in which I provide a rationale for why it is vital to spend time reflecting on issues of character, courage, and self-leadership.

First, self-leadership was a top concern of the executive leaders surveyed for this project. As noted in chapter 1, when the leaders were asked to list the most pressing challenges or issues they face, the category of self-leadership came in second only to challenges related to working with other people and teams. In the second part of the survey—which regards the advice executive leaders offered—self-leadership rose to the top: self-leadership themes represented over 20 percent of the responses offered to the question "*What is the most significant advice you provide (or would provide) to other organizational leaders?*" and the prompt "*Any additional insights or issues you'd note related to organizational leadership.*" In fact, one executive was so bold as to suggest that "effective executives spend over 50% [of their] time in self-leadership."

Second, this finding in the current study is consistent with previous research insights I reported with Mark Strauss in our book *Leadership in Christian Perspective*. In the study we reported on in that book, the presence of leaders who "honestly evaluate themselves before seeking to evaluate others" was a statistically significant predictor of effective leadership practice. In fact, this self-leadership practice had the most dominant predictive effect on leadership effectiveness out of all the leadership practices studied.[2] While self-leadership that involves taking an honest look at ourselves can feel irrelevant to leading larger teams, divisions, and organizations, research shows that both followers and leaders believe it is absolutely relevant.

Third, I argue that the health and well-being of an organization is in many ways an overflow of the health of its members and leaders. Consider how the character of the leader relates to the many organizational leadership priorities we'll engage throughout this book:

- the care and cultivation of team members (chap. 5)
- collaboration and team alignment (chap. 6)
- communication, clarity, and conviction (chap. 7)
- culture and organizational mission (chap. 8)
- crisis leadership (chap. 9)
- change leadership (chap. 10)

Because issues of trust are foundational to each of these priorities, the health and character of the leader is vital for organizational leaders.

A number of the surveyed leaders affirm this logic. One leader, who serves as the executive director for a missions organization, notes, "For Christians, we are to lead others from the overflow of our life with God." Another leader writes that "constantly work[ing] towards improving your ability to lead yourself . . . will pay dividends in your organization." A president in the business world affirms that "a leader's healthy mindset ripples emotional health throughout the organization and creates the two essential elements of effective leadership—trust and respect." These comments support the contention that the health and character of leaders really does matter to the health of those around them and the health of the organizations they lead.

The health and well-being of an organization is in many ways an overflow of the health of its members and leaders.

Finally, as one leader notes, "Generally speaking, people are not doing well. It is more crucial than ever for leaders to show up in a healthy, differentiated way." Although this observation is largely about what leaders need to provide for the people at large in our organizations, the struggle of people not doing well is a leader dynamic as well. A pattern is emerging of leaders either resigning or seriously considering resignation during difficult seasons.[3] Leaders face ongoing stress, work-life imbalances, conflict and criticism, anxiety about global events and the changing cultural landscape, and a general sense of weariness from leading in complex times—complexity that has contributed to many leader resignations.

All of these factors bolster our need to pay close attention to our lives as leaders. One survey participant, who leads in an international organization, writes, "Continually developing yourself as a leader and developing the leaders around you in your organization must be one of your highest ongoing priorities." The work of self-leadership is not easy, but it is essential for Christian leaders. As Paul notes in Acts, we are to "pay careful attention to [ourselves] and to all the flock" (20:28; cf. 1 Tim. 4:16). In fact, the latter is dependent on the former: we care well for others out of the proper attention given to our own character and growth.

In the remainder of this chapter, we will spend time considering the priority of character in the life of the leader.

The Priority of Character in Leadership

Character and Courage: Healthy Leaders Find Courage and Conviction in Their Character

One of the primary reasons character is so important for leaders is that leadership is much more about being than doing. Organizational leaders tend to be people of action. While slowing down to consider the dimension of one's being can be difficult, it is nevertheless vital for leaders with significant responsibility. Consider Warren Bennis's observations on this point: "Leadership is first being, then doing. Everything the leader does reflects what he or she is."[4]

One of the many benefits associated with leaders of character is the courage that tends to flow from virtue and character. While lack of integrity produces leadership insecurity, a beautiful confidence flows out of leaders walking in integrity. Consider the words of Proverbs 10:9: "Whoever walks in integrity walks securely, but he who makes his ways crooked will be found out." Integrity and character provide a foundation for leader confidence and courage.

According to one of my mentors, Mark McCloskey, courage and character go hand in hand. He sees courageous character manifested in three strands of attitudes and behaviors in leaders: love, courage, and moral integrity. It is the thread of integrity that speaks to the power and importance of character for leadership courage. McCloskey asserts that moral integrity is "the strength to live in accord with what one values, to live as one, whole, and morally healthy person, even and especially when a price tag is attached."[5] Leaders need courage in their leadership as much now as ever. Nurturing character provides a solid foundation for developing the type of courage needed for the leadership priorities engaged throughout this book.

Character before Competence: Healthy Leaders Prioritize Character over Charisma and Competence

The challenge is that we regularly see cases where integrity and character are absent in organizational leaders. When leaders compromise their character, organizations and the people connected to them are harmed and human flourishing is violated. One research participant notes this challenge: "The growing number of high-profile leadership failure cases . . . reveals a great deal of leadership dysfunction at the top," and these cases "are worth doing an autopsy on to learn from."

This relates to a theme mentioned by many of the executive leaders surveyed—namely, the danger of leader competence exceeding leader character. Consider the following observations from various leaders:

- "If your competency outstrips your character, it is a dangerous situation to be in."
- "Your character matters more than your competency. Put the root before fruit."
- "Always look for the three C's . . . : character, competency, chemistry; of course, character trumps everything."
- "Competence is important; character is more important."

In his book on character and the leader's work of shepherding like Jesus, Andrew Hébert warns his readers of the danger that a gift for leadership will take people "where their character cannot keep them."[6] It can be easy for leaders to rise in the organizational ranks because they perform their work well and get things done. While this work may be character-based for many, the risk that gifting and skill will outpace character is a very real danger for leaders to watch for in their own lives. This is one of the reasons leadership development scholar J. Robert Clinton emphasizes integrity checks in his leadership development approach. He writes, "The God-given capacity to lead has two parts: giftedness and character. Integrity is the heart of character."[7]

Charles Spurgeon made a similar point in the 1800s. In his *Lectures to My Students*, he notes that "a man in all other respects fitted to be useful may by some small defect be exceedingly hindered, or even rendered utterly useless."[8] Reflecting on Spurgeon's observations, my friend and former colleague Sam Rima writes, "Spurgeon rightly recognized that the ultimate success of a leader will be determined by how well he or she masters the inner life. He saw all other skills, talents, and gifts only as effective as the foundation on which they are built—that foundation being the leader's inner life."[9]

Character and Trust: Healthy Leaders of Character Understand the Priority of Earning and Preserving Trust

In contrast to the trust damaged by competence outstripping character, leader integrity and character build trust within organizations. Although leaders today face new levels of distrust in leaders and institutions, followers still desire leaders they can look to with confidence and trust. Trust is good for followers. Trust is good for our organizations. Max De Pree puts it this way: "Followers too yearn for trust. They want badly to believe their leaders and to trust them to do what they say they will do."[10] This is why the courageous character Mark McCloskey describes is so attractive: "The person with Courageous Character discerns what is right and proper to serve the welfare of others and acts in accordance with what is right, in spite of fear or self-interest. The person with Courageous Character seeks the best for others in the pressure of the moment."[11] Followers delight in trusting such leaders of courageous character.

Although we certainly want to nurture organizational character that people can trust—we'll spend more time on this point in chapter 8—in his book *The Trust Edge*, David Horsager argues that primarily "trust flows from individuals, not organizations."[12] This statement means that, at a minimum, we need to guard the integrity and trustworthiness of both organizations *and their leaders*. Leaders build trust not simply by the words they use but also, and more importantly, by their actions. As one of the CEOs who responded to the survey asserts, "Your root issue is always a Trust issue." Leaders must deal with the root issue of trust through the alignment of their spoken message and their actions.

This is one of the reasons Mark Strauss and I spend so much time focusing on leaders modeling what matters in *Leadership in Christian Perspective*. In that book, we highlight (among other things) the importance of leaders modeling integrity, responsibility, investment, equipping, and empowerment. One of the participants in my more-recent study—the president of a university—argues that "what the leader rewards and what he tolerates will continue unabated." For better or worse, trust is often won or lost for the organization on the basis of how an organizational leader lives before organizational members. Thankfully, a life of integrity has the power to reinforce the character and trust that people desire. While trust can be lost in a moment, the steady and persistent building of trust over years of faithful service is what is needed for both leaders and followers to flourish in their work and service.

Character and the Bottom Line: Healthy Leaders of Character Care about the Bottom Line

One of the leaders who responded to the survey notes, "Character is important regardless of financial bottom lines." I agree. Leaders of character must be willing to do the right thing, even when it is hard for them or for their organizations. Having said that, it is helpful to see that leadership with character does tend to have a positive bottom-line effect. In *Return on Character*, a fascinating book published by Harvard Business Review Press, author Fred Kiel shares his research-based take on the importance of character and the company bottom line. He argues that "people demand character-driven leadership because it delivers higher value to all stakeholders—and because it's the *right* thing to do."[13] I think a similar case can be made for most practices that are faithful to a biblical view of working with people made in the image of God: these approaches end up being both morally right and the right way to go about our work. They end up being both *faithful* and *effective*.

Contrasting CEOs he labels *virtuoso CEOs* (those characterized by integrity, responsibility, forgiveness, and compassion) and *self-centered CEOs*, Kiel notes that "there is an observable and consistent relationship between character-driven leaders and better business results."[14] Kiel found that the return on character—or return on assets in relation to leader character—in organizations was nearly *five times greater* when he compared the leaders of character with the self-centered leaders. For Kiel, this is rooted in a conviction I shared earlier in this chapter: effective executive leaders understand that "*who* they are is just as important as *what* they know how to do."[15] Prioritizing character and integrity over competence and charisma is not only wise for leaders, it also tends to translate into effective bottom-line performance, according to Kiel's research.

Character and Humility: Healthy Leaders of Character Prioritize Humility and Resist Hubris

Although we'll spend additional time focusing on humility in chapter 5, it is important to note here that humility is a sign of the character present in the life of leaders. Note the focus that several of the surveyed leaders place on humility: "Humility is the seedbed for growing in leadership" (an executive pastor); "Humility is the most important attribute of both leadership and followership" (an academic dean); "Humility and curiosity are so helpful in leaders. Narcissism is toxic and lethal" (a lead pastor).

Humility takes many forms and shapes, but it stands in stark contrast to examples of narcissism and hubristic pride. While there can be a positive dimension of authentic pride (e.g., "I'm proud of the hard work this team has done"), pride turns hubristic when the focus turns to the leader. Organizational leaders, by virtue of their positions, are especially vulnerable to hubristic pride. For these leaders, when stories of success are told, the successes are attributed to the leader; when stories of failure are told, the blame tends to be pushed onto others. Another sign that pride might be a problem is when leaders become exceptions to the rule. One president who participated in the survey admonishes, "On a personal level, don't make yourself an exception to the rule." Considering these cautionary examples, it is not only important for leaders to prioritize humility, they also need to actively resist hubris.

Not only is humility important for the contemporary leaders who participated in this study, it also is a biblical value that gets to the very heart and nature of God. For instance, in the book of Philippians, Paul calls Christians to the high standard of taking our cues from Jesus's model of humility. He writes:

> Let each of you look not only to his own interests, but also to the interests of others. Have this mind among yourselves, which is yours in Christ Jesus, who, though he was in the form of God, did not count equality with God a thing to be grasped, but emptied himself, by taking the form of a servant, being born in the likeness of men. And being found in human form, he humbled himself by becoming obedient to the point of death, even death on a cross. (Phil. 2:4–8)

Although humility runs counter to fallen human nature, when we step into a posture of humility and service we are returning to our nature as those made in God's image. In other words, humility and service to others do not find their ultimate foundation in human service; humility and service to others find themselves in the very heart of God.

C. S. Lewis notes in *The Problem of Pain* that when Jesus Christ went to the cross, he was doing what the Father, Son, and Holy Spirit have been doing inside the Trinity throughout eternity past—each deferring to the other, each seeking the glory of the other. Lewis writes, "For the Eternal Word gives Himself in sacrifice; and that not only on Calvary. For when He was crucified He 'did that in the wild weather of his outlying provinces which He had done at home in glory and gladness.'" At the cross, and throughout eternity past, we see the self-giving nature of God on display. Lewis connects this to the human experience of self-giving in the following observation: "In self-giving, if anywhere, we touch the rhythm not only of all creation but of all being."[16]

This points us to deep, profound, and eternal realities. We are made in the image of God. Humility, service, and an other-centered orientation are at the very heart of the triune God we serve. When we embrace this mind and heart of humility that is also in the mind and heart of Jesus Christ, it is in this self-giving, humility, and unselfishness that we experience one of the most central dimensions of what it means for us to bear God's image in our lives and leadership.

Humility, service, and an other-centered orientation are at the very heart of the triune God we serve.

Character and the Gospel: Healthy Leaders of Character Plant Their Roots in the Gospel

But how are dimensions of character, courage, integrity, trust, and humility nurtured in a leader's life? Encouraging positive habits and extinguishing negative habits are certainly part of the story. Fred Kiel writes, "People demonstrate character through habitual behaviors. . . . They can develop habits of strong character and 'unlearn' the habits of poor character."[17] This is helpful. We want our leaders to be people of character in their observed habits and practice. But is there something beyond even behavior that precedes and shapes such important work? I think we need to develop deeper roots if we desire to see sustained change and character in the habits and practices of leaders.

The reality of the fall and sin's curse is not just that humanity is plagued with sinful behavior but that the heart itself is deceitful and distorted: "The heart is deceitful above all things, and desperately sick" (Jer. 17:9). Contextually, this deceitful and desperately sick heart is found in one trusting his own strength (17:5–6) rather than trusting in the Lord (17:7–8). What the heart wants and trusts—for better or for worse—gets at core issues related to our behavior as leaders.

Because of the heart's condition, we need someone outside ourselves to return our heart to its created design. This is what God does for us. In his book *Managing Leadership Anxiety*, Steve Cuss puts it this way: "The miracle of salvation isn't that Jesus stops us from sinning or being tempted to sin, *it is that Jesus changes what our hearts want*."[18] In the words of Paul, "It is God who works in you, both to *will* [heart/desire] and to *work* [habit/behavior] for his good pleasure" (Phil. 2:13). We need a transformation of our habits in the process of character formation, but this behavioral change finds its roots in something deeper: a transformation of our hearts and desires that comes from the gospel at work in us.

Leaders need to work hard on issues of character and integrity in their lives. However, to have the right effect, this work needs to be rooted in the gospel. Tim Keller highlights both the centrality of the gospel in this work and the danger of pursuing right living through a pathway of either moralism (legalism) or relativism (antinomianism), which are devoid of the gospel.[19] Sustained character is found in our lives as leaders when we yield to the heart-changing work of the gospel; it is found when we put ourselves in an active posture of depending on the Lord rather than on ourselves and our deceitful hearts (Jer. 17).

Tim Keller argues that the gospel is central not just as the starting point of the Christian life but to the whole of the Christian life. He writes, "The gospel is not just the ABCs but the A to Z of the Christian life. It is inaccurate to think the gospel is what saves non-Christians, and then Christians mature by trying hard to live according to biblical principles. It is more accurate to say that we are saved by believing the gospel, and then we are transformed in every part of our minds, hearts, and lives by believing the gospel more and more deeply as life goes on (see Rom. 12:1–2; Phil. 1:6; 3:13–14)."[20] One passage that highlights the centrality of the gospel in both our justification and our sanctification is Romans 5.

In Romans 5 Paul declares that "since we have been justified [declared not guilty and declared or counted righteous] by faith" (v. 1), we now have peace with God (right relationship) and access into the grace in which we stand (right standing). We see the gospel at work in our justification. On the heels of this, we also see the gospel at work in our sanctification. Paul goes on to demonstrate the amazing pattern of God using suffering (hardships, obstacles, difficulties) in our lives to bring about endurance (perseverance, resilience), and endurance to bring about character, and character to bring about a hope that does not disappoint us or put us to shame (vv. 3–5).

I think most of us want the dimensions of character and hope described in Romans 5, but we do not always want the hardship, difficulties, and obstacles that God uses in our lives to build the endurance and resilience found on the path to character and hope. But this is the biblical process of sanctification that God is working in our lives. Romans 5 led Christopher Howard and me to conduct an ongoing series of research studies related to leadership development. In these studies, we are seeing how the dynamics Paul is referring to play out in the lives of leaders. Most notably, we are seeing the significant role that hardships and obstacles play in the development of resilience and character.[21]

The work of the gospel in our lives is both immediate and lifelong. In Christ, God has already "delivered us from the domain of darkness and transferred us to the kingdom of his beloved Son" (Col. 1:13), and yet in Christ we continue to "work out [our] own salvation" (Phil. 2:12) and are "being transformed into" (2 Cor. 3:18) the image of the Lord and his character as we grow through the difficulties and sufferings that the Lord uses as he cultivates persevering character and hope in our lives (Rom. 5:3–5). Character really does matter in our lives as leaders. We must lean into this process of gospel renewal as God continues to form us into the image of his beloved Son (Rom. 8:29; 2 Cor. 3:18).

A Word about "Great Man" Theory

As we move toward the close of this chapter, I want to name a potential unintended consequence of focusing so much on the nature of leaders in Part 2 of this book: readers might leave these chapters believing that the health and thriving of organizations rest solely on the shoulders of their leaders.

Such an understanding certainly has roots in the early leadership literature. In the early part of the twentieth century, leadership writers typically focused on the "great" leaders at the center of every story. These leaders were often viewed as being born with distinct traits that qualified them for the significant role they played in their government or organization. Historians have tended to tell the story of leadership in a similar manner, telling the stories of great endeavors and conquests.

Richard Daft describes "Great Man" approaches to leadership in the following manner: "In organizations, social movements, governments, and the military, leadership was often conceptualized as a single 'Great Man' who put everything together. He operated on the macro level, seeing the big picture and how everything fit into the whole."[22] While leaders certainly play an important role in organizations and society, perpetuating a view of leadership centered solely or primarily on the "great" leaders misses other equally important factors in healthy and thriving organizations. And so we have a fine line to walk in our discussion in this book.

On the one hand, your health and character as a leader *does* matter. Leaders who are unhealthy—whether owing to deficits in character or to leadership ineptitude—negatively affect the organizations and people they lead. Generally speaking, organizations do not thrive and people do not flourish when unqualified and unhealthy leaders are at the top. On the other hand, the health and effectiveness of our organizations *are not primarily about their leaders*. Hear these reflections from some of the leaders surveyed for this book:

Generally speaking, organizations do not thrive and people do not flourish when unqualified and unhealthy leaders are at the top.

- "No matter who you are, you are an interim leader. *It's not about you.* Develop others; train, delegate, empower, and affirm. Leave the organization better by building everyone else." (a lead pastor)
- "Protect your mindset. *The success of your organization does not depend on you.* It is dependent on the people you equip. To think otherwise will inevitably lead to some form of self-sabotage, be it perfectionism, the need to please, or eventual avoidance. A leader's healthy mindset ripples emotional health throughout the organization and creates the two essential elements of effective leadership—trust and respect." (a president)

Do you hear both sides of this message? *In humility*, we must embrace the reality that this organization is not about me. We are stewards of that which belongs to another. God is ultimate, and he calls us to prioritize the good of others in the places we serve and lead. Engaging the other side: *with sobriety*, we need to feel the weight of the stewardship responsibility entrusted to us. In the words of one CEO, we need to "be the leader [our] people deserve." The task of leadership is weighty, but at the end of the day, we rest in and rely upon the Lord rather than ourselves. As the national director for a nonprofit reflects, "Stay in God's Word and rely on the Holy Spirit. God provides and works even while we are sleeping." It's not about us. It's about him, and it's about the people God has entrusted into our care to lead.

Recommendations and Reflection

This chapter focused on the importance of character in the life of the leader and how character that is shaped by the gospel provides a basis for courage, competence, trust, an effective bottom line, and humility. We need to understand that who we are, and the character nurtured in our lives, matters much more than what we do. One of the leaders surveyed puts it this way: "One of the most important things to realize is that who I am is more important than what I do. The character of the person I am becoming comes before understanding my identity through the tasks I accomplish."

The leader's essential work of self-leadership begins with the prioritization of character. As character is shaped by the gospel at work in our lives, we have a basis for the courage, competence, trust, bottom-line commitment, and humility that are also vital for the work of organizational leaders.

At the end of each of the remaining chapters you will find questions to help you to reflect on the key topics raised in the chapter. (A summary of the priorities related to these questions can be found in appendix B.) Take a moment to consider the multiple areas of character highlighted in this chapter. Reflect on the following questions that relate to the character of healthy organizational leaders.

Character and courage: Healthy leaders find courage and conviction in their character.

- Do you find yourself investing more time in what you do or in who you are?
- How is the person that you are reflected in what you do as a leader?
- Do you find that your leadership is characterized more by confidence or by insecurity? How does this relate to issues of character in your life?
- What leadership issues are calling for your courageous character in the months ahead?

Character before competence: Healthy leaders prioritize character over charisma and competence.

- What leadership failures have you observed in yourself and in others? Was an issue of character involved in these failures?
- What dangers do you see associated with leaders who prioritize competence and charisma over their character?
- What integrity checks (i.e., challenges related to legal, moral, or ethical choices) have you experienced in your own life and leadership? What do these say about the development of your character?
- Is there an area of your life and leadership that needs to change for the sake of prioritizing your character as a Christian and as a leader? What is your plan to address this area that needs development?

Character and trust: Healthy leaders of character understand the priority of earning and preserving trust.

- Why is trust such an important issue for organizational members?
- Do you agree that trust primarily flows from individuals, not organizations? What does this mean for your leadership?
- How does modeling what matters build trust between leaders and followers?
- Do you see anything in your life or leadership that is compromising trust? What can you change in your life and leadership in the coming months that will help build trust with those you lead?

Character and the bottom line: Healthy leaders of character care about the bottom line.

- Have you ever had to prioritize personal character over the organizational bottom line?
- What helped you to do the right thing, even when it was hard?
- Why do you think that, generally speaking, CEOs with character tend to produce better results for their companies than self-centered CEOs?
- Are there practical steps you can take in your life to nurture the integrity, responsibility, forgiveness, and compassion associated with these more effective CEOs?

Character and humility: Healthy leaders of character prioritize humility and resist hubris.

- Why is leader narcissism and hubristic pride so harmful for leaders and the members of their organizations?
- How can you practically nurture humility in your life as a leader? How can you actively resist hubristic pride?
- Why is the example of Jesus's humility and service to others so important for Christians and Christian leaders?
- Why is it that our human practice of humble self-giving helps us better understand the heart of God?

Character and the gospel: Healthy leaders of character plant their roots in the gospel.

- Why do people need the gospel to nurture character, courage, integrity, trust, and humility in their lives?
- If "the heart is deceitful above all things, and desperately sick" (Jer. 17:9), how can leaders genuinely nurture trust in the Lord (vv. 7–8) over trust in their own strength (vv. 5–6)?
- Steve Cuss writes, "The miracle of salvation isn't that Jesus stops us from sinning or being tempted to sin, *it is that Jesus changes what our hearts want.*" Why is this hopeful for Christians and Christian leaders?
- Tim Keller writes, "The gospel is not just the ABCs but the A to Z of the Christian life." How do you see your life changing over the years as you actively trust in God's work on your behalf in the gospel?

FOUR

The Commitments of Healthy Organizational Leaders

The Priority of Self-Leadership

In his book *Leading from the Inside Out*, Sam Rima argues that all effective, enduring leadership must be built on the foundation of effective self-leadership. He writes, "It is our ability to successfully lead our own life that provides the firm foundation from which we can lead others."[1] Just as any enduring building stands on a firm foundation, so leaders must have a foundation that enables them to endure the weight and challenges associated with the demands of the job. Having such a foundation requires intentionality in the work of self-leadership. I focused on the priority of character in chapter 3, and I turn now to consider the multiple dimensions of self-leadership.

Both historical and contemporary sources place a high value on this work of leading ourselves well. Consider Charles Spurgeon's observation on this point: "We are, in a certain sense, our own tools, and therefore must keep ourselves in order."[2] Just as those in other lines of service must tend to their tools and implements, leaders likewise must keep the tools of their lives in order.

Self-leadership emerged as a dominant theme in my study of executive leaders. I coded at least fifty-five references to self-leadership in the advice given by over two hundred executive leaders. Here's just a sample of these many comments, each of which serves as a reminder of the priority that self-leadership must have.

- "Place a strong emphasis on self-leadership: I am seeing so many leaders who are lacking good self-awareness, and the consequences are becoming pretty alarming—both for the leader and for those they serve." (a president)
- "Work harder on yourself than your job, because when you improve, everyone around you will be automatic beneficiaries of your improvement." (a president)
- "Managing yourself and your insecurities takes a lot of time but shouldn't be ignored. Leadership beyond starts with leading within, by God's grace." (an executive director)
- "A leader's healthy mindset ripples emotional health throughout the organization and creates the two essential elements of effective leadership—trust and respect." (a president)
- "Regularly and humbly self-assess and reflect in light of God's Word." (a senior pastor)
- "Continually developing yourself as a leader and developing the leaders around you in your organization must be one of your highest ongoing priorities." (a director)
- "Work on keeping yourself as emotionally, spiritually, physically healthy as you can." (a senior pastor)
- "Constantly work towards improving your ability to lead yourself; it will pay dividends in your organization." (a CEO)
- "Build your self-awareness and emotional intelligence." (a president)
- "Take care of yourself. . . . Perhaps the most important part of my leadership is managing my own spiritual, physical, relational and mental health. This sounds trite in light of major-league leadership concepts, but leadership starts with my heart. That means I need to be consistently in God's Word. I need to work out 5–7 times a week. I need to have a small group of friends who walk with me, encourage me, and pray for me as I do the same for them. And, more recently, I've learned the need for mental health management." (an executive director)

While the range of self-leadership needs can feel overwhelming, it might be helpful to simply note that the aim is holistic spiritual and personal health. I say holistic in the biblical sense of this concept. We are whole beings. Gregg Allison, in his book *Embodied*, continually calls his readers to consider what it means to live as whole people in a fractured world. We are not designed to live in fragmented ways that dissociate the physical and immaterial parts of our lives.

As Allison puts it, "Scripture affirms that human beings are complex creatures. . . . In this earthly existence, we are a body-soul or body-spirit unity."[3] This logic of living as whole beings translates into embodied leaders caring for the whole of their life in their self-leadership. Leaders must care for the spiritual, emotional, relational, physical, intellectual, and practical dimensions of their lives—not only for their own spiritual and personal flourishing but also for the flourishing of those around them. In the remainder of the chapter, we will focus on each of these areas and consider several important commitments of healthy organizational leaders.

The Spiritual Dimension: Healthy Christian Leaders Prioritize Their Relationship with God

Self-leadership does not begin with oneself. Foundationally, it begins with God. As one leader put it in the survey, "My leadership must grow out of my walk with Christ." Another leader wrote, "Fruitfulness is not the result of hard work, but of abiding in Christ (The True Vine). The first priority of the leader is to draw his/her life from a vital relationship with Jesus." Still other leaders remind fellow leaders to "pay attention to your soul" and to "remember that God has called you and is equipping you for this work; build a team; be as committed to rhythms of soul care as you are to the other things [for which] you're responsible." But, while effectiveness and fruitfulness find their source in abiding in Christ, the True Vine, leaders must be careful to never confuse the ends and the means in their spiritual life.

God is not simply a means to greater organizational ends. He is the ultimate end and the true joy that will satisfy our deepest longings. He is *the* end, not merely the means to some other end. One author I turn to frequently is C. S. Lewis. A common thread in his writing relates to this theme of seeing and embracing God not merely as the means but as the end and goal. For instance, in *The Screwtape Letters*, Lewis writes, "[God] will not be used as a convenience. Men or nations who think they can revive the Faith in order to make a good society might just as well think they can use the stairs of Heaven as a short cut to the nearest chemist's shop."[4] Just as God will not be used to make a "good society," neither will he be used to make a "good person" or a "good leader" and then be cast aside or minimized. Not only is God the means of our sanctification and spiritual transformation, he must also be the primary aim of it.

Further emphasizing this point, in his book *A Grief Observed*, Lewis makes a similar comment about our view of reunions in the life to come. He writes, "[God] can't be used as a road. If you're approaching Him not as the goal, but as a road, not as the end but as the means, you're not really approaching Him at all. That's what was really wrong with all those popular pictures of happy reunions 'on the further shore'; not the simple-minded and very earthly images, but the fact that they make an End of what we can get only as a by-product of the true End"—that is, God.[5]

Lewis's point here is vital. If we approach God simply as a means to our ends—even good ends, such as being reunited with loved ones or pursuing a life of spiritual discipline and transformation—we are not really approaching him at all. When God is not our end, he will not be our means, for, in Lewis's words, God "will not be used as a convenience." But when God genuinely becomes our ultimate end, when he becomes our treasure and infinite delight, then he is ready and willing to graciously give us all things needed to do his will in life and leadership. Such logic resonates with Saint Augustine's beautiful prayer in his *Confessions*: "He loves thee too little who loves anything together with thee which he loves not for thy sake."[6]

In my leadership classes, I often remind students that *we teach what we treasure*; we motivate with what we model; we transform others by what has truly transformed us. In other words, the people we lead do not simply need to hear what we think and know. They need to see and experience what we treasure—what has truly transformed us. The same is true with parenting, isn't it? Children generally don't just follow what they are told by parents. Instead, they learn from what is lived and modeled. The question is, what are we living and modeling for those around us?

***We teach what we treasure*; we motivate with what we model; we transform others by what has truly transformed us.**

We could look to several passages that communicate these truths. I'll point to two. First, a passage that has motivated me since my high school years is Ezra 7:10: "For Ezra had set his heart to study the Law of the Lord, and to do it and to teach his statutes and rules in Israel." Ezra understood that teaching others had to be linked to studying God's Word and *practicing it in his life*. Second, consider Deuteronomy 6:4–9—sometimes referred to as the Shema—which links the ideas of treasuring and teaching:

> Hear, O Israel: The Lord our God, the Lord is one. You shall love the Lord your God with all your heart and with all your soul and with all your might. And these words that I command you today shall be on your heart. You shall teach them diligently to your children, and shall talk of them when you sit in your house, and when you walk by the way, and when you lie down, and when you rise. You shall bind them as a sign on your hand, and they shall be

as frontlets between your eyes. You shall write them on the doorposts of your house and on your gates.

When we are loving God with all our heart, soul, and might (v. 5) and when God's Word is on our heart (v. 6), then we have something to teach diligently to others. Treasuring precedes teaching.

Especially for Christian leaders serving in contexts that are explicitly about ministry, these principles translate into a warning as well. To paraphrase insights I've learned from others, "Make sure to approach the Bible more as a treasure for your heart than as a tool for your ministry." Although ministry contexts often provide occasions to focus on the Bible, there is a danger that the Bible will become a utilitarian means to achieve something apart from treasuring God himself and his Word.

Christian leaders must nurture the spiritual dimension of their life through regular Bible reading and prayer, and all of this must be saturated with a worshipful treasuring of God—the One in whose presence we find "fullness of joy" and "pleasures forevermore" (Ps. 16:11). In *The Imitation of Christ*, Thomas à Kempis often uses the phrase "inordinate affections," challenging us to evaluate the proper ordering of our affections.[7] This is a call to recognize and align ourselves to a view of God as preeminent—a view in which he becomes not only the One through whom we exist, work, live, and lead, but ultimately the One whom we exist to be in relationship with.

The Emotional Dimension: Healthy Leaders Provide a Calm and Courageous Presence

The call to spiritual health in the life of the leader includes various aspects of their mental acuity. Regarding emotions, Peter Scazzero writes, "It is not possible for a Christian to be spiritually mature while remaining emotionally immature."[8] This is not to say that perfection in every area of self-leadership is the standard. Rather, this is a call to see that every area of self-leadership is spiritual because every dimension of our life relates to God. Consider the comment by Abraham Kuyper noted in chapter 1: "There is not a square inch in the whole domain of our human existence over which Christ, who is Sovereign over all, does not cry, 'Mine!'"[9]

As we investigate the emotional dimension of leader health, we will take our cue from some of the survey participants, who named the following as important considerations: self-awareness, emotional intelligence, and the importance of leaders maintaining a calm and non-anxious presence for their organizational members. While self-awareness, emotional intelligence, and a calm and non-anxious presence are important in any era, the complexity and uncertainties of organizational leadership today especially require such emotional character traits.

I note elsewhere that "emotional intelligence is about recognizing emotion and then responding to emotion in ways that limit its negative effects and maximize its positive effects."[10] We are not able to be attentive to the needs and emotions of others—a focus in the next chapter—if we are not first aware of and responsive to the emotions in our own life. While we do not want our emotions to control us, emotion is a gift from God and often is used by God to reinforce or redirect our focus as leaders.

Steve Cuss provides an example of this with anxiety—an emotion that can be especially common among those responsible for leading complex organizations in chaotic and changing times. He writes, "Anxiety can be an early detection system that we're depending on something other than God for our well-being."[11] Anxiety in and of itself is not bad or unhelpful, but it can point to that which *is* bad or unhelpful—especially not trusting God with what concerns us. Anxiety most often is an invitation for leaders to look to the Lord rather than to themselves when they face challenging or undesirable circumstances in their lives or the lives of their organizations.

Emotionally intelligent leaders will be able to recognize when they are experiencing anxiety and then attend to this emotion by offering it to the One who is able to carry the associated concern on their behalf (see Phil. 4:6–7; 1 Pet. 5:7). The same is true for other emotions, such as fear, shame, sadness, and joy. We are emotional beings, and yet we are not designed by God to hold our emotions and burdens in isolation. We are designed by God to share in one another's burdens (Gal. 6:2) and ultimately to bring what is heavy and emotionally burdensome directly to the Lord, where we may find rest for our souls (Matt. 11:28–30).

One of the surveyed leaders notes that "modern organizations need non-anxious leaders who are present with their people." Author Mark Sayers similarly asserts, "In an anxious, crisis-driven environment, the leadership leverage comes from a non-anxious presence."[12] It is important to note that this call for non-anxious leaders does not mean that healthy leaders never deal with anxiety. Rather, it is a call for leaders—even when they face concerns that raise anxiety—to find a way to remain calm on behalf of the people they lead.

As one CEO notes, leaders must provide "clarity of direction and assurance of hope during times of uncertainty, volatility, and turbulence." Part of this assurance of hope comes from the emotional demeanor of the organizational leader. Just as "a leader's healthy mindset ripples emotional health throughout the organization" (a president), the opposite can be true as well. Unhealthy leaders who lack emotional self-awareness can quickly cast ripples of concern and anxiety throughout an organization if they are not mindful of the need followers have for a calm, non-anxious presence in their leaders.

This discussion of non-anxious leadership relates to a concept of self-differentiation that I discuss in more detail in *Leadership in Christian Perspective*.[13] In that discussion Mark Strauss and I note, "Leaders must care and not care at the same time. They must care deeply for the people they lead, but not for the shifting praise or approval of others."[14] Leaders with emotional health are able to provide this blend of care and conviction when they understand their emotions, bring their emotions to the Lord and their immediate community, and then lead out of that place of calmness that is found in a soul that is at peace with the Lord even in the midst of a chaotic world.

Nathan Finn observes the importance of calm and steady leadership: "The world is chaotic. . . . One of the most important everyday virtues a leader can cultivate is steadiness. Your consistency helps to bring order to chaos and contributes to the flourishing of those within your sphere of influence."[15] I argue that it is self-aware, emotionally intelligent, and non-anxious leaders who are able to provide this type of calm steadiness that our organizations desperately need today.

One final consideration in this area is how leaders deal with the pain that inevitably comes with their work as leaders. Whether it is due to criticism for decisions made or to changing market conditions that cause hardship in the lives of volunteers or employees, wise and healthy leaders nurture a calm and courageous presence that is able to face these criticisms and hardships with grace. One of the leaders I have been honored to work with previously is Jay Barnes. He is a humble man who has served as the president of Bethel University and more recently as the president of the Christian College Consortium. One of the insights he shared in the survey is quite profound: "Part of the leader's job is to absorb pain and to return grace." This might not be the part of the job executive leaders love, but it is nevertheless what we are called to do as leaders, and this calling is especially true for Christian leaders. Calm and courageous leaders understand when it is time to absorb pain and to return grace.

"Part of the leader's job is to absorb pain and to return grace." —Jay Barnes

The Relational Dimension: Healthy Leaders Resist Isolation

I noted above that we are not designed by God to hold our emotions and burdens in isolation. Healthy leaders have relationally rich lives—a deep and abiding relationship with God and meaningful relationships with family, friends, mentors, and members of their organizations. Leaders must prioritize not only the people they lead but also the people that God is using to help them mature as well as to help them nurture spiritual and personal wholeness in their lives as leaders. Take mentors as an example. Six of the surveyed executives highlighted the importance of having mentors and advisers throughout the leadership journey. For instance, one executive director noted, "Always have someone with more experience to mentor you in your role! Leaders need leadership from mentors!"

Beyond seeking mentors, prioritizing relationships for leaders especially means putting family first and maintaining friendships that both challenge and encourage you. Here are some of the survey responses on this theme:

- "Nurture and maintain healthy relationships." (a vice president)
- "Keep your priorities straight and don't sacrifice your family or your own soul on the altar of your organization." (a lead pastor)
- "First, work hard to ensure there's a river of grace and peace running through your oversight team (elders, board), your staff/team, and your marriage/family. Each requires intentional cultivating and time, starting first with marriage and family." (an executive director)
- "Family and health first, or you won't get far." (a chief marketing officer)
- "Prioritize your family as you lead." (a vice president)
- "I need to have a small group of friends who walk with me, encourage me and pray for me as I do the same for them." (an executive director)

The theme of relational health and engagement is especially important in this day and age as we observe so many public leadership failures. Leadership failures can take on any number of expressions: ethical (e.g., illegal practices), moral (e.g., sinful behavior), theological (e.g., apostasy), personal (e.g., hubristic pride), or practical (e.g., lack of necessary leadership skill). Though I've not studied this in detail, I would argue that in many cases, failure is tied to leaders slowly becoming isolated over time. Leaders become isolated when they do not regularly and deeply invest in relationships. This includes investing in their relationships with the Lord, with their families, and with friends by whom they may be known, loved, and challenged.

Many executive leaders observe that leadership can be lonely. While this is true for most leaders, I think it is especially true for leaders guiding larger teams, divisions, and organizations. Over time, and in the absence of intentional effort to counteract this pattern, executive leaders can become isolated from deep and meaningful relationships in which they can both challenge and be challenged, love and be loved, know and be known.

This tendency toward isolation is the result of multiple factors. For instance, as organizations grow in size, the structures of organizational hierarchy often produce an isolating effect for leaders. In addition to structural considerations, as the number of organizational members grows, interpersonally it is difficult to nurture and maintain meaningful relationships with a growing number of people. This can result in leaders pulling back from deep connection because their relational capacity has reached a taxing level. Regardless of how you got there, if you find yourself in a situation where you are starting to feel isolated—if it is hard to name friends who know you fully and speak deeply into your life—then it is time to make a commitment to do something about this.

The Bible paints a picture of walking in the light that involves both deep relationship with God and deep relationship with fellow Christians. Note John's exhortations: "If we say we have fellowship with him while we walk in darkness, we lie and do not practice the truth. But if we walk in the light, as he is in the light, we have fellowship with one another, and the blood of Jesus his Son cleanses us from all sin" (1 John 1:6–7). What you need more than leadership strategy is a vital and living relationship with God in Jesus Christ. As we walk with him, this is connected to walking in the light with people who know and love us as well. Do whatever it takes. Take the initiative to find communities and nurture friendships in which you are able to be supported and support others in this journey of life and faith. You, and those you lead, depend on you to get this part of your life right.

The Physical Dimension: Healthy Leaders Care for Their Physical Well-Being

When leaders engage in appropriate time management—a point I will return to later in this chapter—this generally creates time and space for them to care for the bodies within which they live and work. We are embodied people; God designed us this way. In contrast to the ancient gnostics, who saw the material and physical dimensions as essentially evil, Christians affirm the inherent goodness of the physical world God made. In keeping with this view, authors such as Gregg Allison challenge the expression "I have a body." We do not *have* bodies; we *are* embodied humans. Allison points to Frederica Mathewes-Green's offering: "The initial impression that we stand critically apart from our bodies was our first mistake. We are not merely passengers riding around in skintight racecars; we are our bodies. They embody us."[16]

Allison asserts that "God designed and created us to be his embodied image bearers,"[17] and only in eternity "will we be restored to our proper state of human existence, with this twist: our proper state will be that of glorified embodiment."[18] If God has wisely given us an embodied existence, then it is right that we care for the whole of our existence—spiritual, emotional, and physical. We do not care for our bodies as we care for something beyond us, like a home or a yard. We care for our bodies as we care for our souls—something that is part of who we are.

The nature of such holistic care requires leaders to nurture physical health in their lives in multiple ways. This includes attending to our bodies by getting sufficient rest and sleep and regularly exercising. As finite and embodied people, we are not able to work without limits. Limited sleep, the absence of sabbath rhythms, and sedentary and inactive living are not conducive to a flourishing life or sustainable leadership.

Sleep and Rest

On the theme of sleep and rest, God has ordained rhythms of work and rest from the days of creation (Gen. 2:1–3; Exod. 20:8–11). The biblical values of sabbath and sleep are beautifully grounded, both in the example of God resting on the seventh day and in the contrast between his nature and ours. Though we need sleep, we celebrate that "he who keeps Israel will neither slumber nor sleep" (Ps. 121:4). Because God never sleeps and is always at work on our behalf (Heb. 1:3; Col. 1:17), we can say with the psalmist, "In peace I will both lie down and sleep; for you alone, O Lord, make me dwell in safety" (Ps. 4:8).

While diligence in our work and labor is a biblical value, our work and labor are most fruitful as we work with, and not against, the rhythms of rest and work God has established for us. Consider the words of Psalm 127: "Unless the Lord builds the house, those who build it labor in vain. Unless the Lord watches over the city, the watchman stays awake in vain. It is in vain that you rise up early and go late to rest, eating the bread of anxious toil; for he gives to his beloved sleep" (vv. 1–2). Leaders are especially prone to such "bread of anxious toil."

Part of the solution to this life and leadership dilemma is rather simple—*go to sleep*. This is not a call to idleness or laziness. This is a call to embrace our finitude through sleep, understanding that the infinite God is awake and at work even when we are not. In fact, another translation of Psalm 127 reads, "For He gives to His beloved even in his sleep" (v. 2 NASB 1995). Both interpretations of this verse are equally true for Christians: God gives his people sleep; God gives to his people in their sleep. Christian leaders who hope in God have a rich theology that should facilitate sleeping and resting well, because God is at work on our behalf.

Exercise and Fitness

Some of my readers may be familiar with the life and ministry of John Piper. I had the joy of serving with the youth ministry at Bethlehem Baptist Church in the early 1990s, and then my family lived a few blocks from the Pipers in South Minneapolis for nearly twenty years. From the early 1990s to the early 2020s, I caught several glimpses of how John Piper worked to care for his physical well-being. While Piper certainly did not make physical fitness an idol in his life, he did model how to prioritize it along with other meaningful commitments. He stewarded his time and ministry well, in terms of both his pastoral care for the church he led and his ministry to the wider Christian community through more than fifty books. He has lived a very productive and fruitful life, by God's grace.

In the midst of this productivity, Piper carved out time for regular exercise in various forms. In the early '90s, I have fond memories of both early morning prayer and early morning pickup basketball with him and others. I regularly saw him jogging, and then, in more recent years, I regularly saw him walking with his wife, Noël. I admire both the intentionality displayed by his consistent exercise over the years and his willingness to adjust to different forms of exercise during the natural process of aging. As I'm now in my fifties, my exercise routines are starting to change as well. My days of playing basketball are slowly giving way to jogs and walks with my wife, Tasha. I'm grateful for these small lessons learned along the way.

You likely have altogether different routines of exercise and care for your physical well-being. I encourage you to find the time and routines necessary to make caring for your body a regular part of your life as a leader. Include healthy eating as a part of your self-care regimen. As one of the surveyed leaders observed, "Family and health first, or you won't get far." We want to lead well over the long haul; prioritizing care for your physical well-being is part of the process.

The Intellectual Dimension: Healthy Leaders Are Learners

Leadership and the ongoing growth of the leader go together. This brings us to the next dimension in our consideration of self-leadership: *Leaders are learners*. One president observes that "good leaders are always learning, growing, and developing themselves." This is not simply occasional learning; leaders find ways to regularize learning in spite of their busy schedules.

Learning takes many forms, and it can be formal or informal. For over twenty years, it has been a joy for me to partner in the classroom with leaders who are seeking ongoing growth and learning. Some of my most rewarding work has been with congregational and organizational leaders who have come back to the classroom for a season of intentional mid-career learning and growth. Their studies earlier in life helped to launch these leaders in their work serving organizations, but as the demands of their roles grew, they felt prompted to return for a next step in the growth process.

This next step often takes the form of doctoral studies for senior leaders, but—whether the next step is studying for a bachelor's degree, a master's degree, or a doctorate—there are many helpful options available to those seeking growth for the next season of ministry and leadership. My work on a bachelor's degree, two master's degrees, and a doctoral degree spanned three decades of my life. The point was not to rush through the journey. The point was (and remains) to keep growing over the years as I seek to faithfully steward what the Lord has entrusted to my care.

Beyond formal processes of growth and learning, it is important for leaders to regularly lean into informal options. Most of the leaders I know have multiple books they are working through at any given time. One author puts it this way: "When you find a leader, you have found a reader. The reason for this is simple—there is no substitute for effective reading when it comes to developing and maintaining the intelligence necessary to lead."[19] For those constantly on the go, we live in a time where audiobooks and podcasts abound. I personally enjoy the efficiency of caring for both my intellectual and my physical well-being by listening to audiobooks and podcasts while jogging.

Whichever path you use to nurture your growth and learning, the point is simply to make it a priority. The voice of the surveyed leaders was consistent and clear on this point: "Keep learning and growing as a leader" (a senior pastor). "Never stop learning, stay nimble, and be creative" (a vice president). "Never stop learning . . . [read] books, [find] mentors, [ask] questions" (a lead pastor). And why does this matter? It's not just about the growth of the leader. As leaders grow, they become more valuable to the people they lead. As a CEO noted in the survey, growth involves "constantly work[ing] to learn and improve yourself so that you can be the leader your people deserve." Your ongoing growth and learning are all about stewardship—stewarding your learning on behalf of the mission and people entrusted to your care as an organizational leader.

The Practical Dimension: Healthy Leaders Manage Their Time Well, Make Decisions Wisely, and Delegate Effectively

Finally, I want to pause and consider a few practical responsibilities of leadership: managing time well, making wise decisions, and delegating tasks effectively. There are other themes we could explore, but the executive leaders in the study gave special attention to these interrelated areas of self-leadership, so it seems appropriate to focus on them here.

Time Management

In the survey, multiple leaders noted the ever-present danger of letting the tyranny of the urgent take over. Organizational leaders understand that if we do not lead in time management, the latest demands of the day will dictate our schedules for us. One surveyed leader especially laments the "lack of time for deep/strategic thinking." In light of the tyranny of the urgent and an ongoing desire for deep, strategic thinking, leaders must be intentional, ensuring that their priorities are in the right place in terms of both the larger organizational mission and the values that guide what matters most. Consider these encouragements: "Take regular time to assess your priorities." "Keep your priorities straight." Be proactive, "managing [your] schedule to provide a balance of work, rest, exercise, vacation."

Time management includes the prioritization of the spiritual, emotional, relational, physical, and intellectual dimensions noted earlier in this chapter. For instance, multiple survey participants emphasized the importance of devoting time to family and building relationships. Others emphasized the importance of time for thinking, planning, and praying. Not only does effective time management provide space for these previously noted commitments, it also is essential to the creative work for which leaders are responsible.

I think about my days serving as a vice president and dean. The volume of meetings and administrative demands was significant. In that season, it was important for me to pull away from the regular demands to ensure that I had time to look at the big picture and engage in creative work and deeper seasons of study and writing. Deep and creative work does not happen by accident. It happens when leaders are intentional about managing their time in such a way that leaves space for work beyond the normal rhythms of the organization.

Decision Making

Decision making was on the minds of the leaders surveyed for this project. From the weight of organization-level decisions to decision fatigue to staying focused on the strategic and important over the tactical and urgent, organizational leaders understand that part of the job is to make helpful and wise decisions on behalf of the people they lead. Albert Mohler, president of the Southern Baptist Theological Seminary, puts it this way: "Leadership is a blend of roles, responsibility, and expectations. But the one responsibility that often matters most is the ability to make decisions—the right decisions."[20]

Applying reason to decision making is a good starting point. Benjamin Franklin was a proponent of essentially narrowing choices down to the two best options and then rationally deciding between the two by determining which option contains the best associated arguments.[21] In practice, leadership decision making often includes additional nuance and complexity that calls for more than just rationality. Leadership decision making calls for what we've been discussing throughout this book—that is, it calls for wisdom.

If you want to become a better decision maker, focus first on deepening your character and clarifying the foundations that guide you.

One of the leaders surveyed put it this way: "I have become convicted that the character of a leader is the primary determining factor in their ability to make wise decisions on a consistent basis." Wisdom finds roots in the depth of a leader's character. Another administrative leader writes, "The deeper person you become, the better decisions you will make." I think this is helpful. If you want to become a better decision maker, focus first on deepening your character and clarifying the foundations that guide you.

Related to this work of clarifying, the executive leaders who participated in the survey provide key insights regarding the need to stay focused on mission, purpose, priorities, principles, and perspective in the decision-making process. Consider the following statements related to this topic:

- *Mission clarity*: "Keep your mission clear and be singularly focused as you navigate complex and nuanced challenges and decisions." (a president)
- *Mission focus*: "Diligently maintain mission focus and make leadership and organizational decisions based on the few core principles you and your organization are most confident in and committed to." (a vice president and dean)
- *Long-term orientation*: "Make decisions now that serve the long term [needs of the church/organization]." (a lead pastor)
- *Principled decisions and action*: "Know and commit to your principles while being agile tactically." (a CEO)

- *Focus on purpose and priorities*: "Begin with the end in sight (determine and prioritize your outcomes and goals, and then 'back into' your tasks and projects); ask the 'why' that is behind the 'what' and the 'how.'" (a president)
- *Big-picture focus*: "Raise your eyes to the big picture. Let your faith guide your perspective on the future. Don't overreact to anything in the present. Temper your ambition with humility. Remember the words you want to hear from Jesus some day: 'Well done, good and faithful servant.'" (a CEO)

This process of staying focused on what matters most—mission, long-term purpose, principles and values, big-picture priorities—makes some of the more difficult leadership decisions "easy." I put *easy* in quotation marks to acknowledge that, even though some decisions are hard, they nevertheless can be straightforward when set against our purpose, mission, values, and guiding priorities. This step in the decision-making process is all about looking for alignment and misalignment. The answers often become readily apparent and clear when we consider the mission alignment or misalignment of given pathways and options.

In addition to expressing the need for wisdom, character, and an evaluation of mission alignment during the decision-making process, the surveyed leaders also emphasized the importance of exercising due diligence and pursuing wisdom and perspective from others. Although this includes seeking out perspective from trusted team members and wise counsel, for Christian leaders this process should prioritize looking to the Lord for wisdom. Exercising due diligence involves intentionally seeking the Lord's wisdom through prayer and by examining God's Word. One of the Old Testament leaders most frequently held up as a positive example of leadership practice is Joshua. Like all human leaders, however, Joshua had failings, and one of these was neglecting to seek counsel from the Lord at a critical moment (Josh. 9:14–15). Joshua's decision to make a treaty of peace with the Gibeonites in this passage aligned with his due diligence work, but under Joshua's leadership the Israelite leaders failed by not asking "counsel from the Lord." Taking a lesson from Joshua's error, in our decision-making process, we need to both plan and pray; we need to both do our homework and seek the Lord's direction and wisdom.

Many of the surveyed leaders affirmed this vital point about prayer. For instance, a vice president within higher education wrote, "We need an even more cogent vision for the future. That begins and ends in prayer/listening to the Lord." A lead pastor wrote, "Pray, read, and discuss with others about what is most important." This focus on prayer is primary. In the pursuit of leadership wisdom, God is eager to provide for his people.

James reminds us, "If any of you lacks wisdom, let him ask God, who gives generously to all without reproach, and it will be given him" (James 1:5). This passage is not preaching a prosperity gospel that uses God to enrich us and our organizations. It is about Christians humbly and earnestly bringing real needs and questions to the Lord and seeking his will and wisdom.

This approach to prayerful decision making naturally translates into broader due diligence work. One nonprofit president wrote, "Before making decisions or taking action, it is critical to first try to understand the problem as thoroughly as possible. Time is more often your ally." It is vital that decisions are not made in a knee-jerk fashion. One CEO wrote, "Don't overreact to anything in the present." Taking the necessary time to look at the issues behind a problem or question is prudent. We need to take the time to see what has led to the current issue or question, and we need to give care to thinking through the impact of a decision. One leader wisely cautioned, "Do not assume your will is God's will." All of this requires humility and character.

As a part of doing their due diligence, wise leaders are eager to pursue counsel from trusted voices. These include the members of the teams that leaders build around themselves. Survey respondents advised leaders to "build and use a leadership team for decisions and execution" and insisted that "developing your team to make good decisions is critical to organizational success." Although leaders may feel alone in the decision-making process at times, wise leaders do seek the perspectives and insights of others before making key decisions. One senior vice president wrote, "(1) Stay humble; (2) ask questions; (3) have courage/conviction when it's time to make a decision."

This brings us to the final step of the decision-making process—leaders deciding and then acting on their decisions. Consider all the steps that have led to this point in the discussion: pursuing wisdom and character, evaluating mission alignment, consistently praying and seeking God's will about the decision, planning and engaging in effective inquiry, and gaining counsel and perspective from others. While executive leaders would be foolish to avoid or ignore the counsel of others, at the end of the day, leaders need to make and own their decisions. For better or worse, this is one of the primary responsibilities of leadership. Even when the answer is not completely clear, decisions still need to be made. I appreciate the encouragement one vice president provides on this point: "When you don't know what to do, just take the next best step." The key is to not become paralyzed in a state of perpetual indecision.

The decisions leaders make rarely please everyone in the organization. One executive pastor wrote in the survey, "You can lead people or you can please people, but you can't do both." A CEO observed, "[The] art of leadership is learning to be OK with disappointing people." This is where the emotional health and calm, non-anxious presence of the leader (discussed earlier) come into play. While leaders must maintain a spirit of humility in their work, our organizations do need wise and humble leaders who are decisive. One nonprofit director summarized this idea thus: "Do not succumb to a failure of nerve." Once a leader has sought the Lord in prayer, done their due diligence, and sought the counsel of others, it's time to act. We do the best we can in the decision-making process and entrust the organizational decision to the Lord (Ps. 90:17).

Here is one final recommendation before we move on. Wise decision makers take time to review their decisions and to learn from their decisions. Albert Mohler puts it this way: "The stewardship of decision making does not end with the declaration and announcement of the decision. Leaders learn from their decisions and from the process of making them. . . . The leader learns fast, remembers honestly, and moves on."[22] Whether the outcomes of a decision proves helpful or harmful to the health and thriving of organizations, leaders must take time to evaluate decisions. This process of reviewing and learning has the potential to strengthen the quality of decision making in the future, with the aim of facilitating both organizational thriving and human flourishing.

Leader Delegation

The last practical area of self-leadership I will explore here is the responsibility of delegation. Effective leadership involves delegation. One leader wrote in the survey, "Learn to delegate early and often." Although we will focus on delegation in more depth in the next chapter, it also is important to consider the self-leadership dimension of healthy delegation.

From a servant-leadership perspective, delegation is primarily about the identification, development, and empowerment of others. It is not first and foremost about getting work off the plate of a senior leader. But these two functions are intimately connected. When leaders fail to delegate well, they are harming and stunting both themselves and those they lead. While some leaders possess extensive capacity to take on new work and new responsibilities, every leader has limits. Only God is all-knowing, all-powerful, and everywhere present.

A frequently referenced text pointing to the limited nature of human leaders is Exodus 18. In this passage, Jethro, Moses's father-in-law, says, "What you are doing is not good. You and the people with you will certainly wear yourselves out, for the thing is too heavy for you. You are not able to do it alone" (vv. 17–18). Jethro goes on to recommend a strategy for delegating work, with people organized into groups of thousands, hundreds, fifties, and tens.

While there is much more at play in this passage than mere managerial strategy, it nevertheless illustrates the tendency of leaders to take on more than is wise. Delegation not only helps leaders to maintain a healthier approach to work and life, it also ensures that others in the community and organization are able to develop into the leaders God desires them to be. One pastor observed in the survey, "No matter who you are, you are an interim leader. It's not about you. Develop others; train, delegate, empower, and affirm." Your leadership may be for a year, a decade, or multiple decades, but there will be an end to it. Leaders need to delegate for their own health and effectiveness, but—more importantly—they need delegate so that the organization has a healthy and growing group of emerging leaders with experience and skill developed through opportunities given to learn by doing.

Recommendations and Reflection

This chapter focused on the commitments of healthy organizational leaders. Understanding these commitments begins with understanding the sequential priority of self-leadership. Healthy leaders work hard to lead themselves well before they try to lead others. The apostle Paul regularly affirms the importance of practicing care and faithfulness in your personal life as well as faithfully leading others in broader contexts (e.g., Acts 20:28; 1 Tim. 3:2–5, 12; 4:16).

Healthy leaders work hard to lead themselves well before they try to lead others.

Take a moment to consider the multiple areas of healthy self-leadership highlighted in this chapter. Reflect on the following questions related to these vital commitments of healthy organizational leaders:

The spiritual dimension: Healthy Christian leaders prioritize their relationship with God.

- Are you prioritizing your relationship with God?
- Is the Bible a treasure for your heart more than a tool for your ministry or for your leadership responsibilities?
- Are you regularly reading God's Word and seeking God in prayer?
- Is the busyness of leadership or ministry pushing out the greater priority of your relationship with the Lord?

The emotional dimension: Healthy leaders provide a calm and courageous presence.

- Are you nurturing an awareness of your emotions (such as anxiety, anger, shame, sadness, and joy)?
- What do these emotions tell you about your approach to life and leadership?
- Why is it important for you as an organizational leader to maintain a calm and non-anxious presence for those you lead?
- Are you finding ways "to absorb pain and to return grace" with the people you lead?

The relational dimension: Healthy leaders resist isolation.

- Do you have mentors and coaches who are able to support you in your role as a leader?
- Are you working hard to resist the danger of isolation in leadership?
- Do you have deep friendships—friendships where you may support and be supported, challenge and be challenged, love and be loved?
- Are you nurturing deep relationships with those closest to you: spouse, children, family members?

The physical dimension: Healthy leaders care for their physical well-being.

- Are you avoiding both idleness and idolatry in the area of physical well-being—neither avoiding needed exercise and a healthy diet nor letting physical well-being trump other important areas in your life?
- Are you regularly finding time to rest and sleep? Are you scheduling time for exercise and physical movement?
- Are you learning to adjust your exercise patterns for different seasons in your life?
- Are you caring for your embodied life by eating in a manner that is healthy for your body?

The intellectual dimension: Healthy leaders are learners.

- Are you making time for reading and learning?
- Have you identified podcasts or audiobooks that you can bring with you on the go?
- Are you making time for deep reflection and creative thinking?
- Have you considered what your next educational step might be?

The practical dimension: Healthy leaders manage their time well, make decisions wisely, and delegate effectively.

- Are you managing your time, or is the tyranny of the urgent managing it for you?
- Are you seeking appropriate wisdom from others in the decision-making process?
- Are you avoiding difficult decisions (demonstrating indecisiveness), or are you taking the initiative to act when action is needed?
- Are you meaningfully delegating to others? What else should be delegated over the next month?

PART 3

The Role of People and Teams within Thriving Organizations

If you want to go fast, go alone. If you want to go far, go together.
—African proverb

Part 2 focused on how healthy organizational leadership begins with healthy leaders of character. In Part 3 we will explore the importance of the people and teams who are tasked with carrying out the mission of the organization.

To state the obvious: effective organizations do not thrive because of the work of a single leader. Healthy and thriving organizations rely on the coordinated, collaborative, and aligned work of multiple team members. Organizational leaders recruit, develop, and deploy aligned leaders and team members in fulfillment of the organization's mission. Building on this priority of cultivating others, the work of leadership entails both fostering collaboration and ensuring that teams are contributing to the mission of the organization in an aligned manner.

Organizational leadership is not just about speed and efficiency. It is about effectiveness and engaging the mission of the organization in a sustained manner—it is about *going far* together. This orientation toward collaborative and coordinated work is essential for leadership seeking to nurture healthy and thriving organizations where people flourish.

FIVE

The Care and Cultivation of Team Members

In the first four chapters of this book, I covered the nature of organizational leadership, painted a vision for human and organizational flourishing, and described the character and commitments of healthy organizational leaders. Now it is time to turn to the care and cultivation of team members.[1]

As I noted in chapter 1, organizational work is not carried out in isolation by an individual. No matter how talented a leader may be, the work of an organization requires coordinated labor. Leadership requires a network of aligned people and resources. As leaders work toward the fulfillment of an organization's mission, they must prioritize the people with whom they work. This is part of what makes organizations thrive and people flourish.

Mission and the People Who Make It Happen

For leaders, a commitment to the people of the organization must be a priority, for multiple reasons. Let me highlight two. First, this commitment recognizes how people are wired to work with leaders. The president and CEO of a major publishing company explained in the survey, "People want to work with you, not for you." This type of genuine partnership is something that Paul celebrates with the Philippian church: "I thank my God in all my remembrance of you . . . *because of your partnership in the gospel* from the first day until now" (Phil. 1:3, 5). People are willing to work hard for their leaders, teams, and organizations, but most people want to be seen as genuine partners and valuable members of a team—not as expendable hired hands working on someone else's agenda.

Second, leaders of healthy and growing organizations understand that sustained growth and effectiveness is not achieved without engaged and committed team members. One business owner put it this way: "An organization that seeks the health and success of followers is an organization that has a higher potential for long-term buy-in, growth, and team health." Organizational leaders ought to care deeply about the successful fulfillment of the organizational mission. However, faithful and effective organizational leaders understand that mission is best accomplished by qualified and flourishing team members.

The mission of an organization matters—taking care of people is the way to make it happen.

Dondi Costin has learned a lot about leadership during his time serving in the military (he is a retired major general) and as the president of two universities—Charleston Southern University and Liberty University. Noting the importance of caring well for team members, Costin shared the following in one of his survey responses: "The most consequential leadership gem I'd pass on is one of the first I learned during my military career: 'If you take care of the people, the people will take care of the mission.' This reality is especially true in this season of our existence as we navigate the perfect storm wrought by a looming recession, aggressive inflation, and the Great Resignation." The mission of an organization matters—taking care of people is the way to make it happen. Costin continued, "Until you can find a way to make your people your top priority, the mission will never be accomplished the way it should."

Leader Humility and Partnership

Genuinely caring for and partnering with organizational team members calls for the leader to practice humility (unpacked in chap. 3). As one of the surveyed leaders noted, "Growth happens when I put the needs of others and the organization above my own advancement." Not only is humility vital for investing in others, it also plays a key role in the willingness of team members to buy into the mission of the organization. One vice president put it this way: "Humility and authenticity are of utmost importance to truly achieve buy-in and followers that stick together (and [stick] with you)." Leader humility is important for leaders and followers. It is a vital dimension of a leader's character. Leader humility also helps followers learn to trust their leaders and see their own part in the organization's mission.

Although images of rugged individualism have tended to dominate views of leadership in the past, wise leaders quickly learn that they are not called to go it alone. Brian Mowrey—a lead pastor serving within a shared-leadership model—reflects in the survey, "Don't lead alone. Surround yourself with mentors, team members, and positional experts to support and advance the organization." Another leader I respect, who has been president of two significant organizations, wrote, "Don't do life alone—join with others in the body of Christ to have greater wisdom together than anyone has alone." This message is consistent with what we find in the leadership literature. Mark McCloskey argues that a healthy and collaborative leader "embraces the reality that no one person—no matter how talented—can go it alone."[2]

All of this points to the importance of the leader's mindset. Do leaders see themselves at the center of the organizational story, or do they see and understand themselves as one part—among many—in an important story? One leader wrote in the survey, "Narcissism is toxic and lethal." We cannot lead organizations faithfully and effectively—we cannot authentically focus on the care and well-being of team members—unless we have the right mindset. A president in the business world cautioned, "Protect your mindset. The success of your organization does not depend on you. It is dependent on the people you equip." With this mindset—a mindset of humility and authentic partnership—we are ready to dive into the work of caring for and cultivating the members on our team.

A Commitment to Care and Cultivation: Healthy Leaders Focus on the Care and Cultivation of Their Team

The major focus of this chapter is unpacking four key stages in the care and cultivation of organizational members: (1) team member identification, (2) development, (3) empowerment, and (4) motivation. In a business context, these stages relate to the important work of hiring, training, delegating, and retaining. We will spend significant time reflecting on each of these areas. Before doing so, it is important to set the stage by engaging the philosophy of people and leadership that can best facilitate this work. We'll discuss this approach by focusing on the leader's commitment to the care and cultivation of others.

As I write this, my eldest daughter is in a leadership development program at our local church. The program, called Cultivate, is designed to help those exploring potential missions service as they consider how God may be leading them to be a part of international service. Over the course of the program the participants are given two plants that function as a metaphor for the importance of faithfully and effectively cultivating our lives for service. Each week, the group takes time to cultivate and care for one of the plants. The group ensures it is receiving sufficient water, appropriate sunlight, helpful pruning, and rich soil full of the nutrients that plants love. The other plant will be set aside. It will not be cared for or cultivated. Week by week, they observe the stark divergence in the health and vitality of the two plants.

As you can imagine, the fate of these two plants is quite different. The plant that is cared for and cultivated flourishes; the other eventually withers. So it is with human lives. Flourishing comes when lives are intentionally cared for and cultivated. The cultivated plant is a metaphor for anyone aspiring to significant service; it is a reminder to prioritize the care and cultivation of our lives, both spiritually and personally.

This metaphor is not just for missionaries. It is for all of us—it is something our organizational members need. Wise and thoughtful leaders understand that the people of their organizations need intentional care and cultivation. Unfortunately, some models of leadership are overly focused on efficiency and production, missing the importance of care and cultivation. The work of the organization is viewed as more important than the people of the organization. In such organizations, followers are there to do their job and meet the needs of the leader, the organization, or both—not the other way around.

Healthy models of leadership also prioritize organizational mission, but they recognize that organizational mission is not accomplished without sufficient care and cultivation of the people who operationalize the mission. I'm encouraged by the voices of so many of the surveyed leaders who understand this distinction. They emphasize the priority of care, relationship, putting people first, and taking the time to intentionally serve the needs of their teams. Let's explore these threads.

Relational and Caring Leadership

The care and cultivation of organizational members begins with love. We might not always identify "love" as a foundation of leadership. It feels too soft to some organizational leaders. Richard Daft puts it this way: "Despite its power, the 'L' word is often looked upon with suspicion in the business world."[3] Although *love* is not commonly part of leader vocabulary, its effects are powerful as leaders appropriately express and demonstrate genuine care for and cultivation of the people in their organizations.

One executive vice president summed it up beautifully in the survey: "Leading well is loving well." This is grounded in the conviction that another president noted: "People are the most important resource . . . of an organization," and because of this, leaders must "care for and affirm them well." Two other CEOs made similar observations: "Care about your people"; "Truly care for others and show them by your actions that you genuinely value them."

Connecting care and valuing people, James Laub argues in his book *Leveraging the Power of Servant Leadership* that valuing people is the starting point for the practice of servant leadership.[4] Valuing people is not rooted in merely humanistic motivations. Valuing people is a profoundly theological act for Christians. As I noted in chapter 2, people are made in the *image of God*. As those formed and fashioned in the image of God, people have inherent worth, dignity, and value.

We do not primarily value people for what they produce or accomplish; we primarily value people for who they are as bearers of the image of God. While valuing people is consistent with our nature as humans, it is also important for those who desire to cultivate effective and thriving organizations where people flourish. As demonstrated by a study I conducted with Michael McNeff, valuing people has a disproportionately strong effect on the positive culture of companies.[5] Organizational members tend to flourish when leaders value and care for the people they lead.

Because faithful and effective leadership is about caring for and valuing people, healthy leadership is essentially relational. This is a point Mark Strauss and I observe in *Leadership in Christian Perspective*: "In previous eras of coercive, top-down, and directive management, weak relational skills could be tolerated in some cases. In our day of team-oriented and network-style work environments, understanding and working well with others relationally is no longer an optional part of life in the workplace. . . . Leadership is essentially a relational practice."[6] Many of the surveyed leaders likewise emphasize the importance of a relational approach to leadership.

One organizational director put it this way in the survey: "Get the heart of people. Build healthy and ethical relationships. . . . Leading with love yields [the] greatest results." John David Trentham, a dean in higher education, noted: "Invest personally and relationally in the people with whom God has providentially gathered you in your professional organizational life." He went on: "Seek intentionally to be shaped and sharpened by them. You and your team will serve people, your organization, and your mission best when you love and respect one another most."

For some, an overly relational emphasis in leadership seems to deprioritize results. However, for many of the surveyed leaders, it is not about deprioritizing results—it is about recognizing that healthy relational investment helps bring about results that will last. An executive director who participated in the survey points to the difficulty of "balancing leading relationally and leading . . . [the] operations" of an organization. While this balancing task is certainly a challenge, it is nonetheless essential for leaders. One pastor summed it up well: "Focus on results and you'll lose relationships. Build healthy relationships and you'll get results."

A president made a complementary point in the survey: "Lean into relationships and influence rather than positional leadership." While positional power is present for most leaders, the point is that using personal and relational influence rather than resorting to positional power tends to promote better, longer-term effectiveness.

The authors of a *Harvard Business Review* article titled "Connect, Then Lead" similarly argue that while leaders need both warmth (followers can trust the leader) and competence (followers can respect the leader), leaning into strength before warmth often elicits fear from followers. However, when leaders first establish warmth, leader strength and competence is a welcome reassurance for followers. The authors write, "Before people decide what they think of your message, they decide what they think of you."[7] This observation affirms the importance of leaders engaging their followers in both relational and caring ways.

Prioritizing People in Leadership

Healthy leaders act consistently with this emphasis on leaders engaging organizational members with relationship and care when they see the people in their community as the top priority. One CEO wrote in the survey, "Always put others first—actively listen, be empathetic, put yourself in their shoes." This leader went on to note the importance of "assuring clarity of vision, living our values and putting people first." When leaders truly believe that people are the most important aspect of the organization, this changes the way leaders guide their communities.

Again, this is not simply about making people feel good. For organizational leaders charged with a stewardship responsibility—the fulfillment of the organization's mission—prioritizing people is mission-critical work. Here's how one leader expressed this in the survey: "I try to help leaders understand it is vital for them to build their people. Without the manpower the organization will not grow." This leadership work includes "taking the time to help others realize their power, worth, and value to become active carriers of the vision." It is this investment in others that helps bring about mission fulfillment.

Healthy leaders understand that it is not about choosing between people and production. As multiple studies from the middle of the twentieth century affirm, effective leaders focus on both people and results.[8] But this prioritization of both does not rule out a sequential priority. On that front, I argue that the prioritization of people precedes the accomplishment of results in healthy leadership practice. As one director affirmed in the survey, "Tasks are important; people are more important."

Building on this, a COO argued in the survey that "how you go about doing your work and treating people matters far more than getting things done." My addition to this is that *how* one does one's work is intimately related to *what* results are accomplished. Recall Dondi Costin's advice quoted earlier: "Until you can find a way to make your people your top priority, the mission will never be accomplished the way it should."

Transformational and Servant Leadership

So what approaches to leadership best help leaders to prioritize people, relationships, and the care and cultivation of others? A dean of a college of business asserted the following in the survey: "You should believe in your people. If you are in leadership, I recommend Servant Leadership as a philosophy that will carry you through the good and the bad times." I argue elsewhere that servant leadership is not only a good idea—it works.[9]

Alongside the emphasis on servant leaders putting the needs of followers before their own self-interest, transformational leadership principles also are relevant. Complementing the follower focus of servant leadership, transformational leadership is about creating broad and intrinsic ownership of the organization's mission in leaders and followers alike.[10] Both servant leadership and transformational leadership principles become increasingly relevant as the nature of organizations changes and the complexity of organizations grows.

A university provost provided the following observation in the survey about leadership style and the nature of a university: "A university is an ecosystem wherein everything is connected. There are so many areas where I share considerable responsibility for the outcome but do not have the final authority to direct it in a transactional sort of way. I have to balance both 'leading down' (my direct reports) and 'leading over' (my executive-level peers), which at any given time is a matter of 'art' far more than it is 'science.'" As organizational complexity grows, the inspirational nature of transformational and servant leadership becomes vital for those leading significant teams, divisions, and organizations.

In contrast to the highly directive forms of transactional and autocratic leadership, organizational leaders committed to leading effectively in today's dynamic and complex organizations realize the importance of service and inspirational motivation. On this front, a COO challenges organizational leaders to "focus less on control and more on inspiration." While an emphasis on control can feel easy and efficient, the intentional work of inspiring people holds out greater potential for long-term effectiveness.

An executive vice president who responded to the survey gets at these distinctions by contrasting two leadership styles: "We used to refer to [these styles] as a 'cowboy' versus a 'shepherd.' The former is top-down—all of the authority resides at the top. The latter was more focused on 'equipping the saints' to do the work of ministry. I see the same dynamics in the workplace. Employees can respond well to either model, but I think they tend to flourish in the latter environment (which tells you which style of leadership I prefer!)." This image of the leader as shepherd points us to a dominant principle expressed throughout the Bible: those entrusted with leadership responsibilities are called to serve those under their care.

In Ezekiel 34, the human shepherds of Israel are severely corrected for feeding themselves rather than feeding the sheep (v. 2). Rather than caring and providing for the sheep they have been called to shepherd, these "shepherds" are trampling down the pastures in which the sheep should graze and muddying the water from which the sheep should drink (vv. 18–19). In contrast to these shepherds, Jesus comes as the fulfillment of what a true shepherd and servant leader is. In John 10:11, Jesus states, "I am the good shepherd. The good shepherd lays down his life for the sheep."

While some leaders literally put their lives on the line for the people they lead, most organizational leaders must prioritize their followers in other ways. In the survey, one pastor put the importance of leader service this way: "Service and sacrifice are the foundation and lifeblood of leadership." In chapter 3, I noted that "when we embrace this mind and heart of humility that is also the mind and heart of Jesus Christ, it is in this self-giving, humility, and unselfishness that we experience one of the most central dimensions of what it means for us to bear God's image in our lives and leadership." Following in the footsteps of the Good Shepherd allows us to see and experience God's heart in deep and profound ways. Danny Akin, president of Southeastern Baptist Theological Seminary, puts it this way: "You are never more like Christ than when you take on the heart of a servant."[11] As James Laub argues, servant leaders begin the work of serving others by valuing and developing them.[12]

The Four Stages of Caring for and Cultivating Team Members

In the remaining sections of this chapter, we will explore how leaders may (1) identify, (2) develop, (3) empower, and (4) motivate organizational members.

Identifying Team Members: Healthy Leaders Strategically Build Their Team

Among other themes, I have been emphasizing the importance of leaders prioritizing the people of their organizations. This vital work begins with a process of onboarding and building the team of people who will compose the organization. It would be difficult to overstate the importance of this part of an organizational leader's work.

Emphasizing the importance of hiring the right people (those aligned with the mission of the organization), one college president wrote in the survey, "I interview all finalists for all full-time positions. This allows me to explore whether a candidate's experience and/or core competencies fit with the job description. But it also allows me the opportunity to deeply explore missional alignment with our statement of faith and community life covenant. Hiring well is the most important thing I do." Whether or not the size of your organization allows for this type of process, this example points to the high stakes and high priority that organizational leaders need to place on identifying talent and hiring the right people. As I noted in chapter 1, hiring and talent acquisition was a top-level concern for survey participants, with over forty coded occurrences among the listed concerns.

Strategic Identification

The mechanisms for identifying and onboarding team members will differ by organizational sector. However, whether you lead an organization primarily made up of hired employees or serve in a nonprofit or church that is more dependent on interns and volunteers, establishing a strategic plan for the identification, recruiting, and hiring (or volunteer onboarding) processes is essential.

Several survey participants noted the importance of being slow in the hiring process and not settling for just filling slots. While this approach is especially important when hiring for leadership positions, it should also govern building the team at large. Consider these observations: "Be very slow in raising people into leadership." "Choose your leaders wisely. Be slow to hire and quick to fire" (we'll circle back to this comment on firing later in the chapter). And, when you are team building, resist merely "filling a spot [with] a warm body."

I would like to modify the language a bit. The value here is not to be *slow*, but rather to be *strategic*. Even in organizational contexts that require quickly identifying new team members, it is essential to have a clear strategy and values guiding the process.

Identifying the "Right" People

I've already mentioned the importance of finding the "right" people for organizational teams. This word, and similar language, was frequently used in survey responses. Here are some samples:

- "Find the *right* people first, then focus on strategy." (a president)
- "This comes through hiring the *right* people." (a president)
- "Hire the *best* people possible; expect them to push you and make you better." (a provost)
- "Stick with your mission and hire the very *best* people you can find." (an executive director)

I think all of us want to lean into these calls to find the best people we can for our teams. But this raises a question: What makes someone the best or right fit for a team?

One word of caution on this point: The right people are not simply those who fit a personal preference or those who are most similar to you. One of the surveyed executive leaders observed, "When I first started out in leadership, I tried to find people who thought and acted like me because that's what I thought worked best. I quickly realized that was a recipe for disaster. There is significant benefit in a well-rounded team."

Having noted that caution, we still need to answer our question—what makes someone the best or right fit for a team? I encourage leaders to focus on four primary areas as they consider who should be a part of their teams: (1) character and convictions, (2) capacity and competence, (3) chemistry and culture, and (4) context and complement.

Character and Convictions. The first question in the process of identifying, hiring, or onboarding is this: "Is this a person of character who believes in our values and mission?" We spent significant time in chapter 3 examining the importance of character for leaders. All the nuances of character discussed in that chapter apply here. While I do argue that character is even more urgent for leaders owing to the scope of their stewardship responsibility, character also matters for team building in general. Team members need humility and integrity; they need to be characterized by trust.

This emphasis on character was a resoundingly consistent message from the surveyed leaders—hire for character! Note a sample of these comments:

- "Staffing (hiring and firing): . . . Competence is important; character is more important." (a senior pastor)
- "'A' people are those who combine character and competency in carrying out their assignment." (a president)
- "When hiring potential leaders, . . . character trumps everything." (an executive director)

While the survey participants mentioned character along with other important priorities, such as competence, chemistry, and culture fit, there is a sequential priority given to character. Nathan Finn provides a rationale for this sequential priority: "It is not within my power to change someone's character. If he is a person of character, I can often resource him to grow in competence. If he is a person of character and has an appropriate level of competence, I can almost always help him adapt to our culture."[13]

Alongside character are the conviction and values that will guide people as team members pursuing the organization's mission. One provost put it this way: "I think that you need to always make certain that you are hiring for mission." He continued, "It is easier to train folks in their respective areas of work if they are committed to the mission—it is harder to work with talented folks who may not be good mission fits—so don't prioritize other areas over mission." A university president wrote, "Recruit good people who share the vision for the organization and a similar passion for doing the work." We'll give more attention to the importance of mission alignment in chapter 6.

Capacity and Competence. The second question in the process of identifying, hiring, or onboarding is this: "Does this person exhibit present competence—or a significant capacity to learn?" Once you establish that someone is a good fit for your team in terms of character and conviction, it is time to consider the person's capacity and competence. When you are hiring or onboarding seasoned individuals, they may already have a significant track record that affirms their level of competence. When there is no track record available, leaders need to assess a potential team member's capacity to learn the job. In both cases, the point is that competence matters, whether in paid or volunteer roles.

As we consider the importance of competence, the humility of the leader is once again crucial. Organizational leaders need to have enough humility to pursue the very best people they can find, and they need to have the humility to gain the insights of others to better assess the competence of potential team members. One leader puts it this way: "Surround yourself with other leaders who are as gifted or more than you are in a variety of areas. . . . Don't be afraid or intimidated by other gifted people. It makes your organization great." Another leader wrote, "Stick with your mission and hire the very best people you can find." Leaders who are humble and wise are not threatened by competence—they welcome it in their organizations.

Competence includes a potential team member's talent, strengths, knowledge, skills, abilities, experience, and overall work habits. In other words, competence is the interplay of multiple dimensions that collectively contribute to individuals' capacity to effectively carry out their responsibilities. "When it comes to competency," one executive wrote, the people brought into an organization should be "good at what they do or at least show potential that they will be good at what they do. In other words, you don't just settle for anyone because you have to fill a slot or position. Mediocre should not be an option." Assessments of competence will look different in different sectors and in distinct lines of work, but—as with character and convictions—we want our teams to be populated with team members who add value through their capacity and competence.

Chemistry and Culture. The third question in the process of identifying, hiring, or onboarding is this: "Does this person fit with our team culture, and will this person have good chemistry with the team?" As we progress though this sequence of strategic questions in the process of identifying or hiring team members, the question of chemistry and fit for the organization's culture is vital. Having assessed a prospective team member's character, convictions, capacity, and competence, it is now important to assess culture fit and chemistry.

This area can feel less defined at times, but it is vital for thriving organizations and teams. Consider the potential harm to team morale if a person vetted for character and competence comes into a role and unwittingly begins working to make the new team feel just like a previous workplace. While it is helpful for teams to grow and change as new members join, this is different from new members intentionally or unintentionally undermining the culture that has developed in the community.

Though chemistry and culture are not more important than character and competence, leaders should hire—and at times fire—on the basis of culture fit and team chemistry. Protecting and promoting culture is a high-stakes issue for thriving organizations. This does not mean that dissent or challenging voices on the team are unwelcome. We need to be challenged. It does mean that dissent and challenge must maintain a tone that is working *for* the good of the organization and *for* the nurturing of healthy team culture and chemistry. One vice president wrote in the survey, "Build a team that you love to be with. Productivity will follow. Team culture and unity trump strategy."

Protecting and promoting culture is a high-stakes issue for thriving organizations.

Context and Complement. The final question in the process of identifying, hiring, or onboarding is this: "Would this person be a complement to the team, or would adding this person produce a redundancy (too much similarity) or contradiction (too much difference)?" Finding the right people for a team is not simply about personal preference or looking for those who are similar to us. To reiterate this point from one survey participant, finding only people who think and act like the leader is "a recipe for disaster."

In contrast to such an approach, survey participants defended the value of bringing complementary gifts and voices to their team. While we do not want significant contradiction or misalignment—too much difference on our teams—the presence of too much similarity can become toxic or redundant. Consider the following survey responses:

- "I always encourage leaders to surround themselves with an effective, complementary inner circle." (a president)
- "It's important to purposefully build your team with a variety of skills and personalities that can all work together." (a principal)
- "Surround yourself with others whose strengths compensate for your weaknesses, and be generous in giving credit to whom it is due." (a provost)
- "Live into your strengths while surrounding yourself with complementary leaders." (a lead pastor)

This type of logic should not surprise Christians. In multiple books of the New Testament, Paul paints a picture of the church as a body that functions correctly when each part does its work (e.g., Rom. 12; 1 Cor. 12; Eph. 4). As a body is one but has many unique parts, so—Paul argues—individuals within a church bring their diverse gifts together for the growth of the church: "For as in one body we have many members, and the members do not all have the same function, so we, though many, are one body in Christ, and individually members one of another. Having gifts that differ according to the grace given to us, let us use them" (Rom. 12:4–6). We'll spend more time on this theme in chapter 6.

So, as you consider the needs of your team, what additions will help complement what is already present? This work of composing a complementary team involves both avoiding redundancy (which comes from hiring people just like us) and avoiding contradictions or conflict (which come from hiring people who do not share our core commitments and priorities). As you work to build a team in your context that brings complementary—not just complimentary—people together, what types of difference and complement should you consider?

The context of your organization often dictates the nature of needed complements. For instance, if you lead a nonprofit international relief organization, do you have a well-rounded team that represents people with the language skills and cultural know-how to carry out your mission faithfully and effectively? In addition to considerations such as language and culture, it is important to think through issues related to age and generations. This is a point that many survey participants raised.

While some of the survey comments regarding generations focused on the challenging nature of leading multiple generations, the surveyed leaders also expressed genuine concern for leaning into these challenges in an effective manner. Consider the reflections offered by a school district superintendent: "Another leadership challenge is dealing with a multigenerational workforce. In this era, it is not an exaggeration to say that the newest generation to join the workforce is unique. They have grown up in a post-9/11 world that has seen a severe recession, political and social unrest on a scale not seen since the 1960s, and the cherry on top is the pandemic. They're self-centered for a reason. They cannot count on anyone else but themselves." This comment is not meant to disparage a generation but to call those from other generations to invest in younger generations with compassion and intentionality.

An executive pastor at a large church made the following observation: "Generational differences seem to be more prevalent." Reflecting on what he has observed and heard from others, he explained, "This is the first time there are five generations in the workforce. Good leaders have to be able to see beyond their own perspective and bias and understand how to engage and value the strengths and weaknesses of the various generations." This important work of understanding generational differences is not simply a practical issue for managers as they lead a diverse workforce. It is also a matter of sustaining organizational mission.

One survey participant wrote, "Relationships must be built to establish trust, develop leadership skill, and pass responsibility off to the next generation." Another leader challenges us to "always be reaching into the next generation to find the next leader in your organization." Any thriving organization must be investing in the next generation of emerging team members and leaders. This is a practical necessity for sustaining an organizational mission. For Christians, investing in the next generation is also a theological necessity.

One pastor wrote, "No matter who you are, you are an interim leader. It's not about you. Develop others; train, delegate, empower, and affirm." In the Old Testament, Moses is reminded of his interim and temporary status when God reiterates that Moses will not enter the promised land. With this in view, Moses is to "charge Joshua, and encourage and strengthen him, for he shall go over at the head of this people, and he shall put them in possession of the land that you shall see" (Deut. 3:28). The future of God's mission with his people would be continued in Joshua, not Moses.

Consider also Paul's words to his protégé Timothy: "And what you have heard from me in the presence of many witnesses entrust to faithful men, who will be able to teach others also" (2 Tim. 2:2). Do you see the four generations noted in this single verse? Christians who are committed to a biblical vision of discipleship understand the priority of investing in younger generations. Christian leaders who care about whether the communities they lead will thrive and flourish in the future will be intentional about identifying and investing in younger leaders.

All of this points to the next stage in caring for and cultivating team members.

Developing Team Members: Healthy Leaders Equip and Develop Their Team

Now that we've spent time focusing on the importance of identifying, hiring, and onboarding the right kind of people, the next stage in the process of caring for and cultivating leaders is the important work of *developing* team members.

As previously noted, servant leadership begins with a commitment to value and develop people. Developing others is also a central feature in transformational leadership practice. Francis Yammarino captures this in the following statement: "In short, transformational leaders develop their followers to the point where followers are able to take on leadership roles and perform beyond established standards or goals."[14]

In the survey, the topic of equipping and developing people—which is related to the leader's focus on working with people and teams—was second only to questions and concerns about identifying and hiring people. In other words, executive leaders are highly interested in seeing the people of their organizations effectively equipped and developed. Consider just a few of the many encouragements leaders provided in this area:

- "Develop strong teams and trust them. Then get out of the way." (a vice president)
- "Develop leaders and empower volunteers." (a lead pastor)
- "Developing the leaders around you in your organization must be one of your highest ongoing priorities." (a director)
- "Don't go it alone. Develop those around you." (a pastor)
- "Develop others; train, delegate, empower, and affirm. Leave the organization better by building everyone else." (a lead pastor)
- "The success of your organization does not depend on you. It is dependent on the people you equip." (a president)
- "The best leader isn't the smartest person in the room, but the one who is willing to get the best answer from those in the room." (a lead pastor)
- "Developing your team to make good decisions is critical to organizational success." (a senior director of operations)
- "Effective leaders reproduce themselves." (a lead pastor)

This commitment to developing others becomes even more critical when we consider the missional reasons for investing in the next generations, discussed in the previous section. Consider two additional reflections from survey participants on this point. A president wrote, "Spend time, resources and experience to nurture upcoming leaders." A deputy superintendent who guides a district with nearly five thousand employees and thirty-three thousand students wrote, "I would also advise all leaders to remain focused on developing institutional capacity in others and to purposely identify key young leaders among the ranks in whom to invest for [the] short-term and long-term sustainability of our organizations."

While development is vital for any organization, those leading organizations that require a significant number of employees or volunteers especially feel the weight and importance of developing their people. Let's consider several formal and informal ways leaders can invest in equipping and developing their people before moving on to look at spiritual development and leading with patience.

Formal and Informal Processes

People in organizations develop when structures are put in place that support people by both formal and informal means. Organizations offer a wide range of leadership development programs. Some *formal* options include education reimbursement for employees, internal classes, and short-term developmental learning experiences. One of the survey participants recommended regularly inviting people to engage in a six-to-eight-week leadership development experience. The shorter time frame is a manageable addition to the schedules of organizational members, yet it provides the opportunity for meaningful developmental learning. Some organizations may want to adopt an invitation-only approach—focusing on the development of top talent in the community. Other approaches may encourage aspiring leaders to opt in to the leadership development group—a feature that incentivizes personal ownership of the developmental process.

An organization I previously worked for illustrates another possible formalized approach. In this community, the annual review process incorporated intentional developmental conversations between supervisors and employees. While any number of tools could be used to facilitate such conversations, this organization utilized the StrengthsFinder instrument with its employees and had a formalized process during each annual review in which supervisors and employees would reflect on how their strengths were effectively contributing to their work and their professional development. One of the things I appreciated about this annual review approach was that it normalized and regularized developmentally focused conversations in the organization. Instead of encouraging employees to simply review performance and look to the coming year, the developmental model of the annual reviews focused on how employees were owning their personal growth and how supervisors could both advocate for and advise this growth in their employees.

Informal processes often best support growth when executive leaders model mentoring and coaching in an organization. Consider some survey responses: "Surround yourself with a mentor/coach and don't wait too long to start coaching/developing others." "Effective leaders reproduce themselves." "You reproduce who you are." I summarize it this way: developing people develop others.

In *Leadership in Christian Perspective*, Mark Strauss and I argue that the use of teams provides a natural context for this type of developmental work: "Teams provide a unique opportunity for organizations to develop younger or newer talent, because the teams provide an organic environment for leadership development." We continue, "Rather than providing leadership development and mentoring as a side program, teams provide a natural environment in which emerging team members and leaders can observe and interact with tenured team members and leaders in the normal flow of work life."[15]

Spiritual Development and Leading with Patience

Just as the gospel is a priority for our own development as leaders (see chap. 3), so discipleship and gospel growth are necessary for organizational members. Though attending to the spiritual needs of organizational members will likely be different by sector and organization, all humans made in God's image are spiritual beings in need of spiritual care and cultivation. Not all organizational members are open to this need, but it is a need nevertheless. Christian leaders must wisely consider how to approach this need in their unique organizational context.

At the very least, this means modeling care for the whole person. Consider the following leader encouragements: "Pray, stay in the Word, lead by example, and persevere." "Develop the whole person. Leadership development is nothing less than a discipleship process, and involves every aspect of one's life." This focus on whole-person development is part of what this chapter is all about—caring for and cultivating the people of our organizations.

One final note in this section: leaders need to embrace patience with the development process. Consider the encouragement of one of the surveyed leaders: "As leaders, we must be patient with the growth of those we lead. Some will grow quickly, others not so much. But both groups are needed and we must learn to balance it effectively for the overall growth and development of the organization we lead." Patience is relevant not only for quick and slow learners but also for high-capacity and lower-capacity team members. In the survey, an executive director noted the challenge of "keeping high-capacity people from getting bored and low-capacity people from being overwhelmed."

Patience can be hard for leaders to cultivate in themselves, but it bears fruit. It is particularly important while onboarding new team members and developing team members for significant roles. The director of an international airport made the following comment: "When you get a new leader in one of your work areas, give them up to 6 months to meet stakeholders and the right people in the organization, get to know their staff, and to get a good feel of things before they 'do anything.' This frees people up to be more intentionally collaborative and helps prevent early mistakes that cannot be undone." While the length of this learning season may vary across diverse organizational contexts, the point is well taken. We need to be patient with people as we develop them for long-term effectiveness and growth.

Empowering Team Members: Healthy Leaders Delegate to and Empower Their Team

Building on the important work of identifying and developing team members, the next vital stage is to empower these team members. This work of empowerment involves deploying people on the basis of their equipping—that is, the training they have previously received. This involves sufficiently delegating meaningful responsibilities appropriate to their developing competence and capacity.

Mark Strauss and I highlight the intimate connection between equipping and empowerment: "Those who are empowered but not equipped run the danger of failure. . . . Similarly, those who are equipped but not empowered run the danger of frustration."[16] When followers have not been developed through proper direction and equipping, it is unreasonable to expect them to perform as needed. Team members need both proper development and proper equipping, but once they have them, organizational leaders may actually stunt the growth of their people if the leaders don't provide meaningful delegation and empowerment. As leaders seek to reproduce themselves and the values of the organization in others, their work will not be accomplished without significant empowerment.

Empowerment Involves Risk and Trust

Though vital, empowerment may not always be an easy step. It requires leaders and followers to take risks and to trust one another. One director noted in the survey, "If you want people to trust you, you need to trust them." A vice president wrote, "Be nimble; be willing to try and sometimes fail; develop strong teams and trust them. Then get out of the way." A senior partner in a firm encouraged leaders to "hire people you can trust and then trust them, even if their decisions are different than yours." I happen to know some of this senior partner's backstory. Early in his career, he made a mistake that cost a printing company $30,000. He feared he would be fired. Instead, his manager asked him what he had learned from the experience and essentially said to him, "Why would I fire you? I just made a $30,000 investment in your development."

Trusting people is not without risk of mistakes on the part of leaders and followers alike. The art of empowering leadership is deciding when these risks include lots of room for failure and growth and when something becomes an issue that calls for firing someone or removing someone from a role. These are never easy decisions. In the survey, one C-suite leader noted the ever-present issue of "balancing empowerment and the need to ensure excellence."

Empowerment Is Essential for Development

But empowering—risks and all—is part of the process of caring for and cultivating the people in our organizations. Our people don't grow until they are developed and then entrusted with meaningful responsibility. Consider just a few of the dozens of comments survey participants made on this point:

- "Learn to delegate early and often." (a lead pastor)
- "Empower members of your team by using delegation that gives them responsibility." (a president)
- "Delegate sooner than is often comfortable." (a pastor)
- "Delegate tasks that can be done by others." (an executive director)
- "Invest in those leaders around you [and] give away way more than you think you can. You'll be amazed at the capacity of those around you." (a lead pastor)
- "As trust continues to grow, give people the opportunities and resources they need to lead their areas. We have good people; I wasn't hired to do their jobs for them. This means also giving the opportunity to fail and recognizing that their failure may reflect on me, but it's an essential part of growing as a leader, for them and for me." (an executive pastor)

The practice of empowering others and delegating to others is grounded in the logic of delegated authority we see in the Bible. As noted in chapter 2, our stewardship responsibilities as leaders do not originate with us. Stewardship is not ultimate with humans; it is delegated by God to be used in a manner in keeping with his design and purposes for creation. As we humbly receive the delegated responsibilities and opportunities entrusted to us by God and others, we can likewise entrust delegated responsibilities to others. Delegation is not just about trying to get work off a leader's plate. It is about entrusting meaningful responsibility to others in order to see them grow into the people God desires them to be as members of a community.

Empowerment Requires a Culture of Grace

As I noted earlier, decisions to hire and fire are both important and difficult. Before sharing when I think firing or removing someone from a position is in order, let me start with the more important side of the equation. Leaders need to create a culture in their organizations and teams that provides room for failure. Christian leaders often use the language of grace to get at this ideal. In the words of one executive director, "Work hard to ensure there's a river of grace and peace running through your [organization and] team." A CEO wrote in the survey, "Lead with grace. Your people will fail and they need to know their job is not on the line if they fail. Leading with grace also implies that you will empower them to succeed, not set them up to fail." A nonprofit president summarized this idea well: "Provide the space and grace for mistakes."

Grace can feel like "weak" leadership to some. For Christians, it is rooted in the power and beauty of the gospel, as discussed in chapters 2 and 3. One lead pastor wrote in the survey, "The most important thing you do is to create a culture of the gospel so that people can communicate both wins and failures without shame. It is vital that you create this incredible culture within your team so that you can have real team unity." He argues that this culture of the gospel is central to creating a "culture that allows people to flourish."

Leaders need to create a culture in their organizations and teams that provides room for failure.

In his book *Lead*, Paul Tripp highlights that the gospel is both the central message of Christian leaders and the central means for leader formation and practice. He argues that a gospel community is characterized by nurturing, honesty, humility, patience, forgiveness, encouragement, protection, and restoration. Both grace and truth are central to Jesus's life and to the life to which Christians are called (John 1:14, 17). While truth matters (along with excellence and high standards), Christian leaders desiring to walk in the footsteps of Jesus must learn how to appropriately nurture cultures of gospel grace on their teams. As one president put it, "Retain a high bar for excellence and for grace. People need to feel that it is safe to take chances . . . in your organization."

Empowering Leaders Sometimes Need to Fire Team Members

A culture of gospel grace should be primary on our teams and in our organizations. While I certainly see fostering such a culture as a priority for churches, I would argue that it is essential for Christians creating organizational culture in other contexts as well. But, since Jesus is full of grace *and* truth—and since Paul similarly affirms the importance of Christians speaking the truth in love—Christian leaders sometimes reach a point when difficult decisions need to be made about team members.

The decision to remove someone from a role (volunteer or paid) is a weighty decision. It should not be made lightly by a leader. One leader wrote in the survey, "Be slow to hire and quick to fire." I personally don't like the word "quick" here. While some decisions to fire require leaders to be prompt and timely, I don't want to make this decision seem offhand, cavalier, or impulsive. Just as leaders need to have clear strategies and values that guide decisions in hiring, so leaders should be guided by strategy and values in firing.

Some decisions to fire (or remove from a role) are straightforward. These tend to concern cases in which clear legal, ethical, or moral standards have been violated based on the policies and values of the organization. If such situations are not addressed within a team, the results can be destructive to the community. One university president noted, "What the leader rewards and *what he tolerates* will continue unabated" (emphasis mine). A leader who is not willing to fire is engaging in broader organizational communication—the leader's inaction communicates that violated policies and values are not taken seriously.

Other decisions to fire (or remove from a role) are less clear-cut, but they are still important. I see two primary scenarios here: lack of competence and violations of the organizational culture. Let me illustrate. Regarding *lack of competence*, it is in the empowerment stage of the care and cultivation process where lack of competence often becomes clear. In other words, a team member's lack of competence might not be discovered during the earlier stages of identification and development. Sometimes a lack of competence becomes evident only in the course of meaningful delegation and empowerment. When this is the case, a leader in a large organization may be able to reposition a person to a role that fits the person's strengths. But, when repositioning is not an option, maintaining the status quo is generally not helpful for either the team member or the organization.

In the survey, an executive pastor at a large church observed his need to "grow in my trust of [that is, empowerment of and delegation to] the people I serve *and, if the trust cannot be developed,* undertake the difficult work of determining if a personnel change is necessary" (emphasis mine). He continued, "Their failure may reflect on me, but it's an essential part of growing as a leader, for them and for me." While leaders who empower their followers desire to create room for failure and room for growth, there nevertheless comes a time when a team member has demonstrated a consistent inability or unwillingness to meet the needs of a certain role. After a season of intentional development and significant empowerment, a leader may need to make the difficult decision to remove this person from the team.

Regarding *violations of organizational culture*, though the problem may not be as straightforward as dealing with legal, ethical, or moral violations, it is nevertheless a vital issue for leaders to confront. If someone persists in intentional behavior that is eroding organizational culture, this has the potential to act like a cancer on the team or organization. Leaders need to proactively hold people accountable not just for objective work results but also for their subjective attitude and behavior.[17] While such accountability should not be driven simply by personal preference on the part of leaders, leaders must be willing to act when action is needed.

One leader wrote in the survey, "Remove toxic team members once they demonstrate an unwillingness to get on board with the team's mission in a productive way." Again, such decisions should not be made in a cavalier manner, but leaders must be willing to make difficult decisions for the sake of the whole rather than appeasing or accommodating those undermining the culture of the community. Team culture and organizational culture are worth preserving.

In our work of empowering team members, we must take risks to delegate meaningful work, and in that process, we must be willing to both extend significant grace and provide genuine accountability as we steward the teams and the organizational culture entrusted into our care.

Motivating Team Members: Healthy Leaders Retain and Sustain Their Team through Ongoing Motivation and Care

Issues of employee retention, motivation, and care were also significant concerns for survey participants. Once you identify, develop, and empower your team members, it is time to think about how to retain them as valued members of the team over the long haul.

While motivation and retention are always top-level considerations for leaders, the unique dynamics of leading in the current decade add to this. John Coleman, author and frequent contributor to Harvard Business Review, declares that "no topic is as critical right now as employee engagement and motivation."[18] In the survey, one superintendent shared, "As we move out of the pandemic era, the most challenging issues I'm facing as a leader are tied to inspirational motivation." Other leaders noted that they are more frequently "checking in with [their] employees to see how they are doing emotionally" and that leaders need to "get a grasp on how wounded people are" and that, "generally speaking, people are not doing well."

So an important part of leadership these days involves helping team members feel cared for, seen, and valued. This is why several leaders highlight the importance of emotional intelligence. In the survey, one CEO noted his intentionality in ensuring that he is "listening and in tune with the mental health of other leaders in the organization." Highlighting the importance of leaders focusing on the socio-emotional well-being of their staff, a superintendent wrote, "Such leaders easily overachieve in comparison to those who fail to recognize the importance of developing and exercising soft skills and social-emotional intelligence." The care and cultivation of team members necessitates leaders growing in their emotional awareness and emotional intelligence. (See related discussions in chap. 4.)

Another dynamic that relates to this conversation is how to facilitate motivation and care of team members as the nature of work changes. One survey participant noted that hybrid platforms of work are convenient, but that organizational leaders are going to need to develop better approaches to helping workers thrive in these hybrid environments.[19]

The following well-known saying sums up this section well: "Train people well enough so they can leave; treat them well enough so they don't want to." I think this gets to the heart of developing and retaining team members through care and cultivation. We began this chapter by focusing on prioritizing and caring for people, so it's fitting that the chapter's other bookend also involves care. The goal is to build our teams with highly equipped and empowered people of character and then to provide the motivation and care that makes them want to stay with the team for the long haul.

Recommendations and Reflection

This chapter focused on the care and cultivation of team members. This care and cultivation begins with leader humility and with leaders prioritizing the people who make the mission happen. Through servant leadership and transformational leadership practices, healthy leaders who care for their people strategically identify new team members, commit to developing and empowering these team members, and provide sustained motivation and care that retains these team members over the long haul.

Take a moment to consider the multiple areas that healthy leaders attend to in the care and cultivation of their team members. Reflect on the following questions related to these vital team-building priorities of healthy organizational leaders:

A commitment to care and cultivation: Healthy leaders focus on the care and cultivation of their team.

- "Leading well is loving well": Do you agree with this leader's observation? What does appropriate love and care for team members look like in your organization?
- "Tasks are important; people are more important": How can you prioritize your people in the midst of important tasks that need to be accomplished? Why does this matter for the fulfillment of your organization's mission?
- Consider the images of the leader as a "cowboy" and as a "shepherd": Which best reflects your approach to working with your followers? How is this leadership approach affecting your people?

- "You are never more like Christ than when you take on the heart of a servant": Why is this, and how can you better serve your team in the month ahead?

Identifying team members: Healthy leaders strategically build their team.

- As you hire or onboard team members, are you doing so strategically or are you treating each hire in an isolated or ad hoc manner?
- Are you prioritizing character and integrity in your identification and hiring process? How do you balance important considerations related to both character and competence?
- How are you ensuring that potential team members are aligned with the mission and values of the organization? How are you assessing their fit with the organizational culture and team chemistry?
- Are you prone to hire people too similar to you? How can you more effectively build your organizational team by paying attention to characteristics that complement the existing team?

Developing team members: Healthy leaders equip and develop their team.

- Why is it important to include a focus on developing younger team members and leaders? How is your team doing on this front?
- What programs or processes has your organization formalized for developing team members?
- As a leader, how are you personally modeling informal pathways to invest in the development of team members (e.g., coaching or mentoring)?
- How are you incorporating the development of the whole person (professional skills, spiritual well-being, etc.) with team members? Do you feel that you are leading the development of others with appropriate levels of patience, understanding that development takes time and effort?

Empowering team members: Healthy leaders delegate to and empower their team.

- Are you providing meaningful delegation and empowerment for those who you have trained and developed?
- What is the danger if we equip people but do not then empower or deploy them to use this development and training?
- Do you agree that empowering others requires some degree of risk and trust? Is this something that you are comfortable with, or is this something with which you struggle as a leader?

- Why is a culture of grace so important for thriving organizations and flourishing team members? When, and under what circumstances, do you see firing or removing someone from a role as consistent with an overall culture of grace and flourishing? Why is it important to hold both of these principles (grace and accountability) together in leadership?

Motivating team members: Healthy leaders retain and sustain their team through ongoing motivation and care.

- What pressures are team members uniquely facing these days, either due to specific issues in your industry or due to broader societal or global challenges?
- What steps can you take in the next month to better care for and inspire your team members?
- How are issues of morale and employee retention changing because of the increasing use of hybrid work models? How can you provide better support for your team members as the nature of workplaces changes with these dynamics?
- "Train people well enough so they can leave; treat them well enough so they don't want to": Do you agree with this principle of leading organizational members? How can you better facilitate an organizational culture within which this becomes a reality?

SIX

Collaboration and Team Alignment

Thriving organizations include motivated and aligned teams and team members. In chapter 5, I focused on the importance of prioritizing people and intentionally cultivating them through an organizational commitment to the identification, development, empowerment, and motivation of team members. Here in chapter 6, I turn to the value of collaboration in thriving organizations. We will consider strategies for helping the teams of our organizations flourish in a healthy and aligned manner.

Although I have been an advocate for the important role of teams and collaboration in my research, writing, teaching, and practice for more than two decades, the point is not to organize collaboratively through teams just for the sake of following recent trends or preferences. There are more significant considerations that should inform our practice. In this chapter, we explore some of the key reasons why all organizational leaders should prioritize collaboration, and we explore practical advice regarding how to effectively lead teams in thriving organizations.

A Call to Collaboration

Executive leaders of organizations frequently point to the essential nature of collaborative efforts in the life of the institution. Consider Gordon Smith's comments in his book *Institutional Intelligence*: "Institutions thrive quite simply because we learn to exercise our strengths, capacities, and callings in a way that *is mutually dependent on the strengths and capacities of others*."[1] If we want our organizations to thrive—providing a context within which people will flourish—accomplishing this involves mutually dependent, coordinated, and collaborative work by the people of the organization.

While this is true for most every role in an organization, it is uniquely true for top-level organizational leaders. David Gyertson—former president of Taylor University, Asbury University, and Regent University—argues that the university or seminary presidency is essentially a collaborative role: "No single person can possibly do everything a president is expected to do." He wants to know, "Is this person able to build a team?" Is the person able to "identify skill sets that are needed that complement him or her?"[2] For Gyertson, the capacity to build a team is essential for presidential effectiveness.

This call for collaboration reverberates throughout the executive leader comments included in the survey as well. Consider the many calls to prioritize team-oriented and collaborative work:

- "Assemble a trusted, competent core leadership team." (an executive director)
- "Develop strong teams and trust them. Then get out of the way." (a vice president)
- "Don't lead alone. Surround yourself with . . . team members . . . to support and advance the organization. Learn how to walk together with a diversity of people." (a lead pastor)
- "Surround [yourself] with an effective, complementary inner circle." (a president)
- "Focus on building healthy leadership teams. There's no better way to deepen the 'compounding' potential of effective leadership." (a provost and senior vice president)
- "Surround yourself with other leaders who are as gifted or more than you are in a variety of areas." (a senior pastor)
- "Surround yourself with others whose strengths compensate for your weaknesses and be generous in giving credit to whom it is due." (a provost)
- "Build a team that you love to be with. Productivity will follow. Team culture and unity trump strategy." (a vice president)
- "Surround yourself with complementary leaders." (a lead pastor)
- "Build trust with team members and over-communicate on everything with them." (a CEO)

As these leaders repeatedly note, the value of surrounding ourselves with gifted, competent, and complementary team members is high. While collaborative approaches to organizing and leading have been emphasized in recent decades, many see this commitment to team-based work as vital for thriving in the midst of today's complexities. Note one of the surveyed leaders on this point: "Shared leadership has long been seen as one of several paths or styles of leadership. What we are (painfully) learning is that shared leadership is the only way for any organization or leader to survive and thrive." Because organizations are not dependent on the work of an individual, genuine and authentic collaboration becomes essential for organizations to thrive.

Collaborating with Our Eyes Wide Open: Healthy Leaders Understand Both the Challenges and the Benefits of Teams

Challenges in Teamwork

The previous section demonstrated that collaboration and the use of teams in organizations are priorities for today's leaders. But team-based and collaborative work is not easy. This approach to organizing includes both hard work and many challenges. Some of these challenges relate to internal team dynamics (e.g., how people work together and get things done). Other challenges relate to dynamics that are external to teams.

In his book *Group Dynamics for Teams*, Daniel Levi points to one of these external challenges—the potential conflict between team development and the existing expectations or traditional management systems in organizations. When new models of working collaboratively in teams are introduced, Levi argues that this "teamwork requires a supportive organizational context to foster team growth and development."[3]

Reinforcing this challenge, Peter Northouse writes, "For teams to be successful, the organizational culture needs to support member involvement." He continues, "The traditional authority structure of many organizations does not support decision making at lower levels, and this can lead to the failure of many teams."[4] While teams may be functioning in a healthy manner in terms of their internal dynamics, broader organizational expectations and culture can be working against otherwise healthy teams.

Churches may offer one illustration of this. In recent decades, many church leaders have become persuaded by biblical arguments in support of plural eldership in the local church. (We'll spend time reflecting on some of these arguments later in this chapter.) When these convictions have translated into congregations moving to elder-based forms of church leadership, the congregational culture has not always been ready for the new model and structure. Consistent with Daniel Levi's point above, traditional congregational expectations that a single pastor will lead the congregation often conflict with the implementation of a plural form of eldership. New strategies can be helpful—and even biblically rooted—but when new strategies are not paired with a receptive organizational culture, even helpful strategies can struggle.

In addition to the external challenges related to implementing collaborative and team-based models, there are challenges embedded within teams.

- Teams can become *ingrown*: "Groupthink" can become an issue and can work against team innovation and creativity, particularly if team members assume a passive posture on the team and do not assert themselves.
- Teams can be *incompatible*: As noted in chapter 5, a lack of shared values and shared commitments between team members can limit or hinder productive teamwork.
- Teams can suffer from *indecision*: While teams benefit from multiple members providing different perspectives to inform decision making, team dynamics can contribute to confusion about who will act on the discussion in the absence of clarity about decision-making processes.
- Teams can suffer from *inaction*: The problem of inaction is similar to the problem of indecision. Teams can fall into inaction owing to lack of clarity regarding team members' responsibilities.
- Teams can be *inefficient*: Though teams have the potential to perform better than a group of individuals working separately, working within the context of teams generally takes longer and includes additional complexities associated with coordinated work.
- Teams can suffer from *inequity*: The dynamic of "social loafing" can be an issue with teams. While expectations about individual work responsibility tend to be clear, sometimes work responsibilities distributed across a team can translate into some members taking on more responsibility and others taking on less responsibility. When workloads are unevenly distributed, this can also add to relational strain among team members.
- Teams can be *inconsistent*: In association with many of the previous dynamics (indecision, inaction, etc.), teams that are not clearly planning and facilitating their collaborative work can become inconsistent—setting work aside between team meetings.
- Teams can be *inconsiderate*: I use *inconsiderate* in a broad way to note relational and interpersonal challenges that can be present in teams.

As people work closely together, there is the potential for increased substantive conflict or interpersonal conflict.

These challenges present very real and important considerations—particularly for leaders seeking to structure meaningful work for the people of their organizations. Leaders who care about organizational thriving and human flourishing need to engage these challenges in a proactive manner. The point is not to set aside teamwork altogether because of these challenges; rather, leaders need to proactively address these challenges so that organizations may experience the many benefits associated with teams—benefits noted in the following subsection.

One executive pastor at a large church adds some helpful perspective at this point. Noting (in the survey) the unique nature of the church's staff team—a team that emphasizes collaborative approaches and flat organizational structures—this pastor advocated viewing some of the associated complexities as good "tensions to be managed" rather than "problems to be solved." In other words, there are challenges and complexities associated with the collaborative nature of teamwork, but the answer is to lean into these challenges, believing that the work is worth the effort. He summarized the point thus: "True collaboration and plurality is well worth the tensions to be managed."

Benefits of Teamwork

This work of facing challenges becomes worth the effort when we have a better understanding of the benefits associated with teamwork and collaboration. Some of the benefits associated with teams include the potential for greater productivity, more effective use of resources, better decisions and problem-solving, better-quality products and services, and greater innovation and creativity.[5] In *Leadership in Christian Perspective*, Mark Strauss and I highlight the following benefits:

- Teams are best when the stakes are high, and quality is more important than speed.
- Teams provide a context for better ideas and increased insight.
- Teams provide increased courage to face challenges.
- Teams provide a natural presence of peer support.
- Teams provide a context for mentoring and training.[6]

The leaders who responded to the survey also highlight several benefits to teamwork and collaboration, but most of their comments group around three themes: (1) complementary gifts of team members, (2) improved decision making, and (3) increased support and health for the leader and members.

Complementary Gifts

We have been reflecting on the value of finding and working with team members who complement leaders and existing team members. This was a theme in chapter 5 and is an important theme of this chapter as well. One of the survey participants wrote, "It's important to purposefully build your team with a variety of skills and personalities that can all work together." A president encouraged leaders to surround themselves with a "complementary inner circle." And a provost wrote, "Lead confidently from your strengths, be realistic about your weaknesses, surround yourself with others whose strengths compensate for your weaknesses." All of these themes highlight the benefit of team complementarity. As multiple people and multiple gifts come together, this diversity of gifts and strengths raises the capacity of the community.

As we consider the benefit of teams providing a context for complementary gifts, I want to highlight an insight that one of the survey participants reported. In a specific caution for churches and other Christian institutions, one executive pastor remarked, "Biblical/theological competency does not automatically translate to organizational leadership competency." Though focusing on biblical or theological competence is important for an organization, it is important to recognize complementary needs in other areas. If you are a leader of a church or Christian institution largely because of your competence in the areas of theological reflection and biblical exegesis or preaching, be aware that this ability may or may not translate into competence in other important areas your organization needs. Make sure to surround yourself with biblically and theologically faithful people who also have competence in areas where you may be lacking.

Improved Decision Making

In addition to providing a context for complementary gifts, teams also provide a context for improved decision making. Consider the following observations from survey participants: "Build and use a leadership team *for decisions and execution*," and "the best leader isn't the smartest person in the room, but *the one who is willing to get the best answer from those in the room*" (emphasis added). Another leader commented on the challenge of decision fatigue in leadership. Working with others collaboratively in the context of teams helps leaders to share some (though not all) of the weight of decision making. As leaders gain insight and perspective from others, they are able to identify better pathways forward in the decision-making process. As we read in Proverbs, "Where there is no guidance, a people falls, *but in an abundance of counselors there is safety*" (11:14).

Increased Support and Health

Finally, teams provide a natural means for leaders to feel less isolated in their work and responsibilities. While it is true that "sometimes it's lonely at the top" (as one executive notes in the survey), intentional team building can offset this experience. This is a point that multiple executives called to our attention in the survey.

I quoted at least five references to this idea earlier in this chapter. In the survey, I counted over a dozen places where participants referred to the need for leaders to intentionally *surround* themselves with healthy, supportive, and competent team members. Here are a few additional comments from three surveyed pastors that speak to this point:

- "*Surround yourself with* a team. . . . Don't go it alone."
- "*Surround yourself with* emotionally and spiritually healthy [people]."
- "*Surround yourself with* a team of advisers."

One respondent summed it up well: "Leaders are only as good as the people they surround themselves with." This raises a question: Who are the people surrounding you? We need people who care about us, complement us, and challenge us. Developing robust teams in our organizations is not the only way this can happen; however, healthy teams do hold significant potential to provide a context for support and health—both for leaders and for team members.

Collaborating with Conviction: Healthy Leaders Understand Why Collaborative Work and Teams Matter

Earlier in the chapter I noted that our motivation to work collaboratively should not be driven merely by recent trends or preferences. We need more significant reasons to inform our practice. The benefits of teamwork identified in the previous section are helpful in this regard. However, I want to argue here that Scripture and theology also commend team-oriented and collaborative approaches. While the themes in this section have unique relevance for those leading within the context of a church, the biblical and theological insights here are powerful for shaping the convictions of Christians leading teams in any sector. Take time to consider how the nature of God as Trinity and key patterns for organizing observed in the New Testament might inform how you approach collaboration in your organizational context.

The Nature of God as Trinity

The Bible is robustly trinitarian. God exists as three persons—Father, Son, and Spirit; each person is fully God; and there is one God. While God's triune nature is seen in part in the Old Testament (e.g., Gen. 1:26; Ps. 110:1; Isa. 48:16; 63:10; Hosea 1:7), we see a more complete picture of God as Trinity revealed in the New Testament (e.g., Matt. 3:16–17; 28:19; 1 Cor. 12:4–6; 2 Cor. 13:14; Eph. 4:4–6; 1 Pet. 1:2; Jude 20–21).

One of the reasons the triune nature of God is so significant is that it displays the personal and relational aspects of God. Because people are made in the image of God, this personal and relational quality is central to our nature—we are naturally wired for community and relationship.

In their book *Teams That Thrive*, Ryan Hartwig and Warren Bird write, "Christianity is unique among major religions in presenting one God who eternally exists and functions as a divine team."[7] God's team-like nature has implications for leaders—and all people—when we consider our nature as those formed and fashioned in his image.

Consider Stan Ott's reflections for those considering teams in their organizations. Noting that "we need to look no further than the Trinity" to find an ultimate picture for a team, Ott reflects that "the members of the Trinity share a common vision for ministry. They enjoy fellowship in wonderfully loving relationships. And each member of the Trinity has a unique 'task' or role in the process known as salvation history."[8]

While God's relational and triune nature is ultimate—he is not merely a means to help us better understand leadership—it should not surprise us, as those created and sustained by him, that patterns of plurality and unity make their way into human experience. Wayne Grudem observes, "There are many activities that we carry out as human beings (in the labor force, in social organizations, in musical performances, and in athletic teams, for example) in which many distinct individuals contribute to a unity of purpose or activity. As we see in these activities a reflection of the wisdom of God in allowing us both unity and diversity, we can see a faint reflection of the glory of God in his triune existence."[9]

Collaboration is woven into the fabric of our nature and our world.

The nature of God as Trinity is the theological starting point that helps us understand the "why" behind teams and collaboration in the church and in other human organizations. As those made in his image, we are wired for relationship; we are wired for community; we are wired for collaboration. While the presence of sin means that collaborative endeavors include challenges, these approaches nevertheless image God himself. Collaboration is woven into the fabric of our nature and our world.

The Chief Leadership Role of Jesus with His People

The Bible regularly instructs and holds up examples of human leaders. However, the Bible also provides a clear and consistent message that God's leadership is ultimate—the leadership of humans is not.

Chapter 1 unpacked the nature of organizational leaders as *stewards*. In that discussion I noted that in God's economy, Christian leaders must begin by recognizing that they are stewarding people and things that do not ultimately belong to them. Our responsibilities and authority as leaders are delegated responsibilities and delegated authority.

Consider Peter's instruction to church leaders: "Shepherd *the flock of God* that is among you, exercising oversight, not under compulsion, but willingly, as God would have you; not for shameful gain, but eagerly; not domineering over those in your charge, but being examples to the flock. And when *the chief Shepherd* appears, you will receive the unfading crown of glory" (1 Pet. 5:2–4). Peter makes it clear that the church is not ultimately *their* church—it is the flock *of God*. And who is the chief leader in the church of God? It is *the Chief Shepherd*—Jesus Christ.

In contrast to the New Testament, where leadership often takes a plural expression (e.g., elders and deacons; see the related discussion in the next section), major leadership examples in the Old Testament were often solitary or "singular" in nature. These individual leaders in the Old Testament—with small moments of success and significant moments of failure—pointed to the ultimate singular leader to come in Jesus Christ.[10] In the New Testament church, leadership takes its shape and cues by looking back to the ultimate and chief shepherding that Jesus provides. I think this points to one of the primary reasons why we see a shift from Old Testament leadership structures, which often are singular and centralized, to New Testament leadership structures, which often are plural and decentralized. The Old Testament models point forward to the central leadership that Jesus the Messiah provides. The New Testament models, in recognition of the present and central leadership of Jesus, take on plural and distributed forms.

Of course, even in the central leadership that Jesus provides, we come full circle to the plurality and unity of the Trinity once again. While Jesus is the Chief Shepherd, he is the Chief Shepherd over his Father's flock, and human servants of God's flock are ultimately appointed (Acts 20:28) and empowered (Acts 6:2–6) by the Holy Spirit.

Distributed, Plural, and Collaborative Structures in the New Testament

So what are some of the patterns of distributed and plural forms of leadership in the New Testament? Let's consider a few of these before moving on to several practical considerations related to effective teamwork and collaboration.

Distributed Structure

First, because the gospel opens the way for God's people to have direct access to God in Christ, which stands in contrast to the priestly models of the Old Testament, the New Testament points to a distributed *priesthood of all believers*. Consider Peter's reflection on this: "But you are a chosen race, a royal priesthood, a holy nation, a people for his own possession, that you may proclaim the excellencies of him who called you out of darkness into his marvelous light" (1 Pet. 2:9). Rather than relying on a small handful of priestly leaders, God distributes priest-like status to all true believers. In the words of one theologian, "The New Testament allows for no special class of Christians who have greater access to God than others."[11] This theological commitment should help Christian leaders to see the value of partnering with others who broadly have access to God.

Plural Structure

Second, leadership structures in the New Testament church exhibit a remarkably consistent and unified pattern of plurality. This is true with Jesus's approach to leadership and with those of the leaders he personally appointed. Consider Alexander Strauch's observation: "Shared leadership should not be a new concept to a Bible-reading Christian. Shared leadership is rooted in the Old Testament institution of the elders of Israel and in Jesus' founding of the apostolate. It is a highly significant and often overlooked fact that our Lord did not appoint one man to lead His Church. He personally appointed and trained twelve men. *Jesus Christ gave the Church plurality of leadership.*"[12]

The first-century church consistently applied a model of plurality—in accordance with the example set by Jesus—in the leadership structures among apostles, pastors/elders, and deacons. Hartwig and Bird observe, "One consistent pattern across all of these roles and references is the use of plural: not one apostle, but a team of apostles; not one deacon or elder, but elders and deacons, always referred to in the plural. Some churches had multiple elders, while others had multiple elders and deacons."[13] Hartwig and Bird further point out that the "practice of multiple leadership—or teams—existed from the church's birth" and that "at each stage in the early church's structural development, when a new form of leadership shows up, it looks like a team."[14]

While Jesus Christ is the Chief (central and singular) Shepherd of his church, all other leaders find their place joyfully linking arms with peers in their collaborative service to Jesus Christ. These ideas are further reinforced with the New Testament metaphors used of the church.

Collaborative Structure

The metaphors that New Testament writers use when describing the church also reinforce the collaborative nature of the church. While there are many New Testament metaphors for the church that emphasize both plurality and unity (e.g., agricultural, architectural, familial, etc.), my colleague Tom Schreiner observes that the most famous metaphor for the church in Pauline writings is the "body of Christ" metaphor.[15]

As I noted in chapter 5, in multiple books of the New Testament, Paul paints a picture of the church as a body that functions correctly when each part does its work (e.g., Rom. 12; 1 Cor. 12; Eph. 4). As a body is one but has many unique parts, so Paul argues that individuals within a church bring their diverse gifts together for the growth of the whole. Reflecting on this metaphor, Hartwig and Bird write, "A functioning body, whether literally or metaphorically, needs to respect, honor and nurture all its members. And it needs to give what it can and receive what it must from each other member."[16]

This metaphor reminds us of the priority of collaboration in the communities of which we are a part. Grudem notes, "When we see different people doing many different things in the life of a church we ought to thank God that this allows us to glorify him by reflecting something of the unity and diversity of the Trinity."[17] Collaborating well helps us to better see and understand the heart and nature of our triune God.

A Clarification

One quick point of clarification: Having examined these biblical themes of distributed, plural, and collaborative structures in the New Testament, we might assume that this emphasis on distributed plurality means that there really is no place for leaders. In at least two areas, however, we see that plurality and collaboration do not eliminate distinction and authority.

First, while we see in the Trinity that each person is fully God and that there is one God, we nevertheless see the Son submitting to the Father's will in obedience in the face of the cross (e.g., Mark 14:36; Rom. 5:19; Phil. 2:8; Heb. 12:2). Second, while all true Christians represent a distributed priesthood of believers (1 Pet. 2:9) and thus should be treated as genuine partners in a common mission, leaders are nevertheless identified (see 1 Tim. 3; Titus 1), and they are expected to lead with the knowledge that they will give an account for this work (Heb. 13:17). Those in the church are called to honor, respect, and be subject to such leaders (see 1 Thess. 5:12–13; 1 Tim. 5:17; Heb. 13:7; 1 Pet. 5:5).

These examples remind us that, while the Bible regularly exhibits distributed, plural, and collaborative structures, leaders in established roles should exercise appropriate influence and authority as they model the shepherd-servant values of the kingdom.

The Nature of Effective Collaboration and Teamwork: Healthy Leaders Understand What Makes Teams Work within Organizations

Having explored the challenges, practical benefits, and biblical convictions surrounding teams and collaboration, we now turn to some practical matters that contribute to team flourishing in the context of thriving organizations. The items covered here could easily supply material for an entire book. I have enjoyed teaching courses on team-based leadership and shared leadership practices in multiple programs over the years, so I have a lot that I could share. I'll keep this discussion focused on some of the top observations and priorities.

Clarity for Teams

Effective team practice begins with clarity. The next chapter will spend more time on the importance of clarity in leader communication, but clarity is relevant for the work of teams as well. In order for teams to effectively carry out their work in organizations, there must be clarity. Leaders must provide clarity about the mission of the organization, clarity about how teams will operate, clarity about team member roles, and clarity about how team members and teams will coordinate their work. Consider what a few of the survey respondents wrote about this priority:

- "The majority of people in an organization desire clarity about their role and [the roles of] others, as well as the goals of the whole organization." (an executive pastor)

- "Clarity is kindness. This is especially true in the context of . . . overlapping (dotted line and areas of shared ownership) and complex organizational models." (an executive pastor)
- "Define your role and others' roles very clearly from the start." (an executive director)

Let's add clarity about four priorities for those leading organizations with teams: (1) right people and roles, (2) right preparation and training, (3) right processes and culture, and (4) right purpose.

Right People and Roles

In *Leadership in Christian Perspective*, Mark Strauss and I note that "finding the right people for your team is the first step, because leaders and followers are all in the work of the organization together. As team members thrive in their roles and meet their goals, so goes the success and flourishing of the leader and organization."[18] So what characterizes effective team members? While the items noted in the previous chapter—such as character, competence, and chemistry—are relevant here, it also is helpful to consider work from other sources concerning teams specifically. For instance, in his book *The Ideal Team Player*, Patrick Lencioni notes the necessity of having team members who are *humble*, *hungry* (driven), and *smart*.[19]

In another book, *When Teams Work Best*, Frank LaFasto and Carl Larson report findings from their research with six thousand team members and leaders. Among other questions, they asked participants, "What are the attributes or behaviors of individual team members, as seen by their fellow team members, that help the team succeed, or interfere with the team's success?" They landed on six team member attributes organized around the two areas of working knowledge factors and teamwork factors: (1) working knowledge factors: experience and problem-solving ability; (2) teamwork factors: openness, supportiveness, action orientation, and a positive personal style.[20]

In addition to finding the right people on the basis of these characteristics, it is also essential to get these people into the right roles on the team. In my survey, a CEO encouraged fellow executive leaders to "put people in roles that best utilize their gifts and abilities." And the director of an international airport argued for the importance of "having the right people in the right positions and giving them the proper amount of support and guidance to be successful."

All of these comments reinforce themes we've been engaging throughout this book. The people of our organizations matter—and getting the right people working collaboratively in the right roles is key for effective teams. A denominational president summed it up well: "Establish role clarity for everyone on your team (including yourself), then strengthen team alignment and goals through collaboration and respectful listening."

Right Preparation and Training

While there are many benefits associated with working together collaboratively, realizing these benefits often requires intentional learning and preparation on the part of leaders and team members. The African proverb I quoted earlier is helpful on this point: "If you want to go fast, go alone. If you want to go far, go together." While there are faster ways for individuals to work than in teams, learning what contributes to effective team-based and collaborative work helps us to secure better and longer-lasting outcomes.

Approaches to Team Learning

Teams that learn together improve together. A vice president noted in the survey the value of taking time to "teach your managers and leaders how to help teams work collaboratively and effectively toward organizational goals, [how to] nurture and maintain healthy relationships, and how to lead effectively up their organizational structure." Thankfully there are many pathways and approaches to team learning and team development in such areas. I highlight three of these pathways below.

Conversations about books. There are many helpful books on leadership and teamwork. I encourage you to find one that provides an opportunity for thoughtful reflection as a team. Whether you discuss the book chapter by chapter at regularly scheduled meetings or all at once during a single session, find resources with reflective questions (like those at the end of the chapters in this book) that can guide your team conversations. One of the survey participants highlighted a specific book: "Take your entire team through the book *Managing Leadership Anxiety* by Steve Cuss. They will all become more aware of their own forms of anxiety and how to manage it better. It will significantly improve team communication and decision making." Whether you choose this book or another, intentional learning through book conversations is a beneficial practice to nurture on your team.

Teams that learn together improve together.

Conferences and retreats. Conferences and retreats are a helpful approach for team learning as well. Find a conference or retreat with a focus that is right for your team and use this both for increasing the team's knowledge and for improving the team's health. While the topics covered at these events are part of the value, perhaps more important is having a shared and social learning opportunity that is outside the normal flow of work. These opportunities to periodically pull away facilitate learning and team bonding.

Consultants and coaching. While most teams possess the knowledge and skill needed internally to guide team learning experiences—don't sell yourself or your team short—inviting someone from outside the organization to facilitate unique learning opportunities has the added benefit of providing fresh perspective and insight for your team. Whether this takes the form of bringing in a speaker on a specific topic or bringing in someone to provide coaching about a specific team-building tool or instrument, outside voices and perspective provide a unique value to teams. I personally have appreciated interactive team-building experiences that used instruments such as CliftonStrengths (StrengthsFinder) and the Working Genius instruments.[21]

A Few Team Basics

As we consider the nature of teams, I want to draw some helpful distinctions.

Groups versus teams. There is a difference between teams and groups; not every group is a team. Organizations rightly use both groups and teams, but it is important to understand the core distinction. *Groups* tend to organize around individuals bringing together independent work in light of individual goals (consider a group project in a class where work is simply divided up and your grade is not dependent on what others do in the group). *Teams* tend to organize around individuals bringing together coordinated work in light of common goals (consider a team sport like football where eleven players need to coordinate their work on the field as they strive together toward a team goal of winning the game).

When people are considering whether a group or a team is better for a given situation, I encourage them to use the following guideline: *Groups* are better when the stakes are low and speed is essential. Because groups tend to focus more on the individuals, work tends to be faster because coordination is not as central to the process. Conversely, *teams* are better when the stakes are high and quality is more important than speed. While I tend to prioritize teams because of the prioritization of quality, it is important to know the organizational needs in a given area; there are times and places for both groups and teams.

Types of teams. Though I will not unpack types of teams in detail, I do want to acknowledge that organizations have different ways of seeing types of teams in organizations. In other words, not all team types are the same. Some authors categorize team types as problem-resolution teams, creative teams, and tactical teams.[22] In light of these categories, we can see that if a team exists to problem-solve, to create, or to identify and implement solutions, the purpose of the group should shape the dynamics of the group accordingly. Author Gary Yukl highlights another way of looking at team categories or types: functional operating teams, cross-functional teams, self-managed teams, self-defining teams, and top executive teams. This reflects another approach to seeing the function of different types of teams in the organization. Reflecting on such types of teams, Yukl observes that these "types of teams differ with regard to how much influence each has over the mission, the membership, and the continued existence of the team."[23] While we could spend more time reflecting on the unique nature of these team types, my purpose here is simply to acknowledge that there are different ways of categorizing team types and the goals of your organization should determine the types of teams that are selected for your organization.

Team Development

Another important observation is that a team's type can differ by season (i.e., it can shift from one type to another). One of the classic models of team development comes from Bruce Tuckman and describes the process by which teams go through forming, storming, norming, and performing.[24] As teams develop through diverse stages, they may mature in such a way that they adjust and grow.

For instance, a team may begin as an externally led team and over time may grow in its capacity, becoming a self-managed team (that decides *how* the work of the team is accomplished) or a self-led team (that decides both *what* the team should focus on and *how* the work of the team is accomplished). Many organizational leaders seek to help teams mature and grow in ways that improve the teams' capacities to deliver outcomes that are aligned with the organization's mission in a highly autonomous manner. This is why the authors of *Team Work and Group Dynamics* encourage leaders to help their teams mature through empowering leadership.[25] This approach to leadership, they argue, helps team members move toward greater ownership of their work as a team develops from the start-up phase into a well-trained, mature team.

Understanding Board Teams

One president noted in the survey the importance of "building a strong board of directors." Organizational boards are another vital team or group in thriving organizations. Although boards and governing structures look different in different sectors, when organizations have a board, it is essential that these groups function in a healthy manner. Another executive director wrote, "Have a good board. Understand the role of a board and its relationship with the executive director." A pastor noted the importance of churches "aligning [their] staff and board."

It would be difficult to overstate the importance of boards faithfully executing their stewardship responsibilities. At a minimum, boards are responsible for ensuring that the organization is staying true to its organizational ends—avoiding the ever-present danger of mission drift—and that they are hiring, encouraging, and holding accountable the point leader (or leaders) of the organization, whether this be a president, a CEO, an executive director, or another leader or group of leaders. It is imperative that organizational leaders understand the importance of the board's role in their organization and nurture a healthy, productive, and aligned partnership as they work with the board to serve the organizational mission.

For more on boards, particularly those in the nonprofit context, I recommend that readers explore *The Policy Governance Model and the Role of the Board Member* by John and Miriam Carver. The Carver model emphasizes the organizational ends statement, board process policies, board-executive linkage policies, and executive limitation policies.

Right Processes and Culture

In addition to getting the right people in the right roles and facilitating the right preparation and training, leaders must also ensure that teams have the right processes and culture in place to support their work.

Consider the diverse factors Carl Larson and Frank LaFasto identify as related to effective team practice. According to their research, effective teams need (1) a clear, elevating goal; (2) results-driven structures; (3) competent team members; (4) unified commitment; (5) a collaborative climate; (6) standards of excellence; (7) external support and recognition; and (8) principled leadership.[26] While there is much that could be unpacked in these factors, most of them have a face validity to them—we can quickly understand why these themes are important. To complement these factors, I'd like to highlight some additional insights that survey participants noted related to effective team processes and culture.

Team Agreements and Healthy Team Culture

As teams are launched or as members are added to teams, it is helpful to have some basic principles that will guide the team's culture and priorities. One CEO advised leaders to "build relationships and understand your teammates, *build team agreements* on how you will address/include diverse perspectives as well as develop team values to give all safe ways to address conflict/decision making/idea sharing" (emphasis added). This focus on team agreements and team values is not about replacing organizational values. Rather, it is about defining how teams that are aligned with broader organizational values will approach their work together.

As an example of this, one church has adopted the following covenant language to guide its staff team: "As staff, we commit to the core values of unity, honor and excellence, and to creating a culture that glorifies God, expresses integrity to each other, and allows us to lead together with joy." The team's covenant highlights the commitments and biblical values that will support the team members' work together. For instance, under the core value of *unity*, the agreement highlights their commitment to "live and work in unity with God and one another" by (1) enjoying leading together (Rom. 15:13), (2) co-laboring with one another (Rom. 15:5–6; Eph. 4:11–13), and (3) working through disagreements efficiently and agreeably (Matt. 18:15–20; 5:23–24; Col. 3:13; James 1:5; 1 Cor. 1:10).

Such agreements are designed to create a context where healthy team culture may emerge. This desire for healthy team culture points us back to the principles of grace and accountability discussed earlier in the book. Those working on teams need to understand that their work, and the quality of their work, matters. They also need room to take chances within a culture of grace. In the survey one university president expressed the need to hold these themes in appropriate tension, noting the importance of both "a high bar for excellence and for 'grace.' People need to feel that it is safe to take chances . . . in your organization." Another nonprofit president identified the importance of providing "the space and grace for mistakes."

Effective and Productive Meetings

Though I will not spend a lot of time on the nitty-gritty of meetings, multiple leaders used the survey to highlight the importance of leading team meetings well. Here are some of their targeted encouragements:

- "Have great weekly meetings by having staff write out answers to consistent questions ahead of time. So reporting is clear, concise, and accountable. Saves the leader a lot of time. Allows for more personal touches." (a pastor)
- "Listen to those you lead and encourage full expression in team meetings. Help the team to process divergent viewpoints emerging from the

team that will help the team shape a way forward that is wiser and more complete than the vision of any one individual." (a pastor)

- "A proper meeting structure is the best way to manage your leadership teams. Meeting types: (1) daily 10-minute huddle, (2) weekly leadership team meeting [of] 60–90 minutes, (3) monthly financial accountability and Rock [big goals] accountability meeting, (4) quarterly Rock-setting and big issue–solving meeting, (5) annual planning meeting." (a president)

For additional insights on meetings done well, see Patrick Lencioni's *Death by Meeting*.[27]

Leader Priorities

Leaders play a vital role in the teams they lead. Frank LaFasto and Carl Larson asked the following question in their research on teams: "What are the behaviors of team leaders, as seen by members of the team, that help lead the team to success or failure?" Participants in that study highlighted five priorities. They noted that effective leaders (1) focus on the goal, (2) ensure a collaborative climate, (3) build confidence, (4) demonstrate sufficient technical know-how, and (5) set priorities.[28] Following are a few additional insights noted by executive leaders.

Leaders both praise and positively challenge. Leaders celebrate their team members and team member contributions, but they also stir up healthy dialogue by raising important issues and identifying needed solutions. Good dialogue should allow for different perspectives to be heard and considered. Team leaders should encourage team members: "Stay humble and celebrate others actively"; "accept blame and share credit." Team leaders should also stimulate debate and dialogue among team members: "Ask questions"; be a leader "who is willing to get the best answer from those in the room." When a healthy team culture has been nurtured, encouragement and positive reinforcement collectively work together to bring out the best in team members.

Leaders model vulnerability and trust. Consider a few survey responses on this point. One CEO wrote, "Be wisely transparent, especially when it is humbling, to build trust with team members." A vice president noted, "Humility and authenticity are of utmost importance to truly achieve buy-in and followers that stick together." And another CEO wrote, "Your root issue is always a Trust issue." Vulnerability and trust go hand in hand. Jimmy Mellado, president and CEO of Compassion International, affirms that a willingness to be open and vulnerable creates a deeper connection with team members and helps to build trust and speed up the accomplishment of team goals.[29]

Leaders facilitate healthy conflict management. Healthy teams do not avoid hard conversations. In the midst of hard conversations, healthy teams work to nurture a peaceful and productive culture. Healthy teams must be willing to navigate both substantive and interpersonal conflict productively. Helping us understand conflict management from a Christian perspective, Ken Sande, author of *The Peacemaker*, notes that rather than pursuing escape or attack responses, healthy conflict management should look to peacemaking responses. Sande writes, "Peacemakers are people who breathe grace. They draw continually on the goodness and power of Jesus Christ, and then they bring his love, mercy, forgiveness, strength, and wisdom to the conflicts of daily life."[30] Leaders and team members understand that they cannot control the responses of other people, but they can lean into the wisdom of Paul: "If possible, so far as it depends on you, live peaceably with all" (Rom. 12:18).

Healthy teams must be willing to navigate both substantive and interpersonal conflict productively.

Engaging in conflict and accountability conversations with teams requires the calm and courageous presence discussed in chapter 4. Leaders and team members need mutual trust and a non-anxious presence to lean into this important work. One of the lead pastors who participated in the survey encouraged leaders to "address conflict quickly and directly." While a leader must always be ready and willing to address conflict, a CEO observed that "you can't solve every problem, and especially in 24 hours." Sometimes one day's pressing concerns sort themselves out over time. In other words, we should not be conflict-avoidant, but we also need to provide space for people and processes to work through concerns. This is part of the process of leaders trusting and entrusting, though they must always be willing to engage directly when direct engagement is needed.

Right Purpose

Finally, as we consider what makes teams work *in organizations*, I conclude with what might be the most significant reflection: teams and team members must be aligned with organizational priorities and commitments. While there are many factors that contribute to healthy teams, without this final point, we will not have healthy teams working collaboratively within the organizational environment. For teams to be productive and healthy in organizations, team members and teams must be *aligned*. One president and CEO put it this way in the survey: "Alignment is far more important than agreement. Alignment is the leader's work of art!"

Early in an organization's life cycle, the team may in fact be the organization. As organizations grow, their expansion inevitably leads to needed division of labor and the multiplication of team efforts. As the number of teams in an organization grows, the complexity of leading this network of teams also grows. Here's the crux of my argument: among several priorities, the alignment of teams around broader organizational commitments must be a top-level concern for organizational leaders. As the number of teams grows, and as the complexity of an organization grows, alignment becomes even more critical for organizational health and success.

Teams can quickly proliferate in large organizations. The point is not simply to have more teams doing more work. The point is to have *aligned* teams and *aligned* work. This alignment is primarily about purpose and mission. Note these reflections from a university president: "Keep your mission clear and be singularly focused as you navigate complex and nuanced challenges and decisions. Make sure everyone not only knows the mission but [also knows] how committed the institution and the leadership are to it." The alignment I'm referring to is this alignment of purpose, mission, values, and vision. Team practice must be aligned with organizational values and organizational mission. With team members individually and teams collectively, this commitment to and alignment with organizational priorities is essential.

Notice the remarkably unified voices on this issue of alignment from so many of the leaders who responded to the survey:

- "Help teams work collaboratively and effectively toward organizational goals." (a vice president)
- "Unifying these groups around a collective purpose is essential." (a superintendent)
- "It is my responsibility to establish a mission-centric culture . . . and explore missional alignment [with incoming team members]." (a president)
- "Find opportunities to connect every person's position in the building with the big whys of the work—how every person has a role in the mission of the organization." (a principal)
- "Shepherd high-initiative leaders toward mission and value alignment to stay on course and make wise, strategic decisions." (an executive vice president)
- "Meet on a regular basis in order to have the opportunity to keep one another informed of what's going on in their respective areas." (a president)

- "Learn to 'translate the cause' well. . . . [Make] sure people understand the WHY behind their positions . . . so that they have ownership over the difference they're making for the whole organization." (an executive pastor)

This focus on alignment was a key emphasis in chapter 1 as well. I noted there that, as leaders align people and resources behind a common vision of a preferred future, these people and resources may be faithfully and effectively deployed in fulfillment of the organization's mission. So it is with effective teams in the organizational context as well. Without significant alignment of team endeavors, organizations run the risk of having mini kingdoms—isolated teams in the organization—building empires that are at odds with broader organizational priorities. One of the most important jobs of any senior leader is to ensure that individual teams with unique and important responsibilities are all working toward common and aligned mission fulfillment.

The point is not just to have individual teams succeed. The point is to have teams collectively working toward the success and fulfillment of the broader organizational mission in an aligned manner. Once again, "Alignment is far more important than agreement. Alignment is the leader's work of art!"

Recommendations and Reflection

This chapter focused on the priority of collaboration in thriving organizations and considered strategies for helping the teams of our organizations flourish in a healthy and aligned manner. Understanding that teamwork and collaboration have associated challenges and benefits, we explored biblical and theological convictions that support collaborative work. In the final section, we explored how aligned team members and teams may be trained and led in such a way that these teams contribute to thriving organizations.

Take a moment to consider collaboration and team alignment in the organizational context. The following questions will help you to reflect on how you are approaching and prioritizing healthy teamwork and collaboration in your leadership and organization.

Collaborating with our eyes wide open: Healthy leaders understand both the challenges and the benefits of teams.

- One challenge to successful teams is the wider organizational culture. Does your organizational culture support team structures and team member involvement?
- We examined several other team challenges (e.g., groupthink, social loafing, indecision, inaction). What are the top one or two challenges you have experienced when working on or with teams?

- "Teams are best when the stakes are high, and quality is more important than speed": Do you agree with this statement? Why or why not?
- Other benefits of teams include the complementary gifts of members, improved decision making, and increased support and health. Which of these benefits have you seen or experienced in teams?

Collaborating with conviction: Healthy leaders understand why collaborative work and teams matter.

- How does the triune nature of God relate to and inform human collaborative and team-oriented endeavors?
- Why is it important to see God's leadership, rather than the leadership of humans, as ultimate? How does this shape your view of leaders as stewards of the people and teams they lead?
- The apostle Peter identifies true believers as "a royal priesthood" (1 Pet. 2:9). How does this New Testament view of the priesthood of believers shape the way we should work together under the Chief Shepherd leadership of Jesus?
- Leadership structures in the New Testament church exhibit a remarkably consistent and unified pattern of plurality (many leaders rather than one leader). How does this shape the way you look at the value of shared and collaborative leadership?

The nature of effective collaboration and teamwork: Healthy leaders understand what makes teams work within organizations.

- Many leaders emphasize the priority of getting the right people in the right roles. Why is this essential for healthy and aligned teams?
- Recommendations for approaching team learning include book discussions, conferences and retreats, consultants and coaching. Have you experienced any of these team-building methods? Which were the most helpful for your team's growth and development?
- Team agreements can help facilitate healthy team culture. If your team has not developed a set of guidelines to shape your work together, which values and commitments would you like to see included in such an agreement?
- "Alignment is far more important than agreement": Do you agree with this statement? Why is alignment vital for team and organizational thriving? How can the teams in your organization move toward greater alignment?

PART 4

Leadership Priorities for Thriving Organizations

The first responsibility of a leader is to define reality. The last is to say thank you. In between the two, the leader must become a servant.

—Max De Pree, *Leadership Is an Art*

Part 2 focused on how healthy organizational leadership begins with healthy leaders. Based on the character and commitments of healthy organizational leaders, Part 3 explored the importance of the people and teams that compose organizations. This emphasis on people includes a focus on the care and cultivation of team members and the priority of engaging organizational mission through aligned and collaborative work.

Part 4 will focus on four priorities for faithfully and effectively leading organizations: *leadership communication*, *organizational culture*, *crisis leadership*, and *change leadership*. While we could consider many other areas of importance, the four addressed here hold special significance for leaders seeking to faithfully and effectively navigate the practice of organizational leadership. The rapidly changing landscape within which organizational leaders must lead today can feel like a daunting environment. But, as complex and daunting as this reality may be, leaders also have the opportunity and privilege to nurture healthy and thriving organizational environments within which people may flourish and missions may be fulfilled. Communicating well, nurturing organizational culture, leading effectively during crisis, and navigating change are four priorities for organizational thriving in these unique and complex days.

SEVEN

Communication, Clarity, and Conviction in the Thriving Organization

Communication is an essential part of leadership. Although you can be an effective communicator without being an effective leader, it doesn't work the other way around. Effective leaders are *by necessity* effective communicators.[1]

The same can be said of effective and thriving organizations—such organizations do not exist without prioritizing meaningful communication. Consider the following observation: "Communication is the lifeblood of an organization; if we could somehow remove communication flows from an organization, we would not have an organization. Communication pervades all activities in an organization."[2]

One executive leader wrote in the survey, "Effective communication is always a mission-critical issue, both internally as well as externally." Although effective communication is critical, it's also difficult and very complex. An executive pastor of a large, multisite church put it this way: "Communication is incredibly complex as we get further away from each other geographically, add new staff, make changes, and attempt to keep our staff and church aligned."

Other respondents echoed these observations. As noted in chapter 1, communication is one of the top challenges noted by executive leaders in the area of organizational dynamics (see table 1.2). Communication issues noted by participants include technological complexities, the importance of communicating mission and vision clearly, diverse follower communication styles, communication within hybrid and dispersed teams, and the challenge of staying consistent with organizational messaging.

Even though the work of communication is difficult, getting communication right is a vital dynamic in organizations. Communication is key to organizational effectiveness. Research on the topic has demonstrated a link between effective organizational communication and a variety of variables, including "managerial effectiveness, the integration of work units across organizational levels, characteristics of effective supervision, job and communication satisfaction, innovation, adaptability, creativity, and overall organizational effectiveness."[3] If organizational leaders want to see their organizations thriving in areas such as these, they must prioritize effective leadership and organizational communication.

The Nature of God as Communicator: Healthy Christian Leaders Look to God for His Example and Priorities in Communication

Throughout this book, we have been reflecting on how the nature of God and his work in this world shapes our view of people and the work of leadership. As those made in God's image, we should never be surprised when we see how some of his attributes are reflected—even in faint ways—through our lives and work. The nature of human communication provides an example of this.

Jonathan Edwards put it this way: "The great and universal end of God's creating the world was to communicate himself. God is a communicative being."[4] In fact, we are introduced to God's communicative nature in the very first pages of Scripture. As God creates and fills the realms of creation over the six days outlined in Genesis 1, each day begins with the words "God said." Of this work of creation, one commentary notes, "God accomplishes all his work by speaking. 'God said . . .' and everything happened. This lets us know that God's power is more than sufficient to create and maintain creation."[5] Psalm 33:6 likewise affirms the speaking nature of God's work in creation: "By the word of the Lord the heavens were made, and by the breath of his mouth all their host."

From God's work in creation to his ongoing work of sustaining and upholding all things "by the word of his power" (Heb. 1:3), we see God's communicative nature on display throughout the Bible. Tom Schreiner writes, "The one true God is a speaking God, one who communicates with his people and reveals his will and his ways to them."[6] Although humans reflect the spoken and communicative nature of God imperfectly, as those made in God's image, people and leaders likewise approach many dimensions of their lives and leadership through communication.

Looking at the central role that communication plays for the work of leaders, Albert Mohler asks, "So what do leaders actually *do*? The answer to that question is an ever-expanding list of tasks and responsibilities, but one central duty stands out above all others—the leader communicates. . . . Leadership doesn't happen until communication happens."[7] This central job of the leader both mirrors and is different from God's communicative leadership.

Let's turn to creation once again. The communicative work of God in creation was what theologians term *ex nihilo*—out of nothing. God spoke, and nothing became something. To state the obvious, human leaders do not share this power to make something physical out of nothing. But, while leaders are not able to communicate things into existence in the *ex nihilo* sense, they are required to make the intangible tangible.

Concerning this point of making the intangible tangible, James Kouzes and Barry Posner write, "Because visions exist in the future, leaders have to get others in the present to imagine what the future will look like, feel like, sound like, even smell like. . . . Your vision—an intangible—must be made tangible."[8] While leaders do not create with their words in the same way that God creates, leaders nevertheless are responsible for inspiring and motivating the people they work with through effective, compelling, and clear communication. Though done imperfectly by humans, this part of the leader's work finds an ultimate reference point in the nature of God.

Communicating Clearly and with Conviction

The leadership work of providing effective and compelling communication begins with clarity. David Horsager argues that "people trust the clear and distrust the ambiguous."[9] Leaders must give special attention to clarity in their communication work. This focus on clear communication was a consistent theme in the executive leaders' survey comments:

- "Clarify and communicate vision culture for all levels of the organization." (a lead pastor)
- "The larger the scope you lead, the clearer and simpler your communication must be." (an executive vice president)
- "'Clarity is kindness. Clarity is king.' At this particular moment in time, I find myself returning again and again to the issue of clarity—for myself, my team, and our church." (a lead pastor)

- "Organizational clarity and unity is a surer foundation than having all the money in the world." (an executive director)
- "Define your role and others' roles very clearly from the start!" (an executive director)
- "Complexity and risk increase as growth happens. It's the remit of leadership to make sense of [and to communicate] the intersection of those spaces." (a CEO)
- "Lack of clarity is toxic to the health and progress of any organization." (an executive pastor)

The remainder of this section will examine how clarity in communication is central to many of the leadership priorities considered in this book: (1) clarity about organizational culture and commitments, (2) clarity for people and teams, (3) clarity in moments of crisis, and (4) clarity about long-term vision and change.

Healthy Leaders Communicate Clearly about Organizational Culture and Commitments

Organizational leaders must communicate clearly about the organization's culture and commitments. In the survey, one CEO argued that "assuring clarity of vision . . . [and] providing clarity of direction and assurance of hope during times of uncertainty, volatility and turbulence" is a priority in his corporate leadership. Another respondent, a president, charged organizational leaders to "Keep your mission clear. . . . Make sure everyone not only knows the mission but how committed the institution and the leadership are to it."

While communicating clearly about the organization's culture and mission should be a value for all team members, this responsibility is central to the work of senior leaders. Reflecting on this stewardship responsibility for senior leaders, Gordon Smith writes, "Presidents are uniquely positioned to and responsible to foster good conversation about mission and calling." He continues, "They are positioned to equip the trustees both to see and to understand the mission and know what it will take to be trustees of that mission. And they are positioned to communicate that mission to . . . external constituencies and to potential employees and volunteers."[10]

Culture is not only about top organizational priorities, such as mission, but also about setting the tone for how work will be done and what values will guide the work. In the survey, one director expressed a frustration related to organizations that at times "seem to make up their own rules and justify everything by saying they are free to do things different." Such environments create a lack of consistency and clarity that erodes healthy cultural norms in organizations.

Holding out another vision for organizational work cultures, Rob Goffee and Gareth Jones write, "The ideal company is not a company without rules. It is a company with *clear* rules that make sense to the people who follow them."[11] Organizational leaders must ensure that communication about the organization's mission and the organization's approach to work is clear, consistent, and compelling for team members.

Healthy Leaders Communicate Clearly for Their People and Teams

Clarity and Alignment for Team Members

Clarity about organizational culture provides clarity for people and translates into team alignment. John Baldoni, author of *Great Communication Secrets of Great Leaders*, observes that effective "leadership communications emerge from organizational culture and values as well as from the values of the leader. Their ultimate aim is to build, or continue to build, a relationship between leader and follower."[12] When leaders provide clarity to organizational members about who they are, what they're about, and how they approach their work together, this provides a context within which people can flourish. One executive pastor noted in the survey, "Organizational clarity is kindness."

Another executive pastor, who serves in a church with around forty thousand attendees and four hundred staff, reflected on the importance, complexity, and challenges involved with this work of leadership communication: "My main role is to keep 11 campus pastors going the same direction, which will steer the 12–15 people that they [each] oversee, which will impact the direction of each campus." He continued, "Communication is incredibly complex. . . . Dealing with communication challenges is a daily part of leadership." While it is complex work, clarity in communication nevertheless is vital and helps the people of an organization flourish.

According to Ken Blanchard and his colleagues, "If you can teach people your leadership point of view, they will not only have the benefit of understanding where you're coming from, but they'll also be clear on what you expect from them and what they can expect from you."[13] For Patrick Lencioni, this leadership point of view should include clear answers to questions like these: (1) Why do we exist? (2) How do we behave? (3) What do we do? (4) How will we succeed? (5) What is most important right now? (6) Who must do what?[14] Team members thrive with clear and compelling answers to such questions.

Reinforcing the importance of clarity among team members, one of the survey participants noted, "People who thrive in ambiguity are typically in the minority, and the majority of people in an organization desire clarity about their role and others' roles, as well as the goals of the whole organization and progress toward them." Working toward this type of clarity takes time, consistency, and intentionality—often it requires overcommunication and providing redundant pathways to information. Emphasizing the need for overcommunication and multiple pathways in this work, John Baldoni writes, "Communicating the leadership message over and over again in many different circumstances lets employees come to a better understanding of what the leader wants, what the organization needs, and how they fit into the picture. In time, leader and followers form a solidarity that is rooted in mutual respect. When that occurs, leader and followers can pursue organizational goals united in purpose and bonded in mutual trust."[15]

Clarity and Trust for Team Members

As noted above, "People trust the clear and distrust the ambiguous."[16] But trust is not only about clarity of message; it is also about the clarity, consistency, and convictions of the communicator. One business book emphasizes this with its title: *You've Got to Be Believed to Be Heard*.[17] I agree. But this belief has to be rooted in deep conviction on the part of leaders—not just techniques that make one appear believable.

Consider Albert Mohler's reflections on this point: "If a leader has to look for a message, his leadership is doomed. Leaders communicate because they cannot *not* communicate, and their message flows out of them as naturally as a geyser releases its energy. This is the essence of convictional leadership. The message flows out of your deepest convictions and most passionately held beliefs."[18] We spent time reflecting on a similar point in chapter 1. A leader's sense of purpose contributes to faithful and effective leadership and is a significant predictor of higher levels of leadership effectiveness and follower job satisfaction, organizational commitment, and sense of person organization fit.[19] Motivated not just by a broader organizational purpose but by deep and abiding conviction, leaders of purpose and conviction inspire clarity and trust in the leader-follower relationship.

Trust is not only about clarity of message; it is also about the clarity, consistency, and convictions of the communicator.

Trust is also inspired by leaders who demonstrate (1) transparency, (2) honesty, (3) a willingness to listen, and (4) responsiveness. As noted in the previous chapter, in the survey a CEO pointed out the connection between *transparency* and trust, calling organizational leaders to "be wisely transparent, especially when it is humbling, to build trust with team members." Alongside transparency, multiple authors point to the priority of *open* and *honest* communication. Susan Wheelan writes, "High performance teams have an open communication structure that allows all members to participate. Individuals are listened to," and this "increases productivity because all ideas and suggestions get heard."[20]

Frank LaFasto and Carl Larson similarly emphasize open and honest communication as a key factor that distinguishes teams that are good at problem-solving.[21] This type of honest communication is vital because, in its absence, people tend to fill in the blanks with competing narratives. Pat Zigarmi and Judd Hoekstra write, "In the absence of honest, passionate, and empathetic communication, people create their own information . . . and rumors begin to serve as facts."[22]

In addition to transparency and honesty, a willingness to listen and an orientation toward responsiveness are essential in organizational communication. The Bible provides significant wisdom for leaders (and people generally) about *listening*: "If one gives an answer before he hears, it is his folly and shame" (Prov. 18:13). "Know this, my beloved brothers: let every person be *quick to hear*, slow to speak, slow to anger" (James 1:19). While leaders are often called on to speak, wise leaders speak on the basis of thoughtful and proactive listening. Consider many of the survey comments on this point:

- "Listen more than speak. We're not an overly hierarchical organization, but the default for most leaders at all levels is to defer, at least in terms of communications, to the people placed higher in the structure. That can result in more talking than listening, and you can't know what's going on in your church if you're not observing and listening." (an executive pastor)
- "Humility and listening—you don't know everything." (a director)
- "Listen far more than you talk." (a COO)
- "Work to be a good listener." (a vice president)
- "Always put others first—actively listen, be empathetic, put yourself in their shoes." (a CEO)
- "Take the time to make sure the other person . . . truly understands what is being communicated." (an executive pastor)
- "Leaders in general—leading through listening." (a president)

In addition to listening, leader *responsiveness* is also part of building trust in organizational communication. One director of operations put it this way: "Keep your word, be consistent, respond to communications." In organizations with healthy communication practices, executive leaders model responsiveness and there is a system in place that provides a conduit for leaders to receive feedback from their people.

Noting several habits of healthy workplaces, Gordon Smith highlights the priority of organizational mechanisms for communication and feedback: "There is opportunity for each employee to speak to and be heard on working conditions, on what is needed, from their vantage point, to maximize institutional effectiveness." He continues, "Healthy institutions have mechanisms in place for employee communication and feedback."[23] As organizational leaders, we want to create pathways that enable us to hear from our people and respond to them. Without such pathways in place, it is easy to lose perspective on how the people of our organization view the organization and their work within it.

Clarity and Inspiration for Team Members

Because trust is built through clarity, this principle provides a foundation for leading others through inspiration and intrinsic motivation. In the survey, a CEO encouraged leaders to "practice a collaborative servant leadership approach" that provides the basis for leaders to "cast vision, persuade, and not dictate direction." This resonates with something a COO wrote: "Focus less on control and more on inspiration that appeals to emotion."

Our people need this work of inspiration and motivation in both calm and challenging times. Mark McCloskey writes, "Motivating . . . is the work of supporting and sustaining personal and organizational momentum, especially in difficult circumstances." He continues, "The leadership challenge is to impart hope, instill a spirit of optimistic resolution, and infuse individuals, teams and entire organizations with the strength to continue in the face of difficulty."[24] With this, we turn to the role of clear communication during crises.

Healthy Leaders Communicate Clearly in Moments of Crisis

If they learned nothing else in the early 2020s, organizational executives learned much about leading during a crisis. While the pandemic and associated economic realities presented a massive crisis for many organizations, crises can take many forms—we'll explore more of these in chapter 9. But, regardless of the specific crisis that an organization needs to navigate, one of the keys to effective leadership during a crisis is *effective leadership communication*. Let's explore a few communication priorities for those leading an organization through a time of crisis.

Regular and Consistent Crisis Communication

The first communication priority in times of crisis is regular and consistent communication from leaders. Drawing on the example of natural disasters, Margaret Wheatley provides helpful insights on this point: "In a disaster or crisis, the continuous flow of information gives people the capacity to respond intelligently as they seek to rescue and save people and property."[25] At times, this "continuous flow of information" may include only partial information. But when times are confusing and difficult, some information is better than no information. People need to hear from their leaders.

Margaret Wheatley continues, "People deal far better with uncertainty and stress when they know what's going on, even if the information is incomplete and only temporarily correct. . . . The greater the crisis, the more we need to know. The more affected we are by the situation, the more information we need."[26] This notion of "incomplete and only *temporarily* correct" information is difficult for some personalities. But organizational leaders are required to push past this difficulty and assume some risks in their service to others. While leaders cannot speak with complete confidence about every item requiring communication in crisis situations, they nevertheless need to confidently reassure people in the community with what they do know at the time—even if this information is limited. Uncertainty and incomplete information cannot be used as excuses to put people off when they need to hear from their leaders. Leaders should not say more than they are able, but they do need to share openly and honestly about what people need to hear.

In times of crisis, communicate what you can, when you can, and as often as you can.

I still remember where I was on 9/11 when I heard about the attacks on the United States. I felt the need for perspective. I felt the need to be watching a news station or listening to a radio in order to better understand the magnitude of what had taken place. This desire for perspective—a desire that could be only partially satisfied at the time—helped to make sense of the threat my country was facing. Whether the crisis is massive or modest, the people in the organizations we lead likewise need perspective and information to help them make sense of the crisis moment. In times of crisis, communicate what you can, when you can, and as often as you can.

Values-Based Communication and Direct Crisis Communication

Along with regular and consistent communication, leaders need to provide values-based communication and direct communication during crises. Regarding *values-based communication*, leading during a crisis requires leaders to make the culture of the organization clear. Culture is not just for calm moments in the life of the organization; it is also for times of turbulence and crisis.

Reflecting on leadership in the congregational setting, Robert Creech notes the following: "During a crisis, the leader will be careful to connect the actions and responses of the congregation to the vision and values that have become familiar to them." Do you hear that important observation? Organizational action, especially during a crisis, needs to be rooted in the vision and values of the organization. Creech continues, "The message is clear: 'This is how a church with this vision and these values responds to an event like this.'"[27] Such wisdom is valuable for churches, schools, businesses, and nonprofits alike.

While we can never anticipate every dimension of every potential crisis (e.g., how many organizational leaders had a global pandemic on their minds in 2019?), we can run to what we *do* know. We do know what our vision is. We do know what our values are. The leadership responsibility in moments of crisis is to apply the known (vision and values) to the unknown or partially known situation brought about through crisis. According to one CEO who responded to the survey, this is about "providing clarity of direction and assurance of hope during times of uncertainty, volatility and turbulence."

Alongside values-based communication, leaders need to provide *directness*—sometimes even brutal honesty—in moments of crisis. We'll examine this theme further in chapter 9, but Winston Churchill is a helpful model on this point. Reflecting on Churchill's example of crisis communication, John Baldoni notes the importance of brutal honesty. Churchill provided communication that was direct, and he was straight with people. While maintaining a vision of a hopeful future, he did not hide the clear and present dangers that faced the British Empire in the dark days of 1940.[28] In fact, this brutal honesty was just the message that people needed to marshal the moral courage of their nation to face the evil confronting the world.

Planned or Anticipated Crisis Communication

As noted above, we can never anticipate every dimension of every potential crisis. However, this does not mean that leaders and organizations should not do their due diligence to anticipate as many potential crises and scenarios as possible. The larger the organization, the more this type of scenario planning becomes critical to the long-term viability of the organization and its mission.

Reflecting on this priority, Margaret Wheatley writes, "As people engage in processes such as scenario building or disaster simulations, they feel more capable to deal with uncertainty." To some, the effort put into planning for seemingly unlikely possibilities feels like lost time and resources. But such work is critical for operational engagement when the scenarios do arise. Military leaders understand this dynamic, but organizational leaders do not always take potential threats seriously. Noting other benefits of this scenario-building and disaster-simulation work, Wheatley continues: "Individual and collective intelligence increase dramatically, as people become better-informed big-picture thinkers. And trusting relationships develop that make it possible to call on one another when chaos strikes."[29]

Multiple Pathways for and Perspectives on Crisis Communication

Finally, crisis communication takes advantage of multiple pathways and multiple perspectives. Katie Allred comments on the importance of using *pathways* such as social media in addition to more traditional forms of organizational communication: "Social media is virtually essential these days, but it is especially so in crisis communication." Allred also speaks to the value of seeking diverse perspectives as a crisis communication strategy is put in place. She writes, "Have a crisis communication team that is diverse."[30] This is not simply a call to pursue diversity for diversity's sake. It is a warning to make sure that you are looking at the present or potential crisis from as many perspectives as possible.

Allred continues, "If you are sitting around the table with people who look like you, have backgrounds similar to yours, and think like you, it will lead to unforeseen problems."[31] Take diversity of age as one example. How many organizations have run into problems because they missed how a particular abbreviation (LOL, IRL, etc.), expression, or cultural meme lands on a younger generation? I've had plenty of moments with my teenage and adult children when we got a good laugh out of how I had missed the meaning of something. Such situations are humorous around a dinner table, but ignorance in these areas has the potential to create serious problems for organizations that don't have a diversity of voices speaking into a communication plan, whether that be a crisis plan or a wider organizational communication plan.

Healthy Leaders Communicate Clearly about Long-Term Vision and Plans for Change

In this final section on communicating clearly, I want to highlight the importance of clear communication and casting a long-term vision for the organization. Chapter 10 will further examine the importance of connecting change to organizational vision, but I want to note some initial communication-oriented observations here.

Leadership communication is central both to setting the conditions within which a community is receptive to change and to establishing momentum that will guide the community as change is implemented and sustained. Vision is key to each of these factors. As I noted earlier, the work of change is about helping a community to make what feels intangible—a vision—more tangible. As James Kouzes and Barry Posner note, this involves helping people see what the vision will look like, feel like, sound like, and even smell like.[32]

Helping people envision a preferred future with clarity is less about inventing than about reinforcing. We want to tap into the desires, aspirations, and motivations that are already present in the hearts of community members. Through communication that is motivating, we want to help members of the community see the inadequacies in present circumstances and desire to collectively work and move toward the desired change. Tod Bolsinger observes that this is not about "finding a new inspiring vision but *reframing* an original or enduring vision of the organization that allows everyone to see a new, compelling future for their beloved organization that is worth sacrifice and commitment."[33]

The key is to connect this robust, enduring vision to present circumstances and the desired future. Without the presence of key leadership communication in times of change, organizational members will have gaps in their understanding about how this enduring vision relates to present and future needs. Reflecting on the importance of communication during times of change, Pat Zigarmi and Judd Hoekstra argue that "a significant amount of resistance encountered during organizational change is caused by a lack of information."[34] Some organizational resistance may be inevitable, but communicating with clarity and providing information that is connected to an enduring vision helps to offset much of this resistance.

Healthy Leaders Tell the Story of the Organization

Storytelling can help leaders at any level of influence, but telling stories well—stories about the organization and its work—is essential at the organizational level. The importance of stories should come as no surprise to Christian leaders. As noted in chapter 2, the narrative of creation, the fall, redemption, and restoration points us to the ultimate story of God's work in redemptive history with his people.

Telling stories well—stories about the organization and its work—is essential at the organizational level.

Addressing the storied nature of Christianity, Gerald Sittser writes, "History is fundamental to the faith because Christianity tells a story—a true story as it turns out—about how God plans to redeem the world." This story is not just about the past. Sittser continues, "What God initiated with Abraham and accomplished in Jesus he promises to continue in and through people like us, until all things are made well and whole again. We too play a part in this epic story."[35]

Christian leaders of organizations likewise need to get good at telling stories—true stories—about their organizations. These true stories point to the *actual* lived experience of their organizations; they also point to true and convictional *aspirations* for the future of the organizations. James Kouzes and Barry Posner argue that "stories by their nature are public forms of communication"[36] and that "well-told stories reach inside us and pull us along. They give us the actual experience of being there and of learning what is really important about the experience."[37]

Because stories have this power to reach inside people to grab their hearts and minds, they convey key information in meaningful and memorable ways. When information is communicated in the form of a story or example—not just the facts and details—people are able to remember the information with greater accuracy.[38] Well-told stories and examples help people hear what the organization is all about, and this is true both for those inside and for those outside our organizations.

Telling the Story with Team Members

Noting the importance of sharing stories and information with team members, Stephen Denning observes that "a carefully chosen story can help the leader of an organization translate an abstract concept into a meaningful mandate for employees."[39] Kouzes and Posner similarly note that "stories put a human face on success. They tell us that someone just like us can make it happen." They highlight how these stories "create organizational role models that everyone can relate to" and "illustrate what everyone needs to do to live by the organizational standards."[40] Other authors note that high-performing organizations ensure the presence of open communication so that team members are able to work effectively because they have the information they need to engage in informed decision making.[41]

Telling the Story Inside and Outside the Organization

In addition to helping direct team members, storytelling is vital for the wider organization and for communication outside the organization. An executive vice president wrote in the survey, "The larger the scope you lead, the clearer and simpler your communication must be," and a lead pastor noted that "clarifying and communicating vision culture [is a priority] for all levels of the organization." Further, Kouzes and Posner observe that as people advance in organizations and the scope of their leadership expands, this expanded platform will absolutely translate into more presentations with an ever-widening audience.[42]

With this wider audience—both internal and external—storytelling helps to solidify the scenario the leader wishes to convey. Noting the relationship between data and story in such presentations, Stephen Denning writes, "Although good business arguments are *developed through the use of numbers*, they are typically *approved on the basis of a story*—that is, a narrative that links a set of events in some kind of causal sequence."[43]

For instance, organizations often report facts and figures in their annual reports. Those inside and outside the organization deserve access to such details. But wise leaders understand that it is often stories, rather than such facts and figures, that compel people to act. Whether an organizational leader is addressing shareholders, donors, or some other group of stakeholders, stories provide a pathway along which the significance of facts and figures becomes clear and animated for people.

One final note regarding storytelling and communication to external audiences: we have established that communication with individuals requires proactive listening and feedback—but this is also true for wider organizations and organizational leaders. We need to stay connected to those outside our organizations, both through proactive listening and through proactive communication.

Noting the importance of external communication for organizations seeking new ideas and strategies, Kouzes and Posner highlight the problematic pattern of organizational leaders cutting themselves off from sources of critical information over time: "When the pressures of profit and efficiency are greatest, [leaders] may even mistakenly act to eliminate or severely limit the very things that provide the new ideas they need to weather the storms of uncertainty." Kouzes and

Posner continue, "Unless external communication is actively encouraged, people interact with outsiders less and less frequently and new ideas are cut off."[44]

Building on this idea, Mark McCloskey emphasizes the importance of effectively engaging with people both inside and outside the organization through what he calls the steward role of the leader.[45] He observes that this steward role in leadership tells the story of the organization in a manner that matches internal organizational strengths to external commitments. Focusing on important dynamics related to an organization's market (in the case of a business) or mission (in the case of a nonprofit), leaders must become effective listeners and effective storytellers, helping to engage the vital message of the organization in a faithful and effective manner with diverse stakeholders, both inside and outside the organization.

A Word about Communication Basics: Healthy Leaders Understand What Makes Communication Work

Far more could be said about communication theory as it relates to the work of leadership. Mark Strauss and I cover more on leadership communication in chapter 7 of *Leadership in Christian Perspective*, which provides a helpful model that I have included here (see figure 7.1).

In this model we argue that effective communication involves multiple variables: (1) competent *communicators*, on both the sending end and the receiving end; (2) attention to the various *filters* that influence what is communicated and received; (3) the clarity of the *message* to be communicated; (4) awareness of diverse communication *channels* and how to use them effectively; (5) understanding of present and potential *noise or interference* in the communication process; and (6) the priority of *feedback*—emphasizing that effective communication is more about dialogue than monologue. If you are not familiar with these features of effective communication, I encourage you to look at that chapter for additional discussion about how these variables influence the practice of leadership communication.

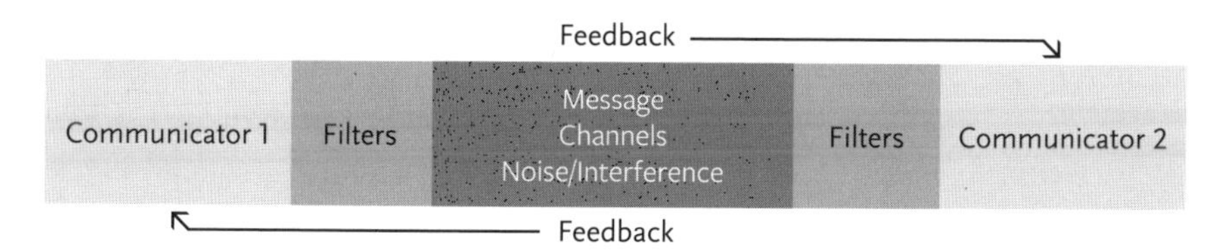

Figure 7.1. Leadership Communication Model

From Justin A. Irving and Mark L. Strauss, *Leadership in Christian Perspective*. Copyright 2019, Baker Academic, a division of Baker Publishing Group. Used by permission.

Recommendations and Reflection

This chapter focused on the nature of communication in organizational leadership. Effective leaders are by necessity effective communicators. After considering the nature of God as communicator—along with the relevance of this attribute to human communication—we focused on communicating with clarity and conviction. This includes communicating clearly about organizational culture and commitments, for people and teams, during crises, and about long-term vision and plans for change. Finally, we considered the importance of organizational storytelling—both within and outside the organization—and briefly noted key variables associated with faithful and effective communication.

Take a moment to consider these principles related to communicating with clarity and conviction in the organizational context. Use the following questions to help you reflect on how you are approaching such communication priorities in your own leadership practice.

The nature of God as communicator: Healthy Christian leaders look to God for his example and priorities in communication.

- God accomplished his creative work in Genesis by speaking things into existence. What does this tell us about God's nature, and how does this provide encouragement to you?
- God not only created but also sustains all things "by the word of his power" (Heb. 1:3). What does this tell us about God's active involvement in the world and in our lives, and why is this an encouragement for leaders?
- "Leadership doesn't happen until communication happens": Do you agree with this statement? How does the leader's central duty as communicator reflect—even faintly—the nature of God as communicator?
- While God uniquely creates *ex nihilo*—out of nothing—human leaders are required to make the intangible tangible. How does effective, compelling, and clear communication help to make a vision of the future tangible for communities?

Healthy leaders communicate clearly about organizational culture and commitments.

- "People trust the clear and distrust the ambiguous": Do you agree with this leadership communication principle? Why or why not?
- "Keep your mission clear. . . . Make sure everyone not only knows the mission but [also knows] how committed the institution and leader-

ship are to it": Why is clarity about the organizational mission such an important starting point for effective leadership communication?

- Why are executive and senior leaders uniquely positioned to provide clarity about organizational culture to a variety of organizational stakeholders, both internal and external to the organization?
- "The ideal company . . . is a company with clear rules that make sense to the people who follow them": Do you agree with this statement? Why is it so important for people to understand healthy norms for work in the organizations of which they are part?

Healthy leaders communicate clearly for their people and teams.

- "Clarity is kindness. Clarity is king": Why is clarity in leader communication so important for people and for the alignment of teams?
- "Leaders communicate because they cannot *not* communicate. . . . The message flows out of your deepest convictions and most passionately held beliefs": Have you seen positive models of this type of communication with conviction? What are the deepest convictions and most passionately held beliefs that shape your leadership?
- Some factors identified with trust and communication are transparency, honesty, a willingness to listen, and responsiveness. Do you find one of these to be more important than the others for building trust as leaders communicate? Why?
- "Motivating . . . is the work of supporting and sustaining personal and organizational momentum": How do leaders effectively provide inspiration and support in their communication with organizational team members?

Healthy leaders communicate clearly in moments of crisis.

- "People deal far better with uncertainty and stress when they know what's going on, even if the information is incomplete or only temporarily correct": Is communicating information that is not complete easy or challenging for you in your leadership? Why do followers need this type of communication in moments of crisis, even if it does not come naturally to you?
- Organizational action, especially in times of crisis, needs to be rooted in vision and values. Why are the organizational vision and values especially important in times of crisis?
- We looked at the value of anticipating potential crises in order to more effectively communicate during times of crises. What crisis issues

are potential concerns for your organization or organizational sector? What priorities could guide your communication response to such crises?

- Why is it important to gain diverse perspectives on crisis situations as your organization plans its response? How can you organize your community or team now to benefit from multiple perspectives as you plan?

Healthy Leaders communicate clearly about long-term vision and plans for change.

- Do you agree that organizational vision is vital for communicating with clarity about plans for change? Why or why not?
- Change is not about "finding a new, inspiring vision but [rather about] *reframing* an original or enduring vision of the organization": Do you agree with this statement? How do enduring visions contribute to clear communication as an organization navigates change?
- "A significant amount of resistance encountered during organizational change is caused by a lack of information": How might your team aim for regular and consistent communication in navigating change?
- Consider some of the stages in a change process—demonstrating the need for change, implementing the change, and sustaining the change. Why is the leader's work of providing clear communication during every stage of the change process so important?

Healthy leaders tell the story of the organization.

- Why is storytelling an especially important skill for executive leaders of an organization? What core stories shape the leadership of your team, division, or organization?
- How does the storied nature of Christianity shape our value of and appreciation for telling true stories—both actual and aspirational—in our organizations?
- While the case for decisions is often built on facts and figures, why is it that stories often solidify people's conviction about the importance of these facts?
- As you consider the work of communication and telling the organization's story, how are you doing, in terms of both internal and external communication? Does one side of this leadership responsibility (communicating *within* the organization or communicating *outside* the organization) come more naturally to you? How can you increase

your capacity and comfort with each side of this senior leadership responsibility?

A word about communication basics: Healthy leaders understand what makes communication work.

- Are you familiar with the elements of communication included in the model shown in figure 7.1? Which elements would you like to learn more about?
- As you communicate as a leader, are you ensuring that your message is clear, are you utilizing multiple pathways and channels for communication, and are you working to minimize potential noise and interference associated with these communication channels?
- When you consider the filters that people have—the things that influence how people speak about and listen to the message—how can you better work toward understanding and being understood?
- Communication is not a monologue. It involves senders and receivers, and it involves pathways for feedback. As an organization, what are some of the systems you have in place that enable you as a leader to regularly hear what others think about your organization—both team members and those outside the community?

EIGHT

Culture and Thriving Organizations

Responsible organizational stewards prioritize organizational culture. Emphasizing just how important culture is, Peter Drucker creatively argues that "culture eats strategy for breakfast."[1] In other words, organizational goals, labors, and investments are doomed to fail when they are not properly aligned with the actual culture of an organization.

To express this positively, "Companies with dynamic cultures full of engaged employees tend to have a leader who sees something much bigger than just a product or service. . . . [They] see why their business exists and how it impacts people."[2] Such healthy organizational cultures are infused with purpose, mission, values, and vision. The leaders and team members of these organizations benefit from a clear and compelling organizational story that motivates aligned and coordinated work.

While contemporary leaders likely hear enough buzz about organizational culture to know that it is a priority, not all leaders and students of leadership really understand what organizational culture is and why it is so important for healthy and thriving communities. The first part of this chapter will explore the nature of organizational culture, probe why it is important, and investigate how to facilitate healthy alignment of the culture within our organizations.

Healthy Leaders Define and Align the Organization's Culture

Max De Pree famously asserts, "The first responsibility of a leader is to define reality."[3] Specifically applying this to organizational culture, Cheryl Bachelder, former CEO of Popeyes Louisiana Kitchen, argues that "defining the principles of the culture and holding the team accountable to those principles is fundamentally the work and responsibility of the leader."[4] But what *is* culture? What is it that the executive leaders of our organizations must define?

At its core, organizational culture defines *who we are*, *what we are about*, and *how we approach our work and life together*. Organizational culture defines these priorities as the leaders and members of the community find clear and compelling answers to core questions such as these:

- *Why* do we exist as an organization?
- *What* is our primary aim and work?
- *How* will we faithfully and effectively accomplish this work?
- *Who* are we as a community? (What values and beliefs define our organizational character?)
- *Where* are we going? (What picture of the future are we striving toward together?)

All organizations have a primary culture, but not every organization understands or readily sees this culture. The organization may not have clear answers to the above questions, perhaps because leaders and organizational members may be unaware of the organization's culture. Whether or not organizational members are aware of the culture, a culture nonetheless is shaping the organization.

Sometimes this culture is healthy and strong; other times it is unhealthy and weak. As Terrence Deal and Allan Kennedy write in their book *Corporate Culture*, "Whether weak or strong, culture has a powerful influence throughout an organization."[5] Leaders often must decide whether the existing culture is what the organization needs to thrive in the years ahead. They must decide whether the organization's answers to the questions listed above are both clear and compelling. When an unhealthy or weak culture dominates the community—perhaps driven by a struggle simply to survive or to maintain the status quo—it takes intentional effort on the part of the leader to diagnose and redirect the culture.

At its core, organizational culture defines *who we are, what we are about,* and *how we approach our work and life together.*

The Complexities of Organizational Culture

What makes this work even more difficult is the fact that culture is a combination of visible and unnoticed (or inconspicuous) dimensions. In his well-known book *Organizational Culture and Leadership*, Edgar Schein sees at least three levels of culture at work: (1) artifacts, (2) espoused values, and (3) basic underlying assumptions. Schein notes that sometimes the basic underlying assumptions—those "unconscious, taken-for-granted beliefs, perceptions, thoughts, and feelings" that are assumed—are the most powerful sources for organizational values and action.[6] The very influences that sometimes shape our organizations the most can remain hidden to those uninterested, unwilling, or unable to observe them.

Discussing the nature of organizational culture, Mark McCloskey writes, "Culture functions like DNA—a hidden, genetic code and . . . blueprint that shapes the collective character of the organization as well as its behaviors and practices."[7] While most of us are unaware of the details of our DNA, our genetic makeup nevertheless shapes and influences us daily. In a similar manner, culture shapes the nature of our organizational behavior and practices in both noticed and unnoticed ways daily. Culture describes the way we think, behave, and work together;[8] culture defines "the way we do things around here."[9]

The Priority of Organizational Culture

The importance of organizational culture was clear among the surveyed executives. Executive leaders noted the value of creating a healthy culture "where there is a shared sense of commitment around mission, vision, and values" and of creating a "culture that allows people to flourish well."

For better or worse, all organizations have a culture, but leaders have the opportunity and stewardship responsibility to ensure that this culture is setting the conditions for organizational thriving and human flourishing. Note a few of the additional comments from survey participants:

- "Stay focused on the mission, not being distracted from it, and raising the necessary support to accomplish the mission." (a president)
- "Keep the main things the main things." (a lead pastor)
- "The main thing is to keep the main thing the main thing." (a program director)
- "Assure clarity of vision." (a CEO)
- "Team culture and unity trump strategy." (a vice president)
- "Do a few things well; have a 'north star.'" (a chief program officer)
- "Work on culture and trust every day." (a provost)
- "Organizational culture seems more important than ever." (a president)

- "Be intentional and prioritize building a healthy culture and work atmosphere, where leaders are work[ing] to build systems and make efforts to make straight the paths of their followers." (a CEO)
- "Make sure culture and vision stays on point." (a pastor)
- "Establish and strengthen the culture of [the] organization." (a president)

While other organizational members (e.g., board members and trustees) are responsible for thinking about the culture of an organization, the primary leader (or leaders) of the organization bears a unique responsibility for this work. Francis Yammarino writes, "As the definers and givers of culture, leaders set the tone, atmosphere, and philosophy for the organization and its subunits."[10] Colin Powell observes, "Great leaders are almost always great simplifiers who can cut through the argument, debate, and doubt to offer a solution everyone can understand."[11] Whether in times of decision or in times of gaining perspective related to the organization's culture, this work requires foresight and clarity of vision as leaders cut through complexity to identify and name the heart of the organization.

The Alignment of Organizational Culture

Central to this work of finding clarity about the organization's culture is the task of identifying or diagnosing what is aligned and misaligned in the organization's culture. Consider the metaphor of the chiropractic adjustment. For those unfamiliar with the process, it is primarily about helping to realign the spine, with the goal of improved motion and decreased pain.[12] Just as we want to properly care for our bodies—helping to align them with conditions that help them flourish and thrive—so organizational culture needs diagnosis and intervention to ensure healthy organizational alignment.

The Danger of a Misaligned Culture

One of the common examples of cultural misalignment within an organization is when there is a gap between stated *values* and actual organizational *practice*. In the Harvard Business Review Press book *The Mind of the Leader*, Rasmus Hougaard and Jacqueline Carter argue that, "far too often, leaders fail to connect espoused values to workplace realities" and that this tends to happen because "the stated values are inconsistent with other important business objectives."[13]

Wells Fargo provided an unfortunate example of the danger of such misaligned values in the past decade. Hougaard and Carter note that, though

Wells Fargo's stated values extolled "ethics" and doing "what's right for customers," the company's values, business objectives, and organizational practices did not align. Hougaard and Carter continue, "In 2016, more than five thousand employees were fired when it was discovered that, due to heavy pressure from supervisors to meet quotas, they created more than 2 million fake accounts collecting at least $2.6 million in fees from unwitting customers."[14] How does such an obvious misalignment of stated values and actual practice take place? Hougaard and Carter see this happening when value statements are not built into daily operations. Values must translate into "how people are rewarded, how policies and procedures are established, or how decisions are made."[15]

Authors Eric Geiger and Kevin Peck take this argument about misalignment a step further. Sometimes the problem in an unhealthy culture is not just that there is a gap between stated values and organizational practice but rather that the practice of the organization is beginning to align with *actual* values and beliefs—unhealthy ones. Geiger and Peck argue that unhealthy culture "is ultimately a theological problem. Eventually, people behave consistently with their most fundamental beliefs."[16] At the end of the day, actual practice typically points to actual values and beliefs. And so, when a practice becomes problematic, sometimes the solution is to identify the actual beliefs and values shaping the practice so that the misalignment between stated values and practice may be addressed.

Alignment with the Lord

For Christian leaders, alignment begins with aligning ourselves and the organizations we influence with the Lord and biblical priorities. Michael Wilder and Timothy Paul Jones associate such alignment with the pursuit of shared goals that are in line with the fulfillment of "the creation mandate and the Great Commission in submission to the Word of God."[17]

As you think back to related discussions in chapters 1 and 2, consider how the biblical story of creation, the fall, redemption, and restoration should guide you in the process of aligning—or realigning—your organizational culture with the priorities and values shaped by this biblical narrative. How is your organization creating a context where people flourish and where they may become all that God has called them to be, and do all that God has called them to do, to the glory of God?

While this work of aligning our communities with biblical priorities may seem most obvious for pastors or those leading within the context of the church, I'm encouraged to see how many of the executive leaders who participated in the survey were thinking about this essential work across diverse organizational sectors. Consider several of their comments:

- "Don't carry your organization. Trust God with it." (a pastor)
- "Raise your eyes to the big picture. Let your faith guide your perspective on the future. Don't overreact to anything in the present. Temper your ambition with humility. Remember the words you want to hear from Jesus some day: 'Well done, good and faithful servant.' As you think ahead to that moment, what are you doing now that he might be referring to?" (a CEO)
- "Stay faithful to God's leading and direction. . . . Act on what God is showing you now." (an executive pastor)
- "Trust the Lord's guidance in the process." (an associate vice president)
- "We need to have a consistent and compelling grasp of God's story in and through our institutional, collective, and individual lives. . . . That begins and ends in prayer/listening to the Lord and collaborating to a space of mutually agreed upon approaches to fulfilling the mission [to which] we have been called." (a vice president)

Christian leaders in diverse sectors need to be wise in their approach to living and leading out of their faith—consider the wisdom needed by leaders such as Joseph in the land of Egypt or Daniel in Babylon. God relates intimately and deeply to our lives of work and leadership in every sector. Whether we undertake responsibilities with high visibility or the humblest of activities, we want to pray with the psalmist: "Let your work be shown to your servants. . . . Establish the work of our hands upon us; yes, establish the work of our hands!" (Ps. 90:16–17). We want to be leaders who ask for the work of our hands to be established as it is aligned with the work of God.

I think of Psalm 90 often throughout my workdays. Today, though I didn't know I'd be focusing on it in my writing, I began my work with the words of Psalm 90 on my lips and heart. I don't know who will eventually read the words of this chapter, but I asked God to establish this work today as I began writing. I asked him to help and guide me as I seek to align a discussion about organizational culture with his even more important priorities and work in the world. I pray that my work will be meaningful to all of you reading this, but I know that the extent of this significance is deeply connected to the infinitely more important work God is doing as he shapes and molds leaders and organizations for his glory.

Our work finds meaning and significance as it falls into line with God's work. Pray to see God's work in the world and in your midst (Ps. 90:16). Ask the Lord to guide your work in such a way that it will be established to the extent that it aligns with his work (Ps. 90:17). While every Christian should pray such prayers, I think leaders have a unique stewardship responsibility to see how the purpose, mission, strategies, values, beliefs, and vision of the organizations they lead align with God's work in the world. Healthy Christian leaders delight in the opportunity to align their work with his.

Aligning Organizational Identity and Culture

In my over twenty years of teaching on the subject of organizational culture, I frequently have emphasized the difference between organizational *identity* and organizational *culture*. Organizational identity is the public face of an organization. It is the part of the organization we see on websites, in advertisements, and in polished annual reports. This public-facing identity often looks like the branding by which an organization desires to be known.

The actual culture of an organization may be either aligned or misaligned with this public identity. The iceberg metaphor is applicable here. Organizational identity lets us know that an organization's culture is present, but we really can't see the "submerged" portions of the culture in the same way that we see an organization's identity. Because of principles related to buoyancy and the nature of pure ice in seawater, it's estimated that only about 10 percent of an iceberg is above water. Adding to the metaphor, it is difficult to judge the contours of the submerged portions of the iceberg simply by looking at the portions above the surface.[18] This is why icebergs present such a threat to ships—think Titanic here.

The visible dimensions of identity and culture are important. But healthy and responsible organizational leaders do not want public branding and reputation to be built on falsehoods. I refer to this dimension of an inauthentic organization as *slogan-based identity*. In contrast to slogan-based organizational identities, we want the public dimensions of the organizations we lead to be aligned with the weightier dimensions of the organization's culture under the surface. We want healthy and wise leaders to guide organizations to a place of authentic thriving. This thriving takes place as the cultures and identities of the community are brought into alignment.

Alignment and Aspiration

What should leaders do when they find a disconnect between the culture and identity of their organizations? The first step is to draw attention to this gap. This relates to the advice from Max De Pree that I highlighted at the beginning of the chapter: "The first responsibility of a leader is to define reality."[19] Defining reality sometimes involves pointing out difficult realities. The point is not that healthy organizations never experience a misaligned culture. The point is that healthy organizations find a way to tell true and hopeful stories about their organizational culture.

Here is where the dimensions of hope and aspiration play a significant role for organizational leaders. Healthy organizations do not always and perfectly live out every dimension of their purpose, mission, values, beliefs, and vision. But healthy organizations are honest about their shortcomings and paint a picture of the aspirational values and vision to which they are called as a community.

Healthy organizations are honest about their shortcomings and paint a picture of the aspirational values and vision to which they are called as a community.

Consider the example of a local church. The church of Jesus Christ has been given a clear mission: "Make disciples of all nations, baptizing them in the name of the Father and of the Son and of the Holy Spirit, teaching them to observe all that I have commanded you" (Matt. 28:19–20). If a church finds itself in a season when the congregation is not engaging in evangelism and global missions, the answer is not to change the mission and move away from the evangelistic and missionary call to make disciples. The better path is to acknowledge the gap between values and practice and then call the community to an aspirational vision of reengaging with these core commitments.

Aligning the Culture of the Organization

As we consider the task of aligning organizational identity and culture, what are some of the key dimensions of organizational culture that shape who we are, what we are about, and how we approach our work and life together?

Earlier in the chapter I pointed to five primary questions that need clear and compelling organizational answers. These five questions relate to five core priorities in an organization's culture: (1) *purpose* (why), (2) *mission* (what), (3) *strategy* (how), (4) *values and beliefs* (who), and (5) *vision* (where).

Figure 8.1 visually depicts these five core priorities and questions using the imagery of an organizational path or roadway guiding an organization on its journey.

As noted in the previous chapter, leaders provide thoughtful and kind leadership when they communicate clearly with their community. In the survey,

Figure 8.1. Organizational Culture

multiple leaders wrote that "clarity is kindness." Among their other responsibilities, leaders must provide clear answers for the community around these five questions and priorities. We'll spend time discussing each of these questions shortly.

A Word of Clarification

Before walking through these priorities for organizational culture, I want to offer one item of clarification. Though I will be addressing five distinct priorities, I do not necessarily encourage organizations to go to work crafting a distinct statement or list for each of these five areas. The point is not to have a *statement* on every element of the organization's purpose, mission, strategy, values and beliefs, and vision. The point is to have *answers* to each of the associated questions.

For example, I know of a church that was guided by the following statement for many years: "We exist to glorify God by making more disciples for Jesus Christ." In this very short and memorable statement, the church provided a clear and compelling answer to both the *why* and the *what* questions related to organizational culture. The church's purpose (the *why*) was to glorify God. What did the members of the congregation do for the sake of glorifying God? They sought to make more disciples for Jesus Christ (the *what*: their mission, which was shaped by the Great Commission).

I observe that organizations frequently use terms such as *purpose*, *mission*, and *vision* in loose and fairly interchangeable ways. Although I think it is helpful to clearly distinguish these terms, I don't think leaders should necessarily reconfigure organizational statements that have been effectively guiding organizations for many years or decades. The point is for leaders to think through the five questions and priorities examined in this chapter and make sure that, as leaders, they indeed have clear and compelling answers to these questions.

Even if organizations have utilized terms and various statements in a manner that differs from what I present in the following sections, it may be that their statements have effectively answered the central questions about organizational culture. If that is the case in your organization, celebrate this achievement and continue telling the organization's story well. If not, the following discussion might help you identify gaps to address and questions that still need clear and compelling answers.

Why: Healthy Leaders Advance the *Purpose* of the Organization

Rick Warren opens his popular book *The Purpose Driven Life* with a short but pointed message: "It's not about you."[20] That's a helpful starting point as we talk about organizational purpose and the role that leaders play in shaping it. Theologically, purpose finds its ultimate starting place in God himself: "Whatever you do, do all to the glory of God" (1 Cor. 10:31). The creation mandate (Gen. 1:28) along with the greatest commandment (Matt. 22:34–40) remind us that we also are to be motivated by human flourishing and love of neighbor. While some organizations are content with the aim of personal financial enrichment, most leaders and team members want more—they want a clear and compelling sense of purpose about the work they do. Christian leaders and team members want to understand how their organization and their work contribute both to glorifying God and to the provision of value and good to others.

Healthy organizations understand and communicate a compelling purpose for their people. Statements of purpose—whether captured in formal documents or woven into the oral and informal communication of an organization—help organizations answer key questions such as these: *Why* do we do what we do? *Why* does this organization exist? *Why* is the story of this organization significant? *Why* don't we just shut our doors?

A healthy understanding of purpose provides answers to such questions. It provides a basis for the organization's work and strategy. It provides a contextual framework for understanding how the parts of the organization fit into the whole. It provides a seedbed for individual and organizational significance. It provides meaning for the mission.

Whether in a nonprofit or for-profit context, understanding the purpose guiding our organizations matters. In their book *Integrating Christian Faith and Work*, authors Sharlene Buszka and Timothy Ewest remind readers that "while within a capitalist economy it may seem the profit motive drives organizations, there are other important reasons organizations exist. Organizations also produce products for human consumption, provide services to support or enhance society, and attempt to resolve social problems."[21] Understanding the purpose driving an organization yields important benefits for leaders, team members, and those served by the organization.

One of the reasons purpose is so important is that it provides the motivation and morale that leaders and team members alike need to sustain their work. David Gergen observes, "Wise leaders understand that regardless of whether a team is formed in the public or the private sector, morale rests heavily upon the degree that its employees—its teammates, if you will—believe they are serving a larger purpose."[22] An executive put it this way in the survey: "Learn to 'translate the cause' well. This is a skill that . . . involves making sure people understand the WHY behind their positions." For this leader, the key is helping team members have ownership of the difference they're making in their respective roles on behalf of the whole organization.

In his book *Start with Why*, Simon Sinek also emphasizes this benefit of morale and inspiration for team members: "Companies with a strong sense of WHY are able to inspire their employees. Those employees are more productive and innovative, and the feeling they bring to work attracts other people eager to work there as well."[23] While other dimensions of the organization's life are critical—*how* we approach our work and *what* work we need to do—the point is that we need to start with purpose. We need to start by answering the *why* question for people.

As this section draws to a close, consider a few of the comments provided by survey participants emphasizing this vital work of getting to the *why* of organizational culture:

- "Keep at it and remind yourself 'why' often!" (a lead pastor)
- "Ask the 'why' that is behind the 'what' and the 'how.' It's not enough to complete a project or task; the ultimate purpose/objective of the project or task must be understood." (a president)
- "Find opportunities to connect every person's position in the building with the big whys of the work—how every person has a role in the mission of the organization." (a principal)
- "Too many leaders in my world just simply 'do church' every Sunday without thinking hard on WHY they are doing what they do." (a lead pastor)
- "Understand your 'why' before figuring out your 'how.'" (a lead pastor)

When it comes to purpose, organizational thinker Patrick Lencioni sums it up well: "Enduring organizations understand the fundamental reason they were founded and why they exist, and they stay true to that reason."[24] As you seek to lead a healthy and enduring organization, insist on building deep and meaningful roots as you provide clear and compelling answers to the why questions of organizational culture.

What: Healthy Leaders Advance the *Mission* of the Organization

Once an organization clearly understands the purpose that is guiding it, the time has come to clarify the organization's mission. *What* does this organization do (its mission) for the reasons stated (its purpose)? Organizational mission is all about answering the *what* question of organizational identity and culture. If, for example, the purpose of an organization is to do all that it does for the glory of God, *what* then is it doing for God's glory?

While I think that an organization's purpose can be effectively communicated orally by senior leaders (though it may be written), the mission of an organization must take the form of a clear and concise written statement. As I mentioned earlier, some organizations call this a purpose statement or a vision statement. The essential thing is that the focus of the mission—what the organization does and the reasons why it does so—must be clear and easily accessible.

Here's a helpful example from Presbyterian Homes & Services, based in Minnesota. The organization offers a range of senior living and care options, including independent living, in-home care, assisted living, memory care, transitional care, and long-term care, and it has a humble and wise Christian leader. Presbyterian Homes & Services captures its purpose and mission in a concise statement of mission: "To honor God by enriching the lives and touching the hearts of older adults."[25]

In this formulation, the mission is not merely a functional statement about providing housing, food, and care for senior adults, it is a statement that gets to the more meaningful and inspirational side of this work: "enriching the lives and touching the hearts of older adults." Note some of the features of a statement of mission like this. It is clear, concise, easy to understand, and easy to remember; it is proactive rather than reactive; it calls people to something of value; and it unifies the multifaceted work of the organization, aligning it to a common mission.

Organizational leaders and team members need what mission statements provide. David Horsager puts it this way: "A simple mission statement gives clarity of purpose. . . . The mission statement gives me direction and helps guide my priorities."[26] Noting the benefit of organizational mission for team members, William Pollard, former CEO of ServiceMaster Company, argues that organizational mission serves as an organizing principle that allows a community of people to care for one another and for those they serve.[27]

Organizational mission was frequently noted as a priority by the executive leaders who participated in the survey. Mission integrity and focus was coded twenty-seven times among top leader concerns. Advice from these leaders clustered around common themes.

Provide a Clear and Focused Mission for Your Organization

- "Keep your mission clear and be singularly focused." (a president)
- "Always ensure that you focus on mission." (a director)
- "Communicate the mission/vision often and in as many ways as possible." (a president)
- "Keep the mission front and center." (a vice president)
- "Mission alignment and relevance is critical." (a senior pastor)
- "I strongly believe that if the mission is not correctly delivered, all outcomes of the organization are selectively affected." (a dean)
- "Make your personal lifestyle choices line up with your organizational mission to facilitate both organizational effectiveness and personal satisfaction/longevity in leadership." (a president)
- "Know who you are, what you are trying to do, and how you plan to accomplish that mission." (a president)

Avoid Mission Drift and Mission Distractions

- "Stick with your mission and hire the very best people you can find." (an executive director)
- "Always ensure that you focus on mission. There can be many distractions that keep leaders and organizations from focusing on their primary mission. It is important that leaders keep themselves and those they lead focused on the primary mission of the organization." (a director)
- "[We want to be sure] that we are staying on mission." (an executive director)
- "We lost so much time focusing on addressing pandemic-related issues that bringing our mission and vision back into focus for our subordinates has been a difficult nut to crack." (a superintendent)

- "Organizations tend toward complexity and chaos. Leaders maneuver that energy into missional momentum." (a lead pastor)
- "Stay focused on the mission [while avoiding distractions] and raising the necessary support to accomplish the mission." (a president)

Use Mission to Guide Hiring and Daily Decisions

- "Diligently maintain mission focus and make leadership and organizational decisions based on the few core principles." (a dean and vice president)
- "Maintain mission discipline by making leadership decisions based on the clearly articulated mission." (a president)
- "Make certain that you are hiring for mission. . . . Don't prioritize other areas over mission." (an associate provost)
- "We focus on 3 internal core values in hiring. They are: (1) *Light heart*. [Candidates] take the mission seriously but not themselves. . . . (2) *Mission focused*. They are committed to our mission. . . . (3) *Servant oriented*. They see our calling to be one of service to others." (a president)
- "It is my responsibility to establish a mission-centric culture. This comes through hiring the right people. . . . Deeply explore missional alignment." (a president)

Mission Focus Requires a People Focus

Finally, the survey participants emphasized that a focus on mission requires a focus on people. Note the following statement by university president Dondi Costin that was quoted earlier in the book: "'If you take care of the people, the people will take care of the mission.' . . . Until you can find a way to make your people your top priority, the mission will never be accomplished the way it should." This is not about deprioritizing mission; rather, it is about emphasizing that organizations exist for the good of people and that caring for people is good business and good organizational strategy.

In *The Mind of the Leader*, Rasmus Hougaard and Jacqueline Carter write, "Creating people-centered cultures is the most logical response to today's organizational crisis of soaring employee disengagement and widespread job dissatisfaction."[28] As I write this book, headlines about the "great resignation" and "quiet quitting" abound. These dynamics connect both to the need to stay focused on mission *and* to the need to support leadership approaches that foster employee engagement through people-centered cultures. The remedy is to treat people in a manner that is consistent with their created nature as image bearers of God. This upholds the dignity and worth that they already possess and translates into inspired mission fulfillment.[29]

How: Healthy Leaders Advance the *Strategy* of the Organization

Having covered the *why* (purpose) and *what* (mission) questions of organizational culture and identity, we turn now to the *how* question, related to strategy.

At the start of this section, I want to emphasize that *strategy is not your primary commitment* as a leader. This is not to argue that strategy is insignificant and unimportant; this is to argue that strategy is insignificant *apart from* sound purpose, mission, values, beliefs, and vision. No matter how flashy or refined an organizational strategy may be, without the guiding compass of other important elements of an organization's culture, this polished strategy really doesn't matter.

With that important clarification noted, *strategy is a vital part of leading organizations faithfully and effectively*. Strategy provides answers to important questions such as these: *How* does the organization intend to accomplish its mission? *How* will the organization implement its mission-directed plans? *How* will processes, people, and resources be maximized in order to see the mission come to life in and through the organization?

Strategic Prayerfulness

One of the first commitments that Christian leaders have regarding *how* to approach their work is an understanding that prayer is the starting point for Christian leadership, precisely because dependence on God is our necessary posture. As noted in chapter 1, leading as stewards of that which does not ultimately belong to us translates into an explicit dependence on God. Michael Wilder and Timothy Paul Jones put it this way: "Precisely because God's purposes will proceed with or without our leadership, we can wait with patience and prayer on the power of the God who goes before us. . . . Through prayerful patience, we recognize that our leadership is meaningless apart from the power of God, and we reject the urge to forge ahead in our own feeble strength."[30]

Leaders in the Bible modeled the centrality of prayer in their work. Consider, as one example, the primary apostolic church leaders in Acts 6 who intentionally implemented a strategy of shared responsibility in order to stay focused on leadership based on prayer and biblical wisdom (vv. 1–7). As for the wider Christian community, James reminds them of the priority of prayer:

"If any of you lacks wisdom, let him ask God, who gives generously to all without reproach, and it will be given him" (James 1:5). As noted in chapter 4, this passage is about Christians humbly and earnestly bringing real needs and questions to the Lord and seeking his will and wisdom.

Many leaders noted in the survey the importance of leading our communities with a prayerful posture:

- "Make time to think, plan, and pray; otherwise the tyranny of the urgent will take over." (a lead pastor)
- "[Praying and] listening to the Lord [helps us to fulfill] the mission we have been called to." (a vice president)
- "Pray, stay in the Word, lead by example, and persevere! God has us in the palm of His hand." (a senior pastor)
- "Pray, do your best, let God do the rest." (a senior pastor)

Leaders tend to be "doers." But the work of prayer helps to remind us that the primary work in God's gospel economy is not done by humans—it is done by God himself. This is the reality to which Isaiah the prophet points us: "From of old no one has heard or perceived by the ear, no eye has seen a God besides you, *who acts for those who wait for him*" (Isa. 64:4). We tend to think that God waits on us to work for him. But Isaiah points us to the exact opposite in God's economy—God *works* for those who *wait* on him. This is not about advancing a pseudo–prosperity gospel by which we seek God simply to advance our organizations. This is about recognizing that God delights to meet us in our posture of dependent waiting on him and his work. Wise and healthy leaders go about their work with a heart oriented toward waiting on the One whose work matters the most.

Strategic Priorities

Emphasizing an approach to leadership that prioritizes strategy along with other commitments, a former colleague of mine articulated several pressing questions that followers implicitly ask their leaders: Do you know where you're going (vision/mission)? *Can you get me there* (*strategy*)? Will you love me along the way (values)? Followers want questions of vision, mission, and values answered, but they also need to know that there is a plan for how we can accomplish what we set out to do together.

As Edgar Stoesz and Chester Raber argue, "Mission statements are little more than fine sounding phrases until they are put into operation through a planning process."[31] Warren Bennis puts it this way: "Vision without action is poverty-stricken poetry."[32] This is where the importance of strategy comes into play. Strategy helps to enact the vision and mission set forth by the community and leaders. Mark McCloskey argues that, at its core, the work of formulating strategy involves "designing a conceptual framework, a series of next best steps, a first level of detail that captures the energy and momentum generated by the vision, and wisely utilizes the assets of the organization to achieve the vision."[33]

The phrase "first level of detail" is important, because leaders should not confuse detailed planning and tactics with the big-picture strategy of the organization. I've pointed to the example of Popeyes Louisiana Kitchen a couple of times already in this book. For Popeyes, such a big-picture strategy may be seen in their five strategic pillars: "These pillars serve as the backbone for the company, guiding their every move to ensure that they stay within their vision."[34] These strategic pillars are as follows:

1. Build a distinctive brand.
2. Create memorable experiences.
3. Grow restaurant profits.
4. Accelerate quality restaurants.
5. Develop servant leaders.

Each organization needs to think through its own strategic priorities, but it is easy to see how detailed planning regarding these five core strategic commitments can help an organization like Popeyes thrive in its work.

While most of this discussion about strategy has been big-picture in nature, it is important to note that details and structure are vital for healthy organizations. David Gergen writes, "It is easy to credit the person at the top of the organization chart for leading a good team, but embedded structures are the supportive tissue that enables a team to succeed."[35] Strategy helps leaders put the right structures in place to create contexts where organizations may thrive and people may flourish.

After I finished college, I spent some time working as a carpenter, framing houses and also helping with some of the "finish work" for custom projects. Framing work and finish work are distinct, but both are important for the finished product. Framing work puts the structure of a building in place; finish work brings the final details of a project together. Using this distinction as a metaphor, the strategic work of leadership involves making sure that the architectural designs of an organization are framed around core strategic priorities. Excellence in finish work is also important, but this detailed planning and work is effective only when it is built upon sound and well-executed framing work.

Let's conclude this section by considering several examples and reflections related to strategy from participants in the survey:

- "Know . . . what you are trying to do and *how* you plan to accomplish that mission/vision." (a president)
- "Focus on your strengths, do them differently than your competitors, and connect relationally with your team and customers." (a CEO)
- "Cut through complexity and identify the decisions and dynamics that require immediate attention and action." (an executive vice president)
- "Find the right people first, then focus on strategy." (a head of school)
- "Understand your 'why' before figuring out your 'how.'" (a lead pastor)
- "Develop the skills of team-based strategic thinking and planning." (an international director)

As noted earlier (in our discussion on prayer), wise leaders go about their work understanding that dependence on God is our necessary posture. The point is not only to work, plan, and strategize, but to hold things before the One who ultimately goes before us and establishes our steps: "The heart of man plans his way, but the LORD establishes his steps" (Prov. 16:9).

Wise leaders go about their work understanding that dependence on God is our necessary posture.

Who: Healthy Leaders Advance the *Values and Beliefs* of the Organization

Getting to the essence of why values and beliefs matter, Cherie Harder, president of the Trinity Forum, states, "The way we pursue our goals should reflect our goals."[36] Healthy leaders not only care about what gets accomplished, they also care about the means used to accomplish it. Values and beliefs rightly situate organizational character alongside the personal character of leaders and team members. Just as the character of individuals tells us something about *who* they are, so the character of an organization—as seen through how beliefs and values are lived out—tells us something about that organization.

Values and beliefs help to answer the *who* questions of organizational culture: *Who* do we want to be known as, as an organization? *Who*—as with individual character, what will be the organizational character with which the organization is identified? *Who*—based on the degree to which the organization lives consistent with its values and beliefs, what will be the organization's "personal" reputation? We turn now to consider the nature of values and beliefs, along with the importance of organizations remaining aligned with their values and beliefs.

The Nature of Values and Beliefs

Authors James Collins and Jerry Porras observe that "corporate values and beliefs are the organization's basic precepts about what is important in both business and life, how business should be conducted, its view of humanity, its role in society, the way the world works, and what is to be inviolate."[37] Authors Joanne Soliday and Rick Mann similarly note that values are foundational, support the mission, and provide principles that guide our work.[38]

I argue that the values and beliefs of an organization provide both clarity and helpful boundaries for organizations. They provide metaphorical guardrails that help organizations stay on the road as they carry out their mission and journey toward their intended destination. While organizations can face many temptations while carrying out their work—consider the Wells Fargo story noted above—taking such shortcuts in pursuit of goals rarely yields long-term benefit to the organization. The guardrails of organizational values and beliefs, when put in place, help ensure that an organization is pursuing its aims in a manner consistent with its convictions.

The authors of the book *Corporate Cultures* contend that "values are the bedrock of any corporate culture." They write, "For those who hold them, shared values define the fundamental character of their organization."[39] John Carver similarly notes, "The essence of any organization lies in what it believes, what it stands for, and what and how it values."[40] So what is an example of values in the business context?

Let's turn again to Popeyes Louisiana Kitchen. Here are the core principles that guided values about working together at Popeyes under Cheryl Bachelder's leadership: (1) We are *passionate* about what we do. (2) We *listen* carefully and *learn* continuously. (3) We are *fact-based* and *planful*. (4) We *coach* and *develop* our people. (5) We are *personally accountable*. (6) We value *humility*.[41] Bachelder sees these principles and values as an important part of the culture that has guided Popeyes to successful results by serving others.

This example limits the number of values to a list that can be operationalized. Patrick Lencioni writes, "When leaders who adopt too many values finally realize what they've done and that there is no hope for actually putting their many values to practical use, they often end up ignoring them altogether."[42] It is also vital that organizational values be *clear* and *authentic*.[43]

I serve as a professor at the Southern Baptist Theological Seminary. I think the school provides a helpful example of how beliefs become authentically operationalized within an organization. Among the several statements of belief affirmed by faculty is the Abstract of Principles, which has guided the school theologically since the seminary's founding in 1859. Each faculty member commits to teaching at the school "in accordance with, and not contrary to, the Abstract of Principles." While administrative leaders and faculty members have changed over the years, these clearly articulated beliefs have remained the same and have provided a foundational standard to guide (and sometimes correct) the course of the institution. I'm thankful for this type of organizational clarity.

Organizational Alignment with Values and Beliefs

The organizational leaders who responded to the survey provide thoughtful perspectives on the importance of values and beliefs in the life of an organization. Rather than simply bolstering the brand of an organization, values and beliefs should translate into aligned organizational behavior. Consider these belief statements from some of the surveyed leaders:

- "Deepen . . . knowledge and application of orthodox biblical theology in light of the radically shifting values in culture." (a vice president)
- "Know and commit to your principles while being agile tactically." (a CEO)
- "Become agile in thinking without losing core values. Lead with integrity regardless of the cost or loss of benefits." (a senior pastor)
- "Make leadership and organizational decisions based on the few core principles." (a pastor)
- "Find partners with shared values with whom to work and share resources." (an executive director)
- "Keep your values and objectives in front of you." (an executive director)
- "How you go about doing your work and treating people matters far more than getting things done." (a CEO)
- "Know who you are." (a president)

Clear values and beliefs—and ones that are authentically lived out in the organization—provide definitional clarity and operational agility. People understand the rules of the road and what lane they occupy in light of these values and beliefs. When values are clear, leaders and organizational members are able to go about their work with a freedom that flows from this clarity.

This observation is consistent with the findings of researchers who compared children at play in fenced and non-fenced areas: "In the first scenario [without a fence], the children remained huddled around their teacher, fearful of leaving out of her sight. The later scenario [with a fence] exhibited drastically different results, with the children feeling free to explore within the given boundaries."[44] Some may argue that fences—or values and beliefs—can feel restrictive. But the opinions of the surveyed leaders and the study about fences affirm that it is freedom rather than restriction that is typically experienced with clarity regarding values and beliefs. In unhealthy organizations, values and beliefs may certainly be weaponized by leaders—used merely as tools to manipulate and control people. However, in healthy organizations, clear values and beliefs provide life-giving and value-adding freedom; these values and beliefs provide the community with clarity that defines the essential character and commitments of the organization.

Where: Healthy Leaders Advance the *Vision* of the Organization

Strategy and planning are vital for healthy organizations, but when it comes to inspiration, organizations need a compelling vision. French author and pioneer aviator Antoine de Saint-Exupéry, from the first part of the twentieth century, put it like this: "If you want to build a ship, don't drum up the men to gather wood, divide the work, and give orders. Instead, *teach them to yearn for the vast and endless sea.*"[45]

Unhealthy and declining organizations tend to be over-managed and under-led; they tend to focus on the details and daily demands of work without taking time to connect these to a compelling vision and the big picture. The leaders who participated in the survey push against this danger. A CEO wrote, "Raise your eyes to the big picture." A president advises, "Begin with the end in sight. . . . Communicate the . . . vision often and in as many ways as possible." And a vice president emphasized, "We need an even more cogent vision for the future."

Healthy and maturing organizations create contexts in which leaders of vision help people focus on the details of today in light of a compelling vision for tomorrow. They look to the long term rather than organizing on the basis of a short-term or reactionary posture. Max De Pree speaks to the value of looking to the future and what *can* be: "We can teach ourselves to see things the way they are. Only with vision can we begin to see things the way they can be."[46] Likewise, David Horsager points to the inspirational value of vision in the life of an organizational team: "Few things inspire trust or hope like every member of a team working together toward a shared vision. A clear vision unifies and motivates."[47]

Unhealthy and declining organizations tend to be over-managed and under-led; they tend to focus on the details and daily demands of work without taking time to connect these to a compelling vision and the big picture.

What *is* vision? Burt Nanus summarizes it as "a realistic, credible, attractive future for the organization."[48] John Kotter adds that it is a picture of the future with some commentary about why people should strive to create the future. I summarize vision as *a picture of a preferred future.*

Vision is visual in nature. Sometimes providing a vision may involve providing literal images for people—consider the value of an architectural mock-up, image, or model to help people envision what a future building might look like. More often, visionary leaders use word pictures and powerful imagery. Through visionary language and figures of speech such as similes and metaphors, leaders help people envision what a preferred future will look like.[49] In *Leadership in Christian Perspective*, Mark Strauss and I point to Martin Luther King Jr.'s speeches as examples of this type of visionary communication:

> Also embedded in these and other speeches by King is the power of vision and word pictures. As King cast a vision for equality and justice to diverse audiences, he intentionally used language that was *visual* in nature. His language awoke the imagination to "*see*" this arc of the moral universe. His language awoke the imagination to "*see*" freedom ringing across the United States. . . . His language awoke the imagination to "*see*" sons of former slaves and sons of former slave owners sitting down together at the table of brotherhood. His language awoke the imagination to "*see*" young black boys and black girls joining hands with young white boys and white girls as sisters and brothers.[50]

An organization's purpose, mission, values, and beliefs should generally remain stable and consistent, but organizational strategy and vision necessarily change over time. Strategies adjust to changing contexts. The vision adjusts to paint a picture of what it will look like for the mission to be lived out over the next five to ten years, as the organization continues to mature.

Because vision adjusts over time, vision does not necessarily need to be captured with a statement. In fact, doing so can be dangerous. Capturing vision in a statement risks taking some of the communicative power out of the vision, since the vision is meant to engage people's imaginations. Consider how you might communicate to your friends the beauty and power of Handel's *Messiah*. You could hand them the sheet music and ask them to consider its beauty. But it would probably be better to bring them to a concert hall where they can hear, see, and experience the beauty of this grand oratorio. Rather than simply parroting words from a written statement, visionary leaders find a thousand different ways to bring a unifying vision to life in and through their regular organizational communication.

Through this type of visionary communication, organizational leaders help to provide answers to the *where* questions of organizational culture. Vision helps to answer questions such as these: *Where* are we heading as an organization? *Where* do we want to be in ten years; what does this preferred future look like? Another related question for organizational vision is "What if . . . ?" *What if* the purpose of the organization is authentically embodied? *What if* our mission and strategy really worked; what would our future look like tomorrow, next year, a decade from now?

Consider a few of the visionary encouragements from executive leaders who responded to the survey:

- "Remain relentlessly focused on what is most essential to advance our vision." (a CEO)
- "Assure clarity of vision." (a CEO)
- "Define [your] vision and values and then carry it out." (a lead pastor)
- "Take the time to help others realize their power, worth, and value to become active carriers of the vision." (a pastor)
- "Make sure [the] culture and vision stays on point." (a pastor)
- "Stay ruthlessly connected to Jesus; seek his vision." (a pastor)
- "Think bigger (small vision is my greatest regret)." (a lead pastor)
- "Develop a vision for the organization and hold people accountable for their contributions [to the vision]." (an executive pastor)

On the theme of visionary leadership looking to the future, Marshall Sashkin writes, "Central to the ability to conceive a vision is the ability to think in terms of a period of time, that is, not just in terms of daily or weekly goals but in terms of actions carried out over a period of years."[51] Making a similar point, Joanne Soliday and Rick Mann encourage leaders to consider what they would like the headlines to say in ten years when people write about their organizations.[52] Or, even better, recall what one CEO wrote in the survey (quoted earlier): "Remember the words you want to hear from Jesus some day:

'Well done, good and faithful servant.' As you think ahead to that moment, what are you doing now that he might be referring to?"

Healthy Christian leaders are people of vision, and they recognize the power and importance of maintaining a clear and compelling visionary direction for their communities. As Jerry Wofford affirms, "Transforming Christian leaders are people of vision. Their visions are the gyros that assure the true course for their organizations. Visions are a shared sense of destiny."[53] This is vital for providing the inspiration, motivation, and hope that the people of your organization desperately need.

Recommendations and Reflection

In this chapter, we focused on the leadership priorities of defining and aligning the culture of the organization. Doing this involves defining *who we are*, *what we are about*, and *how we approach our work and life together*. This task also involves answering five core questions: (1) *why* (organizational purpose), (2) *what* (organizational mission), (3) *how* (organizational strategy), (4) *who* (organizational values and beliefs), and (5) *where* (organizational vision). Although an organization does not need written statements or lists for each of these five areas of organizational culture, leaders *must* provide clear and compelling answers to these questions for their organizations if they desire to create contexts in which people flourish.

Take a moment to consider these key dimensions of organizational culture. Use the following questions to help you reflect on how you are defining and aligning your organization's culture.

Healthy leaders define and align the organization's culture.

- "The first responsibility of a leader is to define reality": Why is the leader's responsibility to define reality and define the culture of an organization so important for organizational team members?
- As you consider the five dimensions of organizational culture and the associated five questions (*why*, *what*, *how*, *who*, *where*), what dimensions of your organizational culture are strong? What dimensions need fresh leadership attention?
- As you reflect on biblical priorities and a biblical vision for flourishing, what about your organization's culture aligns with these biblical priorities and what about your organization's culture is misaligned with these biblical priorities?

- The public identity of an organization can become misaligned with the actual culture of an organization. What are the areas of your organization's identity and culture that are, or may become, misaligned? How might aspirational language be used to bring these areas into better alignment in the organization's future?

Why: *Healthy leaders advance the* purpose *of the organization.*

- Organizations may be motivated by both human and theological purposes. If the purpose of your organization is clear, how does this purpose relate to the aims of glorifying God and being beneficial to people?
- Most organizational members are motivated and inspired when they "believe that they are serving a larger purpose." As a leader, are you positively contributing to morale and motivation through clear communication about the organization's purpose?
- "Understand your 'why' before figuring out your 'how'": Do you agree with this sequential priority in organizations? Why or why not?
- "Enduring organizations understand the fundamental reason they were founded and why they exist, and they stay true to that reason": As you consider a brief conversation with someone (the length of an elevator ride), would you be able to share the purpose of your organization in a concise and compelling manner?

What: *Healthy leaders advance the* mission *of the organization.*

- While all five areas of organizational culture are vital, the organization's mission, values, and beliefs are the most critical to capture in clear, public, and written statements. (Your organization might call its mission statement something else—e.g., a purpose statement or a vision statement.) What is your organization's mission statement: the statement that addresses the "*what*" question about the organization's culture? Does this statement answer more than one of the core questions (e.g., does it address both *what* the organization does and *why* the organization does this)?
- Useful statements of mission tend to be clear, concise, easy to understand, and easy to remember. How does your organization's mission statement measure up against these characteristics?
- Many organizations have struggled with mission drift or mission distraction in the past few decades. Has your organization experienced this? As a leader, how are you working to maintain mission integrity?

- How are you using the organization's mission to guide daily organizational tasks such as hiring, volunteer recruitment, and decision making?

How: Healthy leaders advance the strategy *of the organization.*

- "Strategy is not your primary commitment"; "strategy is a vital part of leading organizations": Do you agree with these two assertions? Why or why not? How can they stand together?
- Is prayer a part of your strategic work? Is prayer viewed as an afterthought to what you do as a leader, or is it a central part of your leadership work and responsibilities?
- "Do you know where you're going (vision/mission)? Can you get me there (strategy)? Will you love me along the way (values)?" Why are all three of these questions important for followers? Do you have clear answers to these questions, including a clear strategy that guides your leadership and organization?
- One leader observed in the survey that many organizations "send out precious cargo in leaky boats." How does having effective strategies and organizational structures contribute to the fulfillment of the organizational purpose, mission, and vision?

Who: Healthy leaders advance the values and beliefs *of the organization.*

- "The way we pursue our goals should reflect our goals": Are values and beliefs effectively guiding and guarding the integrity of your organization's mission and work?
- Values and beliefs both define an organization's character and provide guardrails that keep organizations on the road to their intended destination. Does this image of values and beliefs serving as operational guardrails seem stifling or freeing to your team members? Why?
- In order to meaningfully apply values, organizations should not adopt too many of them. As you consider the values your organization has adopted, is the number manageable? Can you personally name them without looking at a list? Is the list concise and memorable enough that these values inform the daily practice of organizational members?
- Values are not simply for branding. Values should be authentically embraced and lived out within organizations. What are the benefits (to leaders, team members, and the organization) associated with lived values? What are the dangers when organizational values do not align with organizational practice?

Where: *Healthy leaders advance the* vision *of the organization.*

- When organizations are over-managed and under-led, they tend to miss the big picture of where they're heading. Is your organizational temptation to focus more on where you're going or more on the daily work needed to get there (understanding that both are important)?
- Is your picture of a preferred future so clear in your mind that you can speak about it in a dozen unique and fresh ways in the course of your leadership communication?
- "We can teach ourselves to see things the way they are. Only with vision can we begin to see things the way they can be": How are you helping organizational members to "see" the vision of a preferred future for your organization?
- As you consider the articles or headlines that could be written about your organization ten years from now, what do you want those articles and headlines to say? How are you inspiring this vision in the hearts of your people?

NINE

Crisis Leadership and Facing Organizational Challenges and Threats

While the need for crisis leadership is as old as human history, contemporary organizational leaders have understood crisis leadership in fresh ways since the beginning of 2020. As I write this, I'm looking at some past issues of the *Harvard Business Review* sitting on my desk. One is a special issue from 2020, titled "How to Lead in a Time of Crisis." Another is the July–August issue from 2020, titled "Emerging from the Crisis: How to Lead through Uncertainty and Strengthen Your Organization for the Long Haul."

Just like the business leaders in 2020, leaders from all sectors have been seeking to draw out the leadership lessons provided by this unique decade of global pandemics, social unrest, and challenging economic realities. The survey of business, church, educational, and nonprofit leaders I used for this book was conducted in the summer of 2022. Two years out from the *Harvard Business Review* issues I note above, leaders still had similar concerns and challenges on their minds. As I noted in chapter 1, the *changing landscape* leaders face today is among the top five concerns the surveyed leaders expressed (it was number 4, to be precise). Here are some of the observations these leaders provide from this season in their life as leaders:

- "It's been the hardest leadership season of my 33+ years of ministry. But God is no less able now as he was two years ago." (a lead pastor)

- "Leading during this time of history is not easy." (a principal)
- "With the pandemic and sociopolitical climate, this is the most difficult time to be a leader in my lifetime, for sure." (an executive pastor)
- "[We are facing] the perfect storm wrought by a looming recession, aggressive inflation, and the Great Resignation." (a president)
- "There is a fundamental shift in how people relate to work, community, and outreach." (a CEO)
- "[We are facing] a culture that is growing increasingly socially fractured." (a pastor)
- "Many organizational leaders today are not equipped well enough to manage and lead through crisis, criticism, and challenges." (a president)
- "Complexity and uncertainty are at new levels." (a CEO)
- "[We are facing] shifting cultural values that run counter to historic Christian faith, . . . financial models in higher education that no longer work." (a president)
- "In our current climate, there is much national anxiety. Leading through this national anxiety level causes many people to not trust one another, think poorly of each other, or to silo into factions of people who think exactly like they do." (a senior pastor)

The weight of these concerns illustrates the broader need for wise leaders who are proactively preparing themselves to guide their organizations in times of crisis. For those waiting for things to return to "normal," hear this warning from *Harvard Business Review* authors Ronald Heifetz, Alexander Grashow, and Marty Linsky: "Are you waiting for things to return to normal in your organization? Sorry. Leaders will require new skills tailored to an environment of urgency, high stakes, and uncertainty."[1] In order to prepare ourselves for such a new normal, let's consider the following priorities for healthy leaders: (1) understanding the nature of crises, (2) nurturing necessary leader qualities, (3) communicating effectively and proactively, (4) utilizing wise strategies, and (5) embracing values-based leadership.

Healthy Leaders Understand the Nature of Crises

The following observation is attributed to Abigail Adams in a letter she wrote to Thomas Jefferson: "These are hard times in which a genius would wish to live. . . . Great necessity calls forth great leaders."[2] Perhaps such a view represents leaders who seem to be made for the challenging times within which they live—think of Winston Churchill. The fact remains that most organizational leaders do not seek out or wish for the hard times brought about by crisis.

Indeed, "Crises can bring out the best or the worst in organizations and their leaders."[3] Consider just a handful of the well-known crises faced by organizations and the world over the past few decades and how these brought out the best and worst in people and communities: the Three Mile Island nuclear power plant accident in 1979; the tragic story of Tylenol's contamination with cyanide in 1982; the Exxon Valdez oil spill that occurred in Alaska in 1989; the space shuttle *Challenger* disaster in 1986 and the space shuttle *Columbia* disaster in 2003; the 9/11 attacks in 2001; the crisis of sexual abuse exposed among religious communities, Catholic and Protestant, in 2002 and 2019 and among athletic communities such as Penn State in 2011 and USA Gymnastics in 2016; the global financial crisis in 2008; the BP Deepwater Horizon oil spill in 2010; and—last but not least—the pandemic that broke onto the global scene in late 2019 and early 2020 and the associated economic challenges.

Crises take many forms and shapes. Sometimes they are immediate, *exploding* crises; other times they are slower-moving, *unfolding* crises.[4] Additionally, crises can be self-inflicted—issues that arise because an organization did not sufficiently correct a known problem—or they can be brought about by actors or circumstances beyond the control of the organization. Consider the many possible crisis categories noted by the Center for Crisis Management at the University of Southern California: criminal attacks, economic attacks, loss of proprietary information, industrial disasters, natural disasters, breaks in equipment and plants, legal crises, reputational and perceptual crises, human resources–related and occupational crises, health crises, and regulatory crises.[5]

Although the complexities and range of potential crises are extensive, many crises progress through a typical crisis cycle. Stephen Fink provides a model helpful for understanding a common four-stage cycle in organizational crisis. The four stages are the prodromal (or warning) crisis stage, the acute crisis stage, the chronic crisis stage, and the crisis resolution stage.[6] When we think of crisis leadership, our minds often run to the *acute* stage—the stage when the immediate shock of the crisis runs through the organizational system. But effective crisis leadership requires intentionality in each stage.

For instance, healthy and wise leaders proactively guide their organizations in such a way that they intentionally look for warning signs of crises before these crises become acute. This work takes place in the prodromal or warning stage noted above. Writing about this warning stage, Michael Hackman and Craig Johnson argue that catching problems early, before they turn into full-blown crises, is the ultimate goal of crisis management and crisis leadership. They write, "Crisis prevention requires constant vigilance and the determination to respond immediately to [warnings] once they are identified."[7] While healthy leaders seek to wisely lead their communities in each of the four stages identified by Stephen Fink, it is the leader's work during the warning phase that prepares the organization to effectively navigate crises at the other stages as well.

> **Catching problems early, before they turn into full-blown crises, is the ultimate goal of crisis management and crisis leadership.**

As one of the presidents who responded to the survey pointed out, organizational leaders are not typically well equipped to lead through crisis, criticism, and challenge. He noted that it is "character issues and issues of wisdom and judgment" that are vital for leaders guiding organizations through difficulties and crises. In light of this call for character and wisdom, we turn now to core leader qualities that are necessary for leading well in crisis.

Healthy Leaders Nurture Leadership Qualities Necessary for Leading Well during Crises

Tim Johnson, author of *Crisis Leadership*, encourages organizations to develop a "crisis-ready culture." Part of the equation for such a culture is having the kinds of leaders in the organization who are "steady enough to make deliberate, wise decisions even as the world speeds up—which is essentially what happens during a crisis."[8] The speed of a crisis can quickly become overwhelming for a leader without a disposition of steady wisdom. This points back to the aim we discussed in chapter 1—today's leaders need wisdom to face and lead their communities through complex times. Thus, *wisdom for organizational leaders* is our aim for crisis leadership as well.

Although experienced leaders are typically prepared to respond to a variety of problems, crisis creates contexts and scenarios in which the correct responses are not as clear as they are under normal circumstances. Comparing these leadership demands to the work of a first-time chaplain in the intensive care unit, Steve Cuss writes, "No one can prepare you for this. There is no manual, there is no procedure. Leadership in the face of unhinged grief is pure intuition. All you can do is face it, manage yourself, and respond as situations arise."[9] That's a pretty accurate description of crisis leadership and the demands placed on organizational leaders: face the crisis, manage your own anxiety in order to maintain a calm and non-anxious presence, and then respond.

This requires a lot from an executive leader. One of the senior partners who participated in the survey wrote of the need to "grow in humility [and] be ready to step into settings that you will inherently not know the answers to every, or even most, questions." This position of not knowing the answers can be especially difficult for some personalities. But crisis leadership—leadership in scenarios when the appropriate action is unclear or difficult to determine—requires the unique and vital combination of *humility*, *wisdom*, *resilience*, and *calm leadership presence* emphasized in chapters 3 and 4. Let's briefly explore these vital leader qualities.

Healthy Leaders Are Calm and Non-anxious

Crisis tends to elicit a fight-or-flight instinct in people. This is one of the reasons why steady, calm, and non-anxious leadership is vital in times of crisis. Tim Johnson notes how important it is that crisis leaders resist this tendency toward fight-or-flight responses. Daniel McGinn writes, "Actually leading in a crisis . . . requires avoiding these impulses and instead figuring out what's really happening, thinking hard about stakeholders' needs, and creating a purposeful mission to guide the response." Noting that crisis leaders need to resist the urge to do anything immediate, McGinn continues, "Ignore the adrenaline, work with a high-performing team, get the facts, ask questions, and listen; then make a plan."[10]

One of the vice presidents who responded to the survey made a similar point related to decision making: "In stressful situations, take the time to consider your course of action, consult with key advisers or actors in the system, and breathe, before making decisions." There is a lot packed into the word "breathe." Especially in times of crisis, team members need leaders to exhibit a calm and courageous demeanor. Leaders understand that sometimes this calm exterior screens a different internal reality. Leaders still have feelings of anxiety, questions about the right path to pursue, and emotional concerns connected to the weight of their leadership responsibilities. Healthy leaders acknowledge these realities, but they do not let these realities dictate how they relate to their team members. Instead, they pause, gain perspective with close advisers, and then lead their community both calmly and courageously. William Ury reminds his readers that, while objects react, people can choose to calmly respond instead.[11] The authors of *The Leader's Journey* echo this: "During a crisis, leaders need to make an extra effort to calm ourselves so that we can respond rather than react to the crisis."[12]

Healthy Leaders Are Resilient and Persevering

In chapter 3, I noted a series of studies Christopher Howard and I have been conducting that focus on the significant role that hardships and obstacles play in the development of resilience and character.[13] Motivated by the biblical relationships between themes such as hardships, endurance (resilience), and character (see Rom. 5:3–5), we have explored, among other things, how the leadership qualities of endurance and resilience were developed in leaders who display these qualities. Part of this study series highlights how the calm and non-anxious leadership presence noted above—also known as leader differentiation of self—is positively related to leader resilience. In other words, calm and non-anxious leaders also tend to be resilient leaders, and resilience is a character quality vital for crisis leadership.

In his book *Tempered Resilience*, Tod Bolsinger notes the importance of resilience for leading in the midst of change, crisis, and resistance. Bolsinger writes, "To lead, especially in the face of resistance, requires that we develop resilience."[14] He adds the modifier *tempered* to explain that the type of resilience that serves leaders and their organizations well in changing times is a resilience that is both strong *and* flexible. Just as tempered metals are neither too soft nor too brittle, so tempered leaders are both strong and flexible (adaptable) in their resilience. Such adaptability may not be as critical in the normal flow of leadership demands, but in times of crisis this combination of resolve *and* adaptability is essential.

Several of the leaders who participated in the survey underlined the value of enduring and persevering resilience. First, they highlighted the importance of pacing oneself as a leader and maintaining a long-term orientation in the midst of challenging times: "You can't eat the whole elephant—take things one step at a time." "You can't solve every problem, and especially in 24 hours." "Play the long game: build a movement not a moment: ministry is a marathon." "Pace yourself well. Don't be surprised by challenges." Second, as one superintendent noted, it is in times of great need that staying the course and persevering is most relevant: "Stay the course. The grass is not greener and your subordinates need you now more than ever." He continues, "If you are looking for a true leadership challenge, prove to yourself that you can complete the job of climbing the mountaintop after spending time in the valley."

While times of crisis tempt some leaders to throw in the proverbial towel, there is a lot of wisdom in the comments above. Times of crisis are when leaders are likely to be most needed by their team members. Times of crisis are when staying the course is vital. Times of crisis are when the true challenge of leadership awaits us.

Healthy Leaders Are Humble and Wise

In this final section on the type of leader qualities necessary for leading an organization through a crisis, I turn to *humility* and *wisdom*. As noted above, in times of crisis, organizations need leaders who are "steady enough to make deliberate, wise decisions even as the world speeds up."[15] McGinn and Johnson point to the example of President George W. Bush and his initial response to the 9/11 attacks. What was President Bush's response when he heard that New York City was under attack? He continued sitting with Florida schoolchildren. McGinn and Johnson observe that, by not outwardly reacting, President Bush bought himself *space* to think and *time* to respond.[16] Some voices initially criticized the president for this reaction. But as the years have passed, others have noted how his response demonstrated calm in the midst of crisis and chaos.

Although responsiveness in crisis is a high priority noted throughout this chapter, proactive *responsiveness* does not equal immediate *reactiveness*. As noted above, objects react, but people can choose to not react impulsively. Leaders can pause. They can take things in. They can respond with humility and counsel and wisdom. As one nonprofit president put it in the survey, "Before making decisions or taking action, it is critical to first try to understand the problem as thoroughly as possible. Time is more often your ally." Humility allows leaders to value the opinions and perspectives of others. It creates a context within which leaders may gain wisdom from both contemporary and historical advisers. Consider Peter's call to humility: "Clothe yourselves, all of you, with humility toward one another, for 'God opposes the proud but gives grace to the humble'" (1 Pet. 5:5).

Although responsiveness in crisis is a high priority noted throughout this chapter, proactive *responsiveness* does not equal immediate *reactiveness*.

Note two additional comments from the surveyed leaders about humbly gaining perspective from history when facing contemporary crises. One ministry leader noted, "Throughout [the COVID-19 pandemic] I reminded myself of the difficult times church leaders went through [down through history]." Another leader observed, "Understanding historical and current trends is helpful in navigating difficult times." Although times of crisis can make leaders feel as though they are alone—facing a challenge unlike anything experienced by others—students of history tend to see another story. Consider the words of the great teacher in Ecclesiastes: "There is nothing new under the sun" (1:9). Though it was spoken in another era, this enduring wisdom is a helpful reminder for contemporary leaders. Each moment brings new details, but the crises we face often have similarities to crises of the past. Wise and healthy leaders are willing to receive counsel both from contemporary advisers and from the wisdom of history.

Healthy Leaders Communicate Effectively and Proactively during Crises

In chapter 7, we spent time reflecting on communication as one of the keys to effective leadership during crises, so I will not spend too much time going over this topic again here. As a reminder, effective crisis communication from leaders involves several priorities, including making sure that communication is *regular*, *consistent*, *values-based*, *direct*, *planned*, carried out along *multiple pathways*, and informed by *multiple perspectives*. Rather than rehearsing these priorities here, let's look at two crisis leadership examples, focusing on the communication side of these examples.

First, consider the tragic story of Tylenol's contamination with cyanide, mentioned above. In 1982, Tylenol manufacturer Johnson & Johnson and its CEO, Jim Burke, faced a calamity when several people died because of an act beyond the company's immediate control. In the midst of this tragedy and the firestorm that followed, Burke decided to go on the news program *60 Minutes*. Though some, including the company's head of public relations, told Burke this was an awful decision, Burke opted for an approach of openness. He notes, "What it came down to was that if we were *absolutely straight* with them, we'd do fine."[17] From a communication perspective, Johnson & Johnson wisely navigated a painful crisis. Burke continues, "But most important was the fact that we put the public first. We never hid anything from them and were as honest as we know how to be. It just confirmed my belief that if you play it straight, it works."[18]

The second example involves Winston Churchill's leadership as prime minister, especially in 1940. As I noted in chapter 7, Churchill provided communication that was direct and straightforward. John Baldoni writes about him, "He did not hide the dangers that faced the island kingdom in the dark days of 1940."[19] Here's an example of what Baldoni is talking about, drawn from Churchill's first speech to the House of Commons after becoming prime minister.

> I would say to the House, as I said to those who have joined this government: "I have nothing to offer but blood, toil, tears and sweat." We have before us an ordeal of the most grievous kind. We have before us many, many long months of struggle and of suffering.
>
> You ask, what is our policy? I can say: It is to wage war, by sea, land and air, with all our might and with all the strength that God can give us; to wage war

against a monstrous tyranny, never surpassed in the dark, lamentable catalogue of human crime. That is our policy.

You ask, what is our aim? I can answer in one word: It is victory, victory at all costs, victory in spite of all terror, victory, however long and hard the road may be; for without victory, there is no survival.[20]

In the face of the unthinkable evil that Hitler's Germany represented, Churchill chose direct and brutal honesty in his leadership communication. While he paired this with a vision of a hopeful future—"victory at all costs"—his call to action did not back away from the hard truths.

Both Churchill and Burke provide helpful examples of leading during times of weighty crisis. For both of these leaders, direct and honest communication guided them through dark days.

Healthy Leaders Utilize Wise Strategies during Crises

In addition to understanding the nature of crisis and the type of leadership qualities necessary for leading well during a crisis, healthy and effective leaders utilize wise strategies.

Healthy Leaders Are Honest and Proactive

First, healthy leaders opt for a strategy of *honesty* and *proactivity*. We saw the approach of honesty and directness exhibited in the Burke and Churchill examples noted above. Providing additional affirmation for this strategy of honesty, Hackman and Johnson observe, "When it comes to crisis, honesty is the best policy. If your company is at fault, take responsibility. Don't try to hide damaging information (chances are it will be discovered anyway), and correct your mistakes when necessary."[21]

While leaders may be tempted by the desire to conceal damaging information—perhaps out of a partially helpful, though wrongheaded, motivation to protect the organization—the path of concealing generally backfires. For instance, at one time Firestone Wilderness tires were linked to at least 88 deaths and 250 injuries in the US, but recalls were delayed because of financial considerations. Daniel Eisenberg wrote in 2000 that, "thanks to a generally dreadful crisis management, marked primarily by silence and denials, the Firestone brand has very little credibility left."[22]

In addition to honesty, *proactivity* is also vital. One of the survey participants remarked, "We can't continue to be reactionary." Another wrote, "Regardless of the current circumstances, be thinking proactively." This is where proactive work such as scenario planning comes into play. *Harvard Business Review* writer Peter Scoblic notes, "One important element of the practice [of strategic foresight] is scenario planning, which helps leaders navigate uncertainty by teaching them how to anticipate possible futures while still operating in the present."[23] Scoblic argues that managing the uncertainty of the future requires many tools, some of which have similar or even overlapping functions.

Here are some of the tools Scoblic notes beyond scenario planning: *backcasting*, in which participants work backward in time from a particular future to ascertain what in the present caused its emergence; *contingency planning*, which prepares participants for specific scenarios; *crisis simulation*, which involves analyzing participant responses to a specific envisioned scenario; *forecasting*, in which participants make probabilistic predictions about the future; *horizon scanning*, in which participants are asked to consider weak signals of change in the present; *trend analysis*, in which participants are asked to consider the influence of presently visible patterns; and *war games*, in which participants engage an opponent in simulated conflict.[24]

Further emphasizing the importance of planning, McGinn advises companies to create a concise "one-page crisis playbook, similar to what an NFL coach carries on the sidelines." This playbook could include information such as (1) who in the organization (typically not the CEO or equivalent) is the designated person to manage the crisis on behalf of the CEO and organization, (2) which organizational members will form a rapid response team that will assist the designated manager, and (3) the type of scenario-planning training given to this team and specific insights relevant to the organization's sector.[25] While various forms of scenario planning seek insight into potential issues an organization may face, this "crisis playbook" focuses more on who the key players will be in the organization's response to a crisis.

While honesty is the right proactive strategy *after* a crisis arrives, scenario planning and the additional tools of foresight work noted above are the right proactive strategy *before* a crisis arrives. These are themes I stressed in chapter 7 as well, where I emphasized that leaders and organizations should anticipate as many potential crises and scenarios as possible and that this due-diligence work is particularly important in larger organizations, where scenario planning becomes vital to the long-term viability of the organization and its mission.

Healthy Leaders Are Agile and Responsive

As I noted in chapter 7, healthy organizational leaders create pathways for responsiveness in communication. This is part of the process of building trust between leaders and organizations, and it is also vital in times of crisis. People—both within and outside an organization—must see leaders actively responding to rather than ignoring crises. Responsiveness includes being proactive about communication during a crisis, and it includes being proactive about reflecting on lessons learned after the intensity of the crisis has subsided. A posture of active responsiveness is difficult to adopt without strategies that facilitate organizational agility.

This is a point that many organizational leaders highlighted in the survey. One president put it this way: "Leaders must focus on strategic processes that will give them the ability to pivot and change course at any given time." The challenge is that many organizations want to be agile and adaptive but have not created systems and structures that facilitate agility. The other challenge is that organizations need to create systems and cultures that facilitate agility *before* crises hit.

Consider some of the organizations that effectively and rapidly adapted early in the pandemic. One of these organizations was Chick-fil-A. As stores quickly refined their takeout and drive-through service early in the pandemic, Chick-fil-A seemed to find the "secret sauce" to make things work on a large scale. When the US was in its most robust lockdown during the days of "flattening the curve" in the spring of 2020, I remember enjoying one primary family activity outside the house—outings to the Chick-fil-A drive-through. Chick-fil-A acquired such a reputation for efficiency in those days that some public officials sought out advice from Chick-fil-A managers about how to improve drive-through vaccine clinics.[26]

In the realm of education, schools that already had structures and systems in place to shift online outperformed schools that needed to learn these structures and systems. The two schools with which I had connections in 2020 both had a robust model of online education in place. Turning the dial up to serve additional students was a lot of work, but this work was not exacerbated by a need to build the structures and systems themselves. In contrast, the K–12 schools with which my children were engaged were not structurally prepared to make such an agile jump to online education. In a sense, they had to "build the plane while flying." This created painful circumstances, both for educators and for students. The broader educational system is still seeking to recover from the challenges to learning during those days.

Consider the ways leaders emphasized this need for responsive agility in the survey:

- "Never stop learning, stay nimble, and be creative." (a vice president)
- "Create a structure that allows your organization to adapt and change as much as the world around you is changing." (a president)

- "Today's solutions will eventually become tomorrow's limitations. Always adapt to current realities." (a lead pastor)
- "[In] continuing to adapt to an ever-changing world . . . an organization must be structured to constantly adapt, and it is often your newest employees who will lead you in those changes." (a president)

This call to pursue agility and adaptive leadership requires a new approach to collaboration and leading in crisis.

Healthy Leaders Are Adaptive and Collaborative

One of the survey participants called specific attention to what is known as adaptive leadership. This participant advised executives to "find a coach or consultant outside of your context to coach you (and possibly your entire team) in . . . adaptive leadership." Expanding on this idea of adaptive leadership, this leader highlighted the importance of maintaining "the *technical* deliverables that are expected by our community . . . while addressing the most pressing *adaptive* challenges in a rapidly changing" context.

Indeed, adaptive leadership—a concept put forward by Ronald Heifetz in his book *Leadership without Easy Answers*—provides a helpful distinction between technical challenges and adaptive challenges.[27] While *technical* challenges involve problems that are clearly defined with known solutions, *adaptive* challenges are those that are not as clear-cut or easy to identify, and they cannot be addressed "through the normal ways of doing things."[28] For example, while many churches had standard (technical) protocols in place for what to do on a Sunday with an extreme snowfall (in the Midwest) or an incoming hurricane (in the Southeast), these same churches likely did not have protocols for what to do in the face of a global pandemic. Regardless of what response you ended up thinking was best—tight lockdown or continued gathering—the point is that most church leaders had never even thought of this issue before 2020. This type of scenario represents the demands associated with an *adaptive* leadership challenge.

So what are leaders to do in the face of adaptive challenges? Heifetz identifies six strategic leadership priorities for organizations facing crises and adaptive challenges.[29]

1. Get on the balcony (step out of the fray and find perspective).
2. Identify the adaptive challenge (analyze and diagnose the challenge).
3. Regulate distress ("Keep the heat up, without blowing up the vessel").[30]

4. Maintain disciplined attention (keep people focused on the tough work they need to do).
5. Give the work back to the people ("Leaders help others do the work they need to do, in order to adapt to the challenge").[31]
6. Protect leadership voices from below ("Give cover to those who raise hard questions and generate distress").[32]

While many leaders desire to pull in the reins of authority by engaging in highly directive leadership in times of crisis, adaptive leadership provides a counterintuitive perspective. Heifetz emphasizes this with his advice to *give the work back to the people*. Here is a formal definition of *adaptive leadership* that emphasizes this point: "Adaptive leadership is the practice of mobilizing people to tackle tough challenges and thrive."[33]

Collaborative leadership might not be the first thing that comes to mind in times of crisis, but as the complexity of organizational crises increases, so does the wisdom necessary to confront these crises in productive and adaptive ways. One president noted in the survey, "Shared leadership has long been seen as one of several paths or styles of leadership. What we are (painfully) learning is that shared leadership is the only way for any organization or leader to survive and thrive" in today's complex and changing environment. As you navigate organizational crises, consider how a wise and collaborative posture can help you. In contrast to the "old and foolish king who no longer knew how to take advice" (Eccles. 4:13), learn to surround yourself with wisdom and then empower your people to tackle the pressing and adaptive challenges of the day.

Healthy Leaders Provide Values-Based Leadership during Crises

Values-based leadership is essential for times of crisis. As noted previously about a congregational setting, "During a crisis, the leader will be careful to connect the actions and responses of the congregation to the vision and values that have become familiar to them."[34] While values are vital for any stage in the life of an organization (see the related discussions in chap. 8), clarity about *who* we are as an organization is arguably even more important in the push and pull of a crisis.

Values-based leadership is essential for times of crisis.

Just as a sound, seaworthy vessel must have sufficient ballast to keep itself upright in turbulent conditions, so organizations need values, beliefs, and clarity of purpose to provide sufficient organizational ballast in times of crisis. Consider the comments of some of the surveyed leaders who echo this priority:

- "Remain relentlessly focused on what is most essential to advance [the] vision while navigating the ongoing uncertainties that can distract." (a president)
- "The world is always changing, people are always changing: focus on what never changes and be kind." (a head of school)
- "The pandemic proved I don't have control, but at the same time, our mission and focus before the pandemic helped us survive it and recapture the momentum we had beforehand. God indeed determines our steps, though he still wants us to make plans." (a CEO)
- "In this time of rapid change and uncertainty, leaders with a strong moral compass are the best hope organizations have today." (a president)

Such ideas resonate with McGinn's observation that "leading in a crisis . . . requires . . . creating a purposeful mission to guide the response."[35] Clarity about *who* we are as an organization—having a clear sense of the organization's purpose, mission, strategies, values, beliefs, and vision—is precisely what we need when a storm of crisis hits. Heifetz notes, "Defined purposes are the single most important source of orientation in doing both technical and adaptive work, like a ship's compass heading at sea."[36]

As I consider the importance of a values-driven culture to navigating crisis, I think of two phrases, one from a well-known movie and the second from a statement passed down from my wife's family. Perhaps you recall the line spoken by Rafiki to Simba in the 1994 Disney film *The Lion King*: "Remember *who* you are." While organizational leaders might want to pursue quick fixes to crisis problems, times of crisis are when it becomes most important to "remember *who* you are" as a leader and as an organization. Character—individual and organizational—matters most when it is being tested.

The second statement is one my wife heard from her mom frequently: "Remember *whose* you are." The point was for my wife, Tasha, to remember that she was loved and treasured both by her parents and by her God. This is what our children now often hear as they leave the house: "Remember *whose* you are." For Christian leaders, this is affirming what the apostle Paul asserts to the church in Corinth: "You are not your own, for you were bought with a price" (1 Cor. 6:19–20). Paul makes a similar point in 2 Corinthians: "He died for all, that those who live might no longer live for themselves but for him who for their sake died and was raised" (5:15).

For Christian leaders guiding organizations through times of crisis, both statements provide helpful clarity—remember both *who* and *whose* you are. One business thinker reminds us that "when the strategy is uncertain, the best managers acknowledge what's unknown, but also look ahead to what *is* known."[37] In other words, when we are leading during a crisis, our people need to hear us honestly acknowledge and name what is *not* known about the crisis we're facing—but they should also hear a bold, courageous, and confident message about what we *do* know. Our organizational culture—especially our values and beliefs—tell us *who* we are. For Christian leaders who are guiding other Christians, it also is vital to take hope in *whose* we are. While there are plenty of things we don't know about crises, as organizational leaders, we can provide hopeful leadership during crises as we confidently point to the things that we *do* know.

Recommendations and Reflection

This chapter focused on priorities for leading organizations through crises. These priorities include (1) understanding the nature of crises, (2) nurturing necessary leader qualities, (3) communicating effectively and proactively, (4) utilizing wise strategies, and (5) embracing values-based leadership. As leaders face unique organizational challenges and threats—challenges and threats that seem to grow in their complexity each year—learning to face these challenges calmly, collaboratively, and wisely is the order of the day for our new normal of adaptive challenges.

Take a moment to consider these priorities for faithful and effective crisis leadership. Use the following questions to help you reflect on how you may need to grow as a developing crisis leader.

Healthy leaders understand the nature of crises.

- In the survey, several of the leaders noted that the COVID-19 pandemic caused a season of difficulties in leading. Do you agree? What has made this season of leadership difficult, or not, for you?
- Considering the various types of crises noted in this chapter (exploding vs. unfolding; self-inflicted vs. external pressures; the list from the Center for Crisis Management), what are some of the crises faced by your organization?
- Consider a crisis that your organization has faced in the past. As you think about the four stages of crisis noted in this chapter (prodromal/warning, acute, chronic, and resolution), did you see the crisis play out in this typical cycle?

- "Crisis prevention requires constant vigilance and the determination to respond": As you consider potential crises in the future, what steps can your organization take to better prepare the community to see crises at the warning stage rather than at the acute stage?

Healthy leaders nurture leadership qualities necessary for leading well during crises.

- Steve Cuss writes, "Leadership in the face of unhinged grief is pure intuition. All you can do is face it, manage yourself, and respond as situations arise." Do you agree with this? What is helpful about this observation when it comes to crisis leadership?
- Noting the importance of calm and non-anxious leadership during a crisis, one of the cited authors highlights the need to resist the fight-or-flight instinct. Do you tend more toward fight or flight in a crisis? How can you remain calm as a leader so that you respond rather than react?
- Resilience, and a persevering spirit, is a priority for leaders in crisis situations. How can you work on developing the strength and flexibility of tempered resilience?
- Daniel McGinn notes that we need leaders "steady enough to make deliberate, wise decisions even as the world speeds up . . . during a crisis." How are you nurturing the humility and wisdom needed for such demands?

Healthy leaders communicate effectively and proactively during crises.

- Reflecting on the priority of proactive communication noted in both chapter 7 and this chapter, why is regular and consistent information from leaders so important for people during times of crisis?
- Why is delayed communication, or communication that is not straightforward, typically unhelpful or damaging to people and organizations?
- Reflecting on Tylenol's crisis, Johnson & Johnson CEO Jim Burke stated, "What it came down to was that if we were absolutely straight with them, we'd do fine." Do you agree with this approach?
- Considering Churchill's example of pairing brutal honesty with a vision of a hopeful future, how can you better nurture this paradoxical pairing of directness and hope in your organizational communication?

Healthy leaders utilize wise strategies during crises.

- "When it comes to crisis, honesty is the best policy": Assuming you agree with this reflection, why is this so important for leaders and organizations?

- As you consider several of the recommendations for proactivity—scenario planning, contingency planning, trend analysis, and so forth—what practice of strategic foresight work would be helpful for your organization as you consider potential crises that could emerge in your sector?
- "Leaders must focus on strategic processes that will give them the ability to pivot and change course at any given time": As you consider a recent crisis that your organization faced, did you (or did you not) have structures and strategic processes in place that allowed you to pivot with agility? How can you position your organization to have more agility in potential future crises?
- Considering the distinction between technical and adaptive challenges, how might more collaborative approaches to leadership help you navigate adaptive challenges better in the future?

Healthy leaders provide values-based leadership during crises.

- "During a crisis, the leader will be careful to connect the actions and responses of the [organization] to the vision and values that have become familiar to them": Why are values so important for organizations and team members as they navigate crises?
- Considering the metaphor of organizational ballast, how does a clear picture of an organization's culture—particularly its values and beliefs—have a steadying effect amid the turbulent waters of crisis?
- "Remember *who* you are": How can you make your values and beliefs (who you are) clearer for the organization you lead? Why is this work important not only in the midst of crisis but also as you prepare for crises during seasons of calm?
- "Remember *whose* you are": How does reflecting on the nature of God and who we are before God strengthen and encourage Christian leaders facing crisis? How has such reflection been an encouragement to you in the past, helping you to endure through hardship and difficulty?

TEN

Change Leadership and a Thriving Future for the Organization

Throughout this book, and especially in the reflections on organizational culture in chapter 8, we have considered the priority of knowing both *who* we are (think purpose, mission, and values and beliefs) and *where* we are going (think vision). As we work toward a vision of a preferred future for our organizations, change is inevitably a part of the equation.

But for organizations and their leaders, the choice is not one of continuity *or* change; rather, it is about finding the right balance between continuity *and* change. The well-known management thinker Peter Drucker puts it this way: "Change and continuity are thus poles rather than opposites. The more an institution is organized to be a change leader, the more it will need to establish continuity internally and externally, the more it will need to balance change and continuity."[1]

In contrast to change motivated by crisis—the focus of chapter 9—in this chapter we will consider the importance of intentionally providing change leadership that is visionary and future-oriented. While crisis leaders sometimes put the meaningful, though less inspiring, goal of *surviving* front and center, change leaders aim for the vision of a *thriving* future. As one leader wrote in the survey, "The strategies we used to *survive* are not effective for *thriving* and moving ahead."

Can you think of organizations that died off or declined because they were not willing to change? Consider all the shuttered Blockbuster stores after the company failed to switch to streaming services quickly enough and lost out in its competition with Netflix. Or consider the contrast between Sears and Walmart as the two companies competed for market share amid the shift to online retail in light of the growing Amazon platform. Though Blockbuster and Sears both enjoyed a favored position in their respective markets at one time, their approach to change tells organizational leaders a cautionary tale.

Organizational leaders quickly realize that status quo is a myth; the lived reality of the day will change in the days to come. This is why a proactive posture toward change leadership is vital. One president noted in the survey, "We as organizational leaders need to help manage the change and be part of it." Change can be planned (active) or unplanned (passive). Rather than adopting an organizational posture that is *passive*—change happens to the organization in an unplanned manner—healthy and wise leaders lean into the change process with an *active* posture that seeks to further the purpose, mission, and vision of the organization by means of the planned change.

One of the survey participants cautioned leaders, "Resist staying the same and not changing." The desire to stay the same is understandable but is not realistic or sustainable for organizations. As another leader observed, it is simply a reality of life that both people and organizations change. Just as the people of Israel had to resist the desire to return to the familiarity of Egypt when they experienced difficulty while wandering in the wilderness on the way to the promised land (see Num. 14:1–4), so leaders and organizations cannot simply return to the comfort of past successes or familiarities on their journey to a preferred future. Here's how another leader put it in the survey: "Don't go back to normal. Whatever normal was, resist the urge. Even if it's an incremental change, now is the time."

In the remaining sections, we'll explore theological, theoretical, and practical wisdom for leaders seeking to navigate their organizations to a vision of a preferred future. We will consider (1) the theological foundations for change, (2) how leaders can prepare their organizations for change, and (3) how leaders can effectively enact and anchor a change in their organizations.

Healthy Christian Leaders Understand the Theological Foundations for Change

Before considering theoretical and practical matters for change leadership, let's begin with the ultimate foundation for change: "For I the Lord do not change" (Mal. 3:6) and "Jesus Christ is the same yesterday and today and forever" (Heb. 13:8). As one of the survey participants noted, "The world is always changing, people are always changing; focus on what never changes."

The God who never changes is the One who brings about renewal and change in our lives and our communities. Drawing on the insights above from Peter Drucker, I argue that it is the *continuity* of God's unchanging nature that provides a solid foundation upon which we can securely and confidently experience change on a human level.

Throughout the Bible, God calls his people to new realities. He also produces in them a newness and transformation (see Rom. 8:29; 2 Cor. 3:18). In Isaiah, we see God's heart for transformation and newness: "Remember not the former things, nor consider the things of old. Behold, I am doing a new thing" (Isa. 43:18–19). God made a *new* covenant with his people (Jer. 31:31; Heb. 9:15). God puts a *new* heart and *new* spirit in his people (Ezek. 11:19; 36:26). God grants *newness* of life and makes *new* creations of his people (Rom. 6:4; 2 Cor. 5:17). God gives his people a *new* song to sing (Pss. 96:1; 98:1). And, as will be fully realized in the future restoration, God is creating a *new* heavens and a *new* earth for his people (Isa. 65:17; Rev. 21:1–4). Our unchanging God is all about newness and transformation.

The God who never changes is the One who brings about renewal and change in our lives and our communities.

God has been calling his people to newness and change from the first pages of Scripture. Consider God's call to Abraham: "Now the Lord said to Abram, 'Go from your country and your kindred and your father's house to the land that I will show you'" (Gen. 12:1). While the broader passage emphasizes the promise to which Abraham is being called—a promise related to "land, seed, and blessing"[2]—the promise begins with what Abraham needs to leave. This is to be no small change. He is to leave his *country*, his *kindred*, his *father's house*. It is a change of where he will live. It is a change of the family among whom he will live. It is a change in how he will live. In response to this radical call to change, "Abram went, as the Lord had told him" (Gen. 12:4).

Note the contrast between this faith of Abraham and the hardness of heart among the people wandering in the wilderness. Of Abraham we read, "Abraham believed God, and it was counted to him as righteousness" (Rom. 4:3), but the author of Hebrews writes of the "evil, unbelieving heart" represented by those "on the day of testing in the wilderness" (Heb. 3:8, 12). In contrast to those in the wilderness who hardened their hearts and so wanted to turn back to the slavery of their past, our trust in the unchanging and faithful nature of God should inspire us to lean into the future with hope and confidence.

Change leadership requires leaders to step into the future with bold faith. For most leaders—if they are honest—courage can be hard to find when they are leaning into an uncertain future. But Christians have a unique advantage here. We have a wise and sovereign God in whom we are able to ground our hope and confidence. Many of the leaders who responded to the survey note this priority; consider their encouragements:

- "Pray, stay in the Word, lead by example and persevere! God has us in the palm of His hand, and . . . nothing can pluck us out!" (a senior pastor)
- "You have to stay on your knees. If you do not recognize a desperate dependency, you will miss the path that God has prepared for you and all that has been entrusted to you." (a president)
- "Stay faithful to God's leading and direction, . . . act on what God is showing you now!" (an executive pastor)
- "Regain your hope. Part of that comes from simply deciding you won't give up, . . . and you won't give up because God's not done writing your story." (a lead pastor)
- "It is beneficial for me as a pastor to encourage others to keep their eyes on Jesus. . . . Point to how our project or change of approach does not take our focus off of Christ, but better aligns us to serve others and glorify God." (a senior pastor)
- "Trust the Lord's guidance in the process!" (a lead pastor)
- "Raise your eyes to the big picture. Let your faith guide your perspective on the future." (a CEO)

As Christian leaders consider how they will lead their organizations toward a preferred future, the process begins with trust in the wisdom and unchanging nature of God. With this foundation in mind, let's turn to theoretical and practical insights for the demands of change leadership.

Healthy Leaders Prepare Well before Starting a Change Process

This section will explore several change dynamics to help leaders as they prepare for the change journey: (1) common hindrances to change, (2) types of change, (3) how people change, (4) assessing readiness for change, and (5) typical stages in a change process.

Hindrances to Change

Change is hard work, and many people—and organizational structures—are wired to resist change. This is not necessarily unhelpful. Voices and structures that preserve continuity and stability have an anchoring effect on an organization. We need foundations. We need roots. We need anchors. But these values need to be balanced by complementary values of transformation, renewal, and change. Wise organizational leaders understand common hindrances to change; with this understanding, they are able to affirm forces that advocate for continuity while also challenging hindrances that oppose necessary change.

I tend to organize common hindrances to change into four categories: (1) intrapersonal, (2) interpersonal, (3) team and organizational, and (4) environmental dynamics external to the organization.[3] Space limitations make extended discussion on these impractical, but I'll quickly list these common hindrances or barriers to change.

1. *Intrapersonal dynamics (individual hindrances)*: These include personal fear of failure, risk averseness, complacency, fear of increased responsibilities, unwillingness to experience the discomfort of change, threat to personal values and perspectives, comfort with what is familiar, suspicion of new ideas, focus on self-interest, and concerns about job security.
2. *Interpersonal dynamics (relational hindrances)*: These include lack of trust, resentment of interference from others, threat to status, feared loss of power, feared loss of positive personal relationships, being closed off to the ideas of others, feelings of being excluded or left out, and poor communication.
3. *Team and organizational dynamics (group hindrances)*: These include focus on past success and innovation, group self-preservation, institutional focus rather than focus on purpose, a group opinion that change is not feasible, a group opinion that change is not necessary, the rule of a change-averse minority voice, lack of vision or direction from the group leader, perceived high cost to human and financial resources, a punitive view of risk and failure in the organization's culture, misalignment of resources, lack of sponsorship by senior leadership, lack of training about how to approach change, and a change-averse organizational culture.
4. *Environmental dynamics (hindrances external to the organization)*: These include fear of public perception related to change or change failure, uncertain economy, fear of external unknown realities, inordinate concern about organizational competition, lack of environmental (sociocultural) awareness, and ignoring the needs-wants-aspirations of external stakeholders.

The list of potential change hindrances is long. Consider your organizational context and where some of these hindrances may be holding back necessary change in your organization.

Types of Change

Planned, Unplanned, and Emergent

Earlier in this chapter I highlighted how change can be planned (active) or unplanned (passive). I would like to consider several additional factors. First, I would add to this list by noting that change may be *planned*, *unplanned*, or *emergent*. Emergent change is similar to unplanned change, but it generally has a longer timeline associated with it. For instance, while a substantial and unexpected event may quickly change an organization in an unplanned manner—think of organizations that have been affected by natural disasters such as tornados, hurricanes, earthquakes, or flooding—emergent change affects the organization over a longer period. Examples include the adoption of online commerce in business or online learning in higher education.

Technical and Adaptive

Second, change may be *technical* or *adaptive*. I spent some time on this distinction in chapter 9, where I noted that technical challenges are characterized as problems that are clearly defined with known solutions, whereas adaptive challenges are those that are not as clear-cut or easy to identify.[4] While technical changes are fairly routine for organizations, adaptive changes are larger-scale changes that organizational members experience as weightier and more consequential.

First-Order and Second-Order

Finally, it is helpful to note the difference between *first-order changes* and *second-order changes*. This distinction is somewhat parallel to that of technical and adaptive changes: first-order changes represent changes within a system while second-order changes represent changes to the system itself.

For instance, in higher education, an example of a first-order change would be switching a textbook that will be used in a certain course; an example of a second-order change would be switching the course from in-person to fully online. In the context of a church, an example of a first-order change would be adding a second service to the Sunday morning schedule; an example of a second-order change would be moving to a completely different model for services, such as moving to a house church model or a multisite model. In other words, the question is whether you are making a minor adjustment within the system, one that leaves you doing more or less of the same thing (a first-order change), or making a change to the very system and structure within which you are carrying out your work (a second-order change).

Types of Change for Healthy and Unhealthy Organizations

To tie some of these types of changes together: Healthy organizations generally benefit from regular and ongoing *technical* and *first-order* change. If things are going well for the community, the organization will likely need only small adjustments that continue to improve on the already healthy organizational approach. Conversely, unhealthy or declining organizations generally need more *adaptive* and *second-order* change. If things are not going well for the community, bigger and bolder adjustments are likely necessary to bring health and stability back to the community.

How People Change

Lest we forget, organizations are made up of people, so when we talk about change, a primary point of consideration is how *people* change. I'd like to highlight two considerations related to how people are motivated to change.

The Pull, Push, and Pain of Change

First, let's consider the intrinsic, extrinsic, and destabilizing motivations of change. Another way of talking about this is the *pull*, the *push*, and the *pain* of change. The intrinsic motivation, or pull, of change seeks to draw people out with a compelling and inspiring vision. This motivation is the ideal—it's preferable to the others. It is characterized by helping team members personally see and understand the benefits of the desired change. The extrinsic motivation, or push, of change is more transactional. It entails prodding people until they understand that the change is necessary even if they don't personally desire it. The destabilizing motivation, or pain, of change—which sometimes overlaps with intrinsic or extrinsic motivators—is in play when team members recognize that the pain of going through the change process is preferrable to the more painful option of doing nothing.

The Cognitive, Affective, and Behavioral Dimensions of Motivation

Second, it is important to consider the cognitive, affective, and behavioral motivations of change. This means recognizing that we lead whole persons.

As noted in chapter 4, "Scripture affirms that human beings are complex creatures. . . . In this earthly existence, we are a body-soul or body-spirit unity."[5] Because of this, it is important that we consider the whole person and the cognitive, affective, and behavioral dimensions of motivation.

In terms of the *cognitive* dimension of motivation, change rarely happens in the absence of new mental models to guide people. People need new understandings of both their present reality and their desired future to motivate change. Consequently, teaching is valuable to the change process. Teaching can help people understand the value and benefit of the desired change in contrast to present circumstances.

In terms of the *affective* dimension of motivation, change also rarely happens without some affective motivation or disequilibrium. An inspirational picture of the future should help people feel the weight of the needed change in contrast to the felt challenge of present circumstances.

In terms of the *behavioral* dimension of motivation, change is not initiated or implemented without action at the behavioral level of practice. In other words, sometimes organizational leaders need to simply set things in motion to solidify in practice what may not be fully understood yet, either cognitively or affectively.

Readiness for and Timing of Change

Later in this chapter, we will explore a model for implementing change effectively. But effective change is not only about applying the right processes to the change initiative. Organizational leaders are also responsible for considering the readiness of a community before launching a change initiative. I advise leaders to ask two primary questions: Is this the right vision? Is this the right time?[6]

Determining the organization's readiness for change involves carefully evaluating the quality of the vision for change and the organization's readiness to undertake the necessary change process. The following model (figure 10.1) may be useful for discerning whether you and your organization are ready for change. The model is structured around the two primary questions noted above.

The first question—*Is this the right vision?*—should be considered from several angles. Is the vision aligned with biblical values and commitments? Will this vision enable the organization to thrive in the months and years ahead? Does this vision fit with what you and your key advisers see through your due-diligence assessment? Will this vision facilitate organizational team members' flourishing? Is this the right vision for organizational stakeholders?

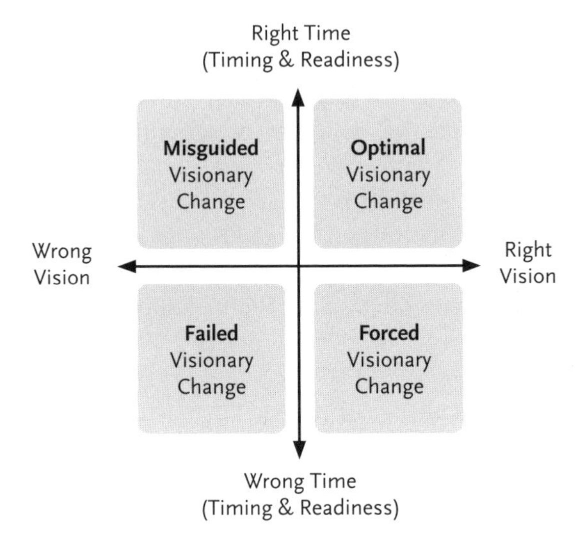

Figure 10.1. Readiness for and Timing of Change

Each organization and organizational sector will have its own angles on this question, but—in brief—you want to take the time to understand whether this is the vision that will best facilitate organizational well-being and human flourishing.

The second question—*Is this the right time?*—should be considered in a similar manner. Are there any biblical and theological factors that will help you discern whether this is the right season for this change? As I write this chapter, I'm reading through Ecclesiastes in my morning devotions; I am struck afresh by the importance of times and seasons: "For everything there is a season, and a time for every matter under heaven" (Eccles. 3:1). Are the structures and systems of your organization ready to take on this change? Are you as a leader ready to take on the practical and emotional work of this change? Are your team members—employees or volunteers—ready to take on the work of making this change happen? Are organizational stakeholders ready to experience the desired change? In other words, having the right vision is not enough. Effective change processes must take into account both whether the vision is right and whether the time is right.

As you can see in figure 10.1, the different answers to these two questions translate into four alternative organizational responses. First, if you find yourself with both the *wrong vision* and the *wrong time*, put up the STOP sign.

When both the vision and the time are wrong, as leaders we need to hit the brakes on change. Pressing for change when the vision is wrong and the time is wrong will lead to *failed visionary change*. Do not change simply for the sake of changing.

Second, if you find yourself with the *wrong vision* but the *right time*, put up the U-TURN sign. When the vision is wrong but the time is right, leaders need to find a safe place to pull over and turn around. Pressing for change when the vision is wrong but the time is right will lead to *misguided visionary change*. Leaders who recognize this unique situation of organizational readiness and misfit vision will have the courage to make a U-turn and get the organization headed in a new direction with a new vision.

Third, if you find yourself with the *right vision* but the *wrong time*, put up the YIELD sign. When the vision is right but the time is wrong, leaders must see and respond to the yield sign. This means recognizing that, while the vision is right, the organization and its people may not be ready. This is often the hardest signal for leaders to identify and follow, because waiting for the right time is difficult. However, pressing for change when the vision is right but the time is wrong will lead to a *forced visionary change*. Forced change often results in failed change. Leaders in this situation must exercise patience and put people before agendas.

Forced change often results in failed change. Leaders in this situation must exercise patience and put people before agendas.

Fourth, if you find yourself with the *right vision* and the *right time*, put up the GO sign or the GREEN LIGHT signal. When both the vision and the time are right, it is time for leaders to hit the accelerator and navigate along a planned path of change at the pace appropriate for their community. When the vision is right and the time is right, you have a moment of *optimal visionary change*.

Stages in the Change Process and Iterative Change

After determining that the time is right for change and that the organization is ready to successfully navigate a change process, it's time to think through what process you will use to lead the organizational change. In the next section I will share a model I recommend, but here I want to provide an overview of a few other models and concepts in the change literature. Most of these models recognize three core movements in the change process: (1) *before change*: what is needed to prepare a community for change; (2) *during change*: what is needed to implement change; and (3) *after change*: what is needed to anchor the change in the life of the community. Let's consider a few of these models.

Kurt Lewin's Three-Step Process

First, Kurt Lewin's change theory includes three primary stages that parallel the three movements noted above. Lewin's stages are (1) *unfreezing*: disconfirming the status quo; (2) *changing*: enacting the processes that produce the desired change; and (3) *refreezing*: honing the new approach. I appreciate the simplicity and clarity of Lewin's approach. The language of unfreezing and refreezing reminds leaders that change is not instantaneous. We need to be patient with communities during each of these stages.

Lewin also highlights that communities have both *driving forces* (forces working toward change) and *restraining forces* (forces working to maintain the status quo). Wise leaders help the community make slight adjustments to these forces in order to see change implemented. This requires leaders to wisely and patiently prepare a community for change, helping the community adjust to the idea that the status quo will be changing. Similarly, it also requires leaders to wisely and patiently work with a community after a change has been implemented to ensure that the new approach is solidifying or "refreezing" in the community. Change is not limited to the second step of implementing change. Change leadership requires wisdom and patience during all three stages in the model.

Everett Rogers's Five-Step Process

Second, in Everett Rogers's well-known book *Diffusion of Innovations*, he puts forward a change theory with five primary stages connected to the two primary movements of initiation and implementation. The decision about which change path is right for the organization or team is made between stage 2 and stage 3. The five stages are (1) *agenda setting* (initiation): identifying problems and brainstorming ways to address them; (2) *matching* (initiation): fitting an organization problem with a potential innovation; (3) *redefining/restructuring* (implementation): modifying the innovation to fit the organization and altering the organizational structures as needed; (4) *clarifying* (implementation): clearly defining the relationship between the organization and the innovation; and (5) *routinizing* (implementation): ensuring that the innovation becomes an ongoing element in the organization's activities and loses its identity as an innovation.[7]

John Kotter's Eight-Step Process

There are other helpful models, such as those put forward by William Bridges, Warner Burke, Jim Herrington, and others,[8] but in this section I'll highlight one final change model, put forward by John Kotter. John Kotter's eight-step model of change is probably the best-known model, at least among business leaders.[9] Here are the steps:

1. Establishing a sense of urgency
2. Creating the guiding coalition
3. Developing a vision and strategy
4. Communicating the change vision
5. Empowering employees for broad-based action
6. Generating short-term wins
7. Consolidating gains and producing more change
8. Anchoring new approaches in the culture

I appreciate the Kotter change model and think it is a helpful guide. A minor critique is that it can be difficult to remember all these steps without referring to the list. In practice, I prefer to have memorable tools that I can quickly recall in any situation. This is why I teach a six-step model that uses the acronym "CHANGE" for the sake of memorability. I'll share the details of this model below.

Iterative Thinking

I'd like to highlight one final point before sharing the CHANGE model. *Iterative thinking* is helpful for leaders and organizations navigating change processes. Iterative processes—often emphasized more in design thinking circles than in change theory circles—highlight the benefit of multiple prototypes in the process of moving toward final project execution. In contrast to approaches that emphasize finding the single best plan in a two-stage process—*plan*, then *execute*—iterative thinking encourages multiple iterations of planning and executing in which each cycle and prototype provides additional opportunities for learning and improvement.[10]

I provide a similar logic to this point in a post I shared titled "Macro Change through Micro Improvements."[11] Sometimes the biggest wins and changes come from a series of small wins and small changes. Rather than putting all the proverbial eggs in one basket, sometimes it is helpful to experiment and try out new things on a small scale before rolling them out on an organization-wide scale. Consider the wisdom of Ecclesiastes: "Invest in seven ventures, yes, in eight; you do not know what disaster may come upon the land" (11:2 NIV). Harvard Business School professor Stefan Thomke affirms the value of such logic, noting that "it's actually less risky to run a large number of experiments than a small number. If a company does only a handful of experiments a year, it may have only one success—or none. Then failure is a big deal."[12] Iterative processes and experimentation with small changes are not always the right fit for an organization, but consider how they might provide a helpful pathway for your organization's journey toward bold, visionary change.

Healthy Leaders Enact and Anchor Visionary Change

Now that we have considered both the theological foundations for change and how leaders may prepare well before starting the change process, let's turn to how leaders may *enact* and *anchor* visionary change into the culture. You have likely already recognized that I've been linking change with vision throughout this chapter. The goal is not simply for leaders to enact change in their organizations—what our organizations need is the enactment of *visionary* change. In other words, we need change that is oriented to a compelling picture of a preferred future for the organization.

When leaders and organizations have a picture of what Burt Nanus refers to as "a realistic, credible, attractive future for the organization,"[13] the work and effort required by change become worth it. Vision is vital to the practice of leadership in general. It also is central to faithfully and effectively guiding a change process. Leaders today must build community around a shared vision and then empower a community of partners to own and enact the vision of change together.[14] David Horsager writes, "Few things inspire trust or hope like every member of a team working together toward a shared vision. A clear vision unifies and motivates."[15]

Vision really is central to each stage in the change process. This includes *initiating* visionary change, *implementing* visionary change, and *reinforcing* visionary change. Consider what is absent when there is no clear vision driving the process. Without vision, organizations tend toward motion without progress, reactivity over proactivity, a short-term focus over a long-term focus, managerial organizing without effective vision fulfillment, and tactical organizational behaviors in place of broader strategies aligned with a visionary direction.

With the priority of vision in view, let's now consider a six-step model for enacting and anchoring visionary changes into the culture of organizations (see fig. 10.2).

Figure 10.2. The Visionary CHANGE Model

C: Create Vision-Based Urgency

The first step in the change process is to *create vision-based urgency*. As noted above regarding how people change, most organizational members are not willing to put in the hard work associated with change unless there are clear reasons and motivations driving the visionary change process. While vision ideally is connected to a *compelling* outlook for the future (the "pull"), sometimes people also feel urgency when they recognize that they are standing on *a burning platform* (the "push" or the "pain"). The point is that, by whatever means, leaders and organizations need to make sure their people understand and feel the weight of the circumstances calling for change in the organization.

While I use the word *create*, the point is not for leaders to manufacture a crisis. Wise leaders understand that this work is not about inventing urgencies but rather about pointing to them. Effective leaders wisely assess their organization and the environmental conditions in which the organization operates in order to diagnose problems and issues that require organizational changes. While risk will always be part of the equation in change processes, when team members feel the facts of their present reality, this experience creates a sense of urgency that helps them understand that the risk is both necessary and required.

Consider the reflections of one president who responded to the survey: "Be willing to risk failure—not recklessly, but with the recognition that what has been successful in the past is likely not the way to the future." As noted above, this recognition can arise from either a burning platform or a compelling vision of the future. However it arises, recognition of the urgency of the present moment is the starting point for leaders and team members alike in the change process.

H: Harness a Guiding Coalition to a Vision

The second step in the change process is to *harness a guiding coalition to a vision*. I intentionally refer to "a" vision rather than "the" vision here because I see this wider group of people surrounding the leader—the guiding coalition—as part of the essential team that will assist the leader to summon the right vision to respond appropriately to the identified crisis. Though most senior organizational leaders will have a vision already in mind by this point, wise leaders will seek out perspective and insight from trusted advisers. Kotter encourages leaders to do so, noting that "creating the vision" is the step that follows "forming a powerful guiding coalition."[16] In other words, the vision comes together in partnership with others.

Consider the reflections on collaboration highlighted in chapter 6—these insights apply here as well. Visionary change typically does not fit a "Mount Sinai" model. The New Testament replaces the image of an individual descending from the mountain to share the vision with the people, in the manner of Moses, with the image of a priesthood of believers, emphasizing the value of collaboration and a plurality of people seeking wisdom and direction together. (Consider the example of the church in Jerusalem in Acts 15:28: "It has seemed good to the Holy Spirit and to us . . .") Drawing from this approach, the leader and the surrounding team work together to develop, deepen, and decide on the vision that will guide the visionary change process.

So what type of people should be part of a guiding coalition? Kotter emphasizes that the guiding coalition should be a team based on trust and a common goal. With these primary considerations in place, organizational leaders likely need to gather people with a combination of four key characteristics: (1) proven leadership ability, (2) good reputation and credibility, (3) expertise and a variety of points of view, and (4) influence and positional power.[17] It is also important to have team members who represent both leadership *and* managerial ability—so that together they can both head in the right direction and do so in an efficient manner.

Once this team is in place, it is time to make vital decisions that will guide the remainder of the steps. This team will do the work of agenda setting and matching that Everett Rogers identifies, and it will do the work of vision and strategy development that John Kotter identifies. In this step, the vision moves from the glimpse seen in the first step (creating urgency) to a well-developed, refined, and deepening vision. Together with the senior leader (or leaders), the guiding coalition shapes the vision, owns the vision, and advocates and influences on the basis of the vision. At this point, it is time to bring the vision to the wider organizational community.

A: Align the Majority to the Vision

The third step in the change process is to *align the majority to the vision.* Here is where the time spent on leadership communication in chapter 7 becomes significant. As noted in that chapter, leadership communication is central both in setting the conditions within which a community is receptive to change and in establishing momentum that will guide the community as change is implemented and sustained. Vision is essential in this communication work. As the leader's confidence in the vision is strengthened owing to the work of the guiding coalition, this confidence allows the leader to boldly paint a compelling picture of the vision in the minds of community members. This change vision includes a picture of where the community is going in the process and clear communication regarding the strategy that will be utilized to make this future both feasible and attainable.

This step is all about communicating the vision for change with clarity, frequency (repetition), simplicity, and methodological diversity (i.e., communicated in multiple forms). It is about articulating the destination, the path, and the rationale for the vision. It is about celebrating the past and saying a fitting goodbye to whatever the community is leaving behind. It is also about opening up meaningful pathways for feedback about the change vision in order to develop broad-based ownership of the vision within the wider organizational community. As leaders grow in their capacity to tell the story of the organization and to communicate the change vision well (see insights from chap. 7), this provides the basis for the vital leadership communication work required in this step of the change process.

One additional point is helpful here. In *Diffusion of Innovations*, Everett Rogers categorizes people into five groups on the basis of their orientation toward adopting innovation: (1) innovators (typically about 2.5 percent of the population), (2) early adopters (13.5 percent), (3) early majority (34 percent), (4) late majority (34 percent), and (5) laggards (16 percent).[18] Rogers's book provides a detailed discussion of these categories; here I'll give you some of my own opinions about them.

First, the guiding coalition members will typically be made up of people in the innovator and early adopter categories, though if there are people in the organization who have significant positional or personal influence, you likely will want to pull them into the planning process early regardless of their innovation-adoption categorization. Second, this step of *aligning the majority* is seeking to influence those outside the initial guiding coalition. As innovators, early adopters, the early majority, and the late majority see the vision and are persuaded—each in their own time and process—by the change vision's value, these groups represent the momentum needed to see the vision successfully enacted in the organization.

Finally, while visionary change communication is also provided to the "laggards," successful change implementation should not necessarily wait for 100 percent buy-in. Not everyone from this final category may come along for the journey. Rogers acknowledges that the term "laggards" has a negative feel to it. Because of this, Alan Nelson and Gene Appel opt for the term "anchors" instead.[19] I think this is a preferable term. While most leaders—particularly leaders who have a compassionate heart that longs to serve each of the members of their community—want to see the whole organization joyfully participating in and owning the change process, sometimes this will not happen. One pastor reflected soberly in the survey, "It's OK to lose some in order to save the whole." This is not ideal—but sometimes change processes need to move forward because the vision and time are right for the majority even if they are not right for every individual. This is part of what makes organizational stewardship a weighty responsibility for leaders.

N: Navigate the Course of the Vision

Now that the urgency is recognized, the guiding coalition is in place, and the vision is effectively communicated to the organization, it is time for the fourth step in the change process: to *navigate the course of the vision*. The actual process of change involves an empowered community enacting the change vision together. Leaders do not carry out change visions in isolation. John Kotter emphasizes *empowering others to act on the vision* and *planning for and creating short-term wins*. Part of this work of empowering others includes getting rid of obstacles to change, changing systems or structures that seriously undermine the vision, and encouraging risk-taking as well as nontraditional ideas, activities, and actions.[20]

Emphasizing other features of leadership as the change vision is enacted, Jeff Iorg, in his book *Leading Major Change in Your Ministry*, focuses on what followers need during the change process: (1) clear, consistent communication; (2) resources to help them accomplish the change; and (3) recognition of the sacrifices they are making for the mission. Highlighting one of these—resources to help them accomplish the change—Iorg emphasizes the importance of *time* (a reasonable timeline for the community), *tracks* (a reasonable path and strategy for the community), and *tools* (reasonable training, consulting, and human and material resources).[21] In other words, as those in the community who will act on the envisioned change, team members need the time, strategies, and resources to implement the planned change process. As Mark Strauss and I note in *Leadership in Christian Perspective*, "After finding the right people, it is time for leaders really to go to work by coming alongside followers with needed support and resourcing," doing everything they can to see their team succeed in bringing the envisioned change to reality.[22]

G: Galvanize the Vision through Routine

After the change vision has been enacted—and this likely will take place over an extended period of time, depending on the nature of the targeted change—it is time for the next step: to *galvanize the vision through routine.* Routine can sound boring, but I remind you of Peter Drucker's conviction—organizations need both continuity and change. Note some of Drucker's additional reflections on this point: "Change leaders are . . . designed for change. And yet they still require continuity. People need to know where they stand. They need to know the people with whom they work. They need to know what they can expect. They need to know the values and the rules of the organization. They do not function if the environment is not predictable, not understandable, not known."[23]

The goal is not to keep a community in a state of perpetual change with no continuity or stability. Rather, the goal is to set new norms for the future. The goal of the change process is to see what was once new become an established part of the organization's life and culture. John Kotter refers to this as "institutionalizing new approaches."[24] Everett Rogers refers to it as "routinizing," when "the innovation becomes an ongoing element in the organization's activities and loses its identity" as an innovation.[25]

The goal of the change process is to see what was once new become an established part of the organization's life and culture.

This step is about strengthening the change vision. It is about moving from vision implementation to vision reinforcement. It is about turning a vision that feels new into a vision that is part of the organizational norm. It is about owning and living in the new organizational reality developed through the change vision's enactment. Just as metals need to undergo a process of galvanization in order to be seaworthy, so organizational changes are strengthened and galvanized as the change that once was new becomes an established part of the culture—a matter of routine in the organization's life.

E: Establish a Culture of Visionary Change

The sixth and final step in the change process is to *establish a culture of visionary change*. While I noted above that organizations are not designed to thrive in a state of perpetual change, organizations do gain from establishing a culture that recognizes the benefit of regular and periodic change as they continue to work toward their vision of a preferred organizational future.

This step is all about advancing the visionary culture of the community. The best time to see the value of change in a community is after a successful change has been enacted and anchored in the culture. Building on this momentum, wise organizational leaders will help their community enjoy the fruits associated with the labor that went into the change and will also help the community to keep dreaming together about the future. Organizations are living realities. This is the time to weave a culture of healthy change into the fabric of the community in a manner consistent with the core purpose, mission, values, and beliefs that ground and root the community.

Nelson and Appel note that most organizational visions have a life cycle that tracks with human life cycles: conception, birth, childhood, adolescence, adulthood, old age, and death.[26] While our current life as Christians has a glorious end—as Paul reminds us, "Yes, we are of good courage, and we would rather be away from the body and at home with the Lord" (2 Cor. 5:8)—healthy organizations and institutions can experience renewal and ongoing life from generation to generation. This necessitates a long-term perspective. One survey participant noted, "Less will happen in a year than you want, but more will happen in 5 years than you would have hoped for." We need to keep looking five, ten, fifteen, and even fifty years out. While we may not be part of that future story directly, we can set the organizational conditions that will help future generations flourish and thrive.

Good organizational leaders guide visionary change on an ongoing basis. The value of creating thriving organizations where people can flourish is a value worth passing on to future generations. As we establish a culture of ongoing visionary change, we create paths for visionary renewal that enable the purpose and mission of our organizations to outlive our days as leaders. As you consider your temporary assignment as the leader of the community within which God has planted you, recognize that this essential work of leading visionary change is central to your responsibilities as a steward and leader. In so doing, you will provide healthy leadership for thriving organizations as you create contexts where people may flourish both today and in the years and decades to come.

Recommendations and Reflection

This chapter focused on the nature of visionary change and how change leadership is part of nurturing thriving organizations. Christian leaders attend to these principles when they understand (1) the theological foundations for change, (2) how leaders can prepare their organizations for change, and (3) how leaders can effectively enact and anchor a new change in their organizations. As leaders understand and apply theological, theoretical, and practical wisdom for change leadership, they will help their organizations navigate toward a vision of a preferred future.

Take a moment to consider these priorities for faithful and effective change leadership. Use the following questions to help you reflect on how you may need to grow as a leader of visionary change for your organization.

Healthy Christian leaders understand the theological foundations for change.

- Why and how is God's unchanging nature an encouragement to people who are experiencing change and leaders who are guiding change?
- God is about "making all things new" (Rev. 21:5), including his covenant, his people, and his heavens and earth. How does God's transforming work in our lives and our world give us strength and hope for the changes and transitions we need to face in organizations?
- Abraham is commended for believing and obeying the Lord's call to radical change ("Abraham believed God, and it was counted to him as righteousness," Rom. 4:3). How does this model of faith and dependence on God provide an example and encouragement for our own faith and dependence on God in all things, including in the midst of significant changes and transitions?
- "Change leadership requires leaders to step into the future with bold faith": How does the wisdom and sovereignty of God ground leaders as they step into the future God has planned for his people?

Healthy leaders prepare well before starting a change process.

- As you consider your life and organization, what are some of the significant hindrances to change that you face?
- "Healthy organizations generally benefit from . . . technical and first-order change. . . . Unhealthy or declining organizations . . . need more adaptive and second-order change": How do these various types of change relate to your organizational situation?

- Before launching into a change process, wise leaders ask whether the organization has the *right vision* and whether it is the *right time*. How would you assess your organization or team's readiness for change?
- Has your organization utilized iterative thinking or iterative processes? How might some of the larger changes your organization needs be accomplished through a series of many smaller changes?

Healthy leaders enact and anchor visionary change.

- As you look back on a previous change process you have (or your organization has) experienced, was it led well in each of the three primary phases—*initiating* and *preparing* for change, *implementing* and *enacting* change, *reinforcing* and *anchoring* change? What went well? What could have been done better?
- Why is urgency—through either a "compelling vision" or a "burning platform"—so vital to the process of motivating organizational members at the beginning of a change process?
- As you consider the steps of *harnessing a guiding coalition* and *aligning the majority*, why is having a committed collective of competent influencers (rather than a single leader) important in the process of helping the majority of organizational members buy into the change vision?
- As the change vision is implemented, why is anchoring this vision in the culture of the community through routine a priority near the end of the change process? (Consider Peter Drucker's comments on the importance of both continuity and change.) Have you experienced a community that has effectively *established a culture of visionary change* in an organization? How did this contribute to the ongoing health and thriving of the organization?

APPENDIX A

Overview of Codes, Categories, and Themes for the First Survey Question

Question: "What are the most pressing (or most significant) challenges/issues you face in your leadership responsibilities?"

216 Executive Leaders on Reported Challenges
(605 coded items; occurrences noted above 10)
Top Five Themes: (1) People, (2) Self-Leadership, (3) Mission and Vision, (4) Changing Landscape, (5) Financial Margin

---

#1 PEOPLE: Staff and Volunteers (212)

alignment (people in right seat)
balancing people and mission
effective models, hybrid work
emotional immaturity
empowering/leading through influence
equipping/developing (26)
equipping/resourcing
executive change/search
executive team development
executive team dynamics
generational differences
hiring (41)
  limited resources
  mission focused
managing/evaluating (14)
mental health
mission alignment (19)
motivation/care (22)
motivation/commitment (12)
people/excellence balance
putting people first
retaining/retention (13)
silos
team cohesion (16)
unity
  challenges to
  maintaining
what is rewarded/tolerated

#2 SELF-LEADERSHIP (100)

building trust as a new leader
complexity of leadership
decision making (13)
  fatigue
  mission-focused
  problem solving
  tactical vs. strategic
  urgent vs. important
  weight of
dependence on the Lord, need for
diverse leadership responsibilities
emotional health
managing leadership anxiety and criticism
personal shortcomings and sin
staying current/learning
stress management
time management (36)
  delegation
  for balanced life
  for long-term/strategic planning
  urgent vs. important (12)
values, living authentically
weight/responsibility of leadership
work-life balance

#3 MISSION and VISION (94)

balancing people and mission
clarity of vision (15)
compelling vision casting (11)
establish and strengthen culture
goal prioritization (11)
growth/momentum
health of staff culture
mission discipline
mission integrity/focus (27)
staying focused on culture
strategic planning

#4 CHANGING LANDSCAPE (88)

consumeristic culture
culture, societal (27)
  change in
  division/tension/factions (19)
  ethically/morally challenging
distrust of institutions and churches
industry shifts
inflation
legal complexities and regulation
macroeconomics
market pressures
pandemic (18)
uncertain/turbulent

#5 FINANCIAL MARGIN (39)

allocation
business/revenue/p&l
donor cultivation
establish effective model
financial goals
fund development
limited resources (17)
  resources, general
  for changing technology
revenue generation

Other Categories (72)

boards
  board/staff alignment
  building strong boards
  managing
  managing board dynamics
bureaucracy, organizational
change (17)
  leading/managing
  speed of
communication (14)
  inconsistency
  dispersed team
  mission/vision clarity
  styles for diverse followers
  technological complexities
complexity of organizations
constituency/stakeholders (15)
  expectations
  balancing internal/external focus
crisis management
scaling
succession planning

APPENDIX B

Priorities for Healthy Leaders

The Character of Healthy Organizational Leaders (chap. 3)

- Healthy leaders find courage and conviction in their character.
- Healthy leaders prioritize character over charisma and competence.
- Healthy leaders of character understand the priority of earning and preserving trust.
- Healthy leaders of character care about the bottom line.
- Healthy leaders of character prioritize humility and resist hubris.
- Healthy leaders of character plant their roots in the gospel.

The Commitments of Healthy Organizational Leaders (chap. 4)

- Spiritual: Healthy Christian leaders prioritize their relationship with God.
- Emotional: Healthy leaders provide a calm and courageous presence.
- Relational: Healthy leaders resist isolation.
- Physical: Healthy leaders care for their physical well-being.
- Intellectual: Healthy leaders are learners.
- Practical: Healthy leaders manage their time well, make decisions wisely, and delegate effectively.

The Care and Cultivation of Team Members (chap. 5)

- Healthy leaders focus on the care and cultivation of their team.
- Healthy leaders strategically build their team.
- Healthy leaders equip and develop their team.
- Healthy leaders delegate to and empower their team.
- Healthy leaders retain and sustain their team through ongoing motivation and care.

Collaboration and Team Alignment (chap. 6)

- Healthy leaders understand both the challenges and the benefits of teams.
- Healthy leaders understand why collaborative work and teams matter.
- Healthy leaders understand what makes teams work within organizations.

Communication, Clarity, and Conviction in the Thriving Organization (chap. 7)

- Healthy Christian leaders look to God for his example and priorities in communication.
- Healthy leaders communicate clearly about organizational culture and commitments.
- Healthy leaders communicate clearly for their people and teams.
- Healthy leaders communicate clearly in moments of crisis.
- Healthy leaders communicate clearly about long-term vision and plans for change.
- Healthy leaders tell the story of the organization.
- Healthy leaders understand what makes communication work.

Culture and Thriving Organizations (chap. 8)

- Healthy leaders define and align the organization's culture.
- *Why*: Healthy leaders advance the *purpose* of the organization.
- *What*: Healthy leaders advance the *mission* of the organization.
- *How*: Healthy leaders advance the *strategy* of the organization.

- *Who*: Healthy leaders advance the *values and beliefs* of the organization.
- *Where*: Healthy leaders advance the *vision* of the organization.

Crisis Leadership and Facing Organizational Challenges and Threats (chap. 9)

- Healthy leaders understand the nature of crises.
- Healthy leaders nurture leadership qualities necessary for leading well during crises.
- Healthy leaders communicate effectively and proactively during crises.
- Healthy leaders utilize wise strategies during crises.
- Healthy leaders provide values-based leadership during crises.

Change Leadership and a Thriving Future for the Organization (chap. 10)

- Healthy Christian leaders understand the theological foundations for change.
- Healthy leaders prepare well before starting a change process.
- Healthy leaders enact and anchor visionary change.

NOTES

Chapter 1 Defining Organizational Leadership

1. John David Trentham, "Reading the Social Sciences Theologically (Part 1): Approaching and Qualifying Models of Human Development," *Christian Education Journal: Research on Educational Ministry* 16, no. 3 (2019): 458–75, https://doi.org/10.1177/0739891319885463; John David Trentham, "Reading the Social Sciences Theologically (Part 2): Engaging and Appropriating Models of Human Development," *Christian Education Journal: Research on Educational Ministry* 16, no. 3 (2019): 476–94, https://doi.org/10.1177/0739891319882699.

2. Richard Stearns, *Lead Like It Matters to God: Values-Driven Leadership in a Success-Driven World* (Downers Grove, IL: InterVarsity, 2021), 4.

3. See Justin A. Irving, "Don't Confuse Motion with Progress," *Purpose in Leadership* (blog), August 25, 2014, https://purposeinleadership.com/2014/08/25/motion-vs-progress/.

4. Max De Pree, *Leadership Is an Art* (New York: Dell, 1989), 19.

5. See Abraham Kuyper, "Sphere Sovereignty," in *Abraham Kuyper: A Centennial Reader*, ed. James D. Bratt (Grand Rapids: Eerdmans, 1998), 488.

6. For a helpful discussion of the creation mandate and the Great Commission and how they shape Christian leaders, see Michael Wilder and Timothy Paul Jones, *The God Who Goes before You: Pastoral Leadership as Christ-Centered Followership* (Nashville: B&H Academic, 2018).

7. Justin A. Irving, "Leader Purposefulness and Servant Leadership," in *Practicing Servant Leadership*, ed. Dirk van Dierendonck and Kathleen Patterson (New York: Palgrave Macmillan, 2018).

8. Bill George, *Authentic Leadership: Rediscovering the Secrets to Creating Lasting Value* (San Francisco: Wiley & Sons, 2003), 19.

9. Justin A. Irving and Julie Berndt, "Leader Purposefulness within Servant Leadership: Examining the Effect of Servant Leadership, Leader Follower-Focus, Leader Goal-Orientation, and Leader Purposefulness in a Large U.S. Healthcare Organization," *Administrative Sciences* 7, no. 2 (2017): 10, https://doi.org/10.3390/admsci7020010.

10. John Kotter, "What Leaders Really Do," in *The Leader's Companion: Insights on Leadership through the Ages*, ed. J. Thomas Wren (New York: Free Press, 1995), 118.

11. Kotter, "What Leaders Really Do," 119.

12. Talisker Whisky Atlantic Challenge website, accessed February 15, 2023, https://www.taliskerwhiskyatlanticchallenge.com/.

13. David Gergen, "Bad News for Bullies," *U.S. News & World Report*, June 19, 2006, 54. Gergen affirms this observation drawn from Peter Drucker.

14. Those who want to explore these topics further will find valuable resources in Sid Kemp and Eric Dunbar, *Budgeting for Managers* (New York: McGraw Hill, 2003); Kalpesh Ashar, *Financial Management Essentials You Always Wanted to Know* (Colorado: Vibrant Publishers, 2019); Bruce P. Powers, ed., *Church Administration Handbook* (Nashville: B&H Academic, 2008); Gordon T. Smith, *Institutional Intelligence: How to Build an Effective Organization* (Downers Grove, IL: IVP Academic, 2017); David S. Dockery, ed., *Christian Leadership Essentials: A Handbook for Managing Christian Organizations* (Nashville: B&H Academic, 2011); Darian Rodriguez Heyman and Laila Brenner, *Nonprofit Management 101: A Complete and Practical Guide for Leaders and Professionals*, 2nd ed. (New York: Wiley & Sons, 2019).

15. De Pree, *Leadership Is an Art*, 19.

16. Smith, *Institutional Intelligence*, 131.

17. Smith, *Institutional Intelligence*, 132.

18. Smith, *Institutional Intelligence*, 131.

19. Smith, *Institutional Intelligence*, 150.

20. Smith, *Institutional Intelligence*, 154.

21. Smith, *Institutional Intelligence*, 154–55.

22. Price Harding, "Hiring Well, Hiring Right," August 16, 2022, episode 26 in *In Trust Center Podcast*, produced by In Trust Center for Theological Schools, 44:11, https://intrust.org/Resources/Podcasts.

23. Thomas J. Watson Jr., *Business and Its Beliefs* (New York: McGraw Hill, 1963), 4–5.

24. Stearns, *Lead Like It Matters to God*, 5.

Chapter 2 A Vision for Human and Organizational Flourishing

1. Jonathan T. Pennington, *Jesus the Great Philosopher: Rediscovering the Wisdom Needed for the Good Life* (Grand Rapids: Brazos, 2020), 206.

2. Jonathan T. Pennington, *The Sermon on the Mount and Human Flourishing: A Theological Commentary* (Grand Rapids: Baker Academic, 2017).

3. Miroslav Volf, *Flourishing: Why We Need Religion in a Globalized World* (New Haven: Yale University Press, 2015), ix; Christian Smith, *To Flourish or Destruct: A Personality Theory of Human Goods, Motivations, Failure, and Evil* (Chicago: University of Chicago Press, 2015), 202.

4. Smith, *To Flourish or Destruct*, 204.

5. Smith, *To Flourish or Destruct*, 202.

6. Drew Cleveland and Greg Forster, *The Pastor's Guide to Fruitful Work & Economic Wisdom: Understanding What Your People Do All Day* (n.c.: Made to Flourish, 2012), 126.

7. Rick Langer, "Toward a Biblical Theology of Leadership," in *Organizational Leadership: Foundations & Practices for Christians*, ed. John S. Burns, John R. Shoup, and Donald C. Simmons Jr. (Downers Grove, IL: InterVarsity, 2014), 69.

8. Timothy Keller and Kathrine Leary Alsdorf, *Every Good Endeavor: Connecting Your Work to God's Work* (New York: Dutton, 2012), 48.

9. Keller and Alsdorf, *Every Good Endeavor*, 50.

10. Michael Wilder and Timothy Paul Jones, *The God Who Goes before You: Pastoral Leadership as Christ-Centered Followership* (Nashville: B&H Academic, 2018), 31.

11. Pennington, *Jesus the Great Philosopher*, 212.

12. Andy Crouch, *Strong and Weak: Embracing a Life of Love, Risk & True Flourishing* (Downers Grove, IL: InterVarsity, 2016), 19.

13. Cleveland and Forster, *Pastor's Guide to Fruitful Work & Economic Wisdom*, 126.

14. Pennington, *Jesus the Great Philosopher*, 213.

15. Anthony A. Hoekema, "The Reformed Perspective," in *Five Views on Sanctification* (Grand Rapids: Zondervan, 1987), 74.

16. Volf, *Flourishing*, x.

17. Pennington, *Jesus the Great Philosopher*, 228.

18. Pennington, *The Sermon on the Mount and Human Flourishing*, 40.

19. Volf, *Flourishing*, 203.

20. Amy Sherman, *Agents of Flourishing: Pursuing Shalom in Every Corner of Society* (Downers Grove, IL: InterVarsity, 2022), 18.

21. Smith, *To Flourish or Destruct*, 11.

22. Volf, *Flourishing*, 17.

23. Smith, *To Flourish or Destruct*, 210.

24. Tom Nelson, *The Economics of Neighborly Love: Investing in Your Community's Compassion and Capacity* (Downers Grove, IL: InterVarsity, 2017), 30.

25. Volf, *Flourishing*, 16.

26. Gordon T. Smith, *Institutional Intelligence: How to Build an Effective Organization* (Downers Grove, IL: IVP Academic, 2017), 4.

27. Richard Stearns, *Lead Like It Matters to God: Values-Driven Leadership in a Success-Driven World* (Downers Grove, IL: InterVarsity, 2021), 18.

28. Matthew J. Hall, "Leadership and Thinking Institutionally," personal website, January 20, 2022, https://www.matthewjhall.net/articles/leadership-and-thinking-institutionally.

29. Volf, *Flourishing*, 16.

30. Smith, *To Flourish or Destruct*, 10.

31. Cheryl Bachelder, *Dare to Serve: How to Drive Superior Results by Serving Others* (Oakland: Berrett-Koehler, 2018), 175.

32. Mike Linville and Mark Rennaker, *Essentials of Followership: Rethinking the Leadership Paradigm with Purpose* (Dubuque, IA: Kendall-Hunt, 2022); Barbara Kellerman, *Followership: How Followers Are Creating Change and Changing Leaders* (Boston: Harvard Business School Press, 2008); Robert E. Kelley, *Power of Followership* (New York: Doubleday Business, 1992).

33. Stearns, *Lead Like It Matters to God*, 18.

Chapter 3 The Character of Healthy Organizational Leaders

1. Quotations not otherwise attributed are taken directly from survey responses.

2. Justin A. Irving and Mark L. Strauss, *Leadership in Christian Perspective: Biblical Foundations and Contemporary Practices for Servant Leaders* (Grand Rapids: Baker Academic, 2019), 41. See also Justin A. Irving, "A Model for Effective Servant Leadership Practice: A Biblically-Consistent and Research-Based Approach to Leadership," *Journal of Biblical Perspectives in Leadership* 3, no. 2 (2011): 118–28; Justin A. Irving and Gail J. Longbotham, "Leading Effective Teams through Servant Leadership: An Expanded Regression Model of Essential Servant Leadership Themes," *Proceedings of the American Society of Business and Behavioral Sciences* 14, no. 1 (2007): 806–17.

3. "38% of U.S. Pastors Have Thought about Quitting Full-Time Ministry in the Past Year," Barna Group, November 16, 2021, https://www.barna.com/research/pastors-well-being/; "Navigating the Pandemic: A First Look at Congregational Responses," Exploring the Pandemic Impact on Congregations, November 2021, https://www.covidreligionresearch.org/wp-content/uploads/2021/11/Navigating-the-Pandemic_A-First-Look-at-Congregational-Responses_Nov-2021.pdf. For a broader perspective and data on the great resignation, see Maury Gittleman, "The 'Great Resignation' in Perspective," *Monthly Labor Review* (US Bureau of Labor Statistics), July 2022, https://www.bls.gov/opub/mlr/2022/article/the-great-resignation-in-perspective.htm.

4. Warren Bennis, *On Becoming a Leader* (New York: Addison Wesley, 1989), 141.

5. Mark W. McCloskey, *Learning Leadership in a Changing World: Virtue and Effective Leadership in the 21st Century* (New York: Palgrave Macmillan, 2014), 112–13.

6. Andrew Hébert, *Shepherding Like Jesus: Returning to the Wild Idea That Character Matters in Ministry* (Nashville: B&H, 2022), 4.

7. J. Robert Clinton, *The Making of a Leader* (Colorado Springs: NavPress, 1988), 58.

8. Charles Haddon Spurgeon, *Lectures to My Students* (Grand Rapids: Zondervan, 1972), 7–8.

9. Samuel D. Rima, *Leading from the Inside Out: The Art of Self-Leadership* (Grand Rapids: Baker Books, 2000), 14.

10. Max De Pree, *Leading without Power: Finding Hope in Serving Community* (San Francisco: Jossey-Bass, 1997), 123.

11. McCloskey, *Learning Leadership in a Changing World*, 113.

12. David Horsager, *The Trust Edge: How Top Leaders Gain Faster Results, Deeper Relationships, and a Stronger Bottom Line* (Minneapolis: Summerside, 2010), 313.

13. Fred Kiel, *Return on Character: The Real Reason Leaders and Their Companies Win* (Boston: Harvard Business Review Press, 2015), xiii.

14. Kiel, *Return on Character*, 3.

15. Kiel, *Return on Character*, xi.

16. C. S. Lewis, *The Problem of Pain*, in *The Complete C. S. Lewis Signature Classics* (New York: HarperCollins, 2007), 643. My thinking in this paragraph is also shaped by related preaching by Tim Keller.

17. Kiel, *Return on Character*, 3.

18. Steve Cuss, *Managing Leadership Anxiety: Yours and Theirs* (Nashville: Thomas Nelson, 2019), 25 (emphasis added).

19. Timothy Keller, *Center Church: Doing Balanced, Gospel-Centered Ministry in Your City* (Grand Rapids: Zondervan, 2012), 48.

20. Keller, *Center Church*, 48.

21. Christopher S. Howard and Justin A. Irving, "The Impact of Obstacles Defined by Developmental Antecedents on Resilience in Leadership Formation," *Management Research Review* 37, no. 5 (2014): 466–78, https://doi.org/10.1108/MRR-03-2013-0072; Christopher S. Howard and Justin A. Irving, "A Cross-Cultural Study of the Role of Obstacles on Resilience in Leadership Formation," *Management Research Review* 44, no. 4 (2020): 533–46, https://doi.org/10.1108/MRR-02-2020-0067; additional studies in process.

22. Richard Daft, *Leadership: Theory and Practice* (Fort Worth: Dryden, 1999), 48.

Chapter 4 The Commitments of Healthy Organizational Leaders

1. Samuel D. Rima, *Leading from the Inside Out: The Art of Self-Leadership* (Grand Rapids: Baker Books, 2000), 17.

2. Charles Haddon Spurgeon, *Lectures to My Students* (Grand Rapids: Zondervan, 1972), 7–8.

3. Gregg R. Allison, *Embodied: Living as Whole People in a Fractured World* (Grand Rapids: Baker Books, 2021), 16n2.

4. C. S. Lewis, *The Screwtape Letters* (New York: Macmillan, 1982), 108–9.

5. C. S. Lewis, *A Grief Observed* (New York: Bantam, 1976), 79.

6. Henry Bettenson and Chris Maunder, eds., *Documents of the Christian Church* (Oxford: Oxford University Press, 2011), 54.

7. Thomas à Kempis, *The Imitation of Christ* (Chicago: Moody, 1980).

8. Peter Scazzero, *The Emotionally Healthy Church: A Strategy for Discipleship That Actually Changes Lives* (Grand Rapids: Zondervan, 2003), 50.

9. Abraham Kuyper, "Sphere Sovereignty," in *Abraham Kuyper: A Centennial Reader*, ed. James D. Bratt (Grand Rapids: Eerdmans, 1998), 488.

10. Justin A. Irving and Mark L. Strauss, *Leadership in Christian Perspective: Biblical Foundations and Contemporary Practices for Servant Leaders* (Grand Rapids: Baker Academic, 2019), 44. See that book for a fuller discussion of emotional intelligence.

11. Steve Cuss, *Managing Leadership Anxiety: Yours and Theirs* (Nashville: Thomas Nelson, 2019), 17.

12. Mark Sayers, *A Non-Anxious Presence: How a Changing and Complex World Will Create a Remnant of Renewed Christian Leaders* (Chicago: Moody, 2022), 100.

13. Irving and Strauss, *Leadership in Christian Perspective*, 47–48.

14. Irving and Strauss, *Leadership in Christian Perspective*, 48.

15. Nathan Finn, LinkedIn post, accessed September 1, 2022, https://www.linkedin.com/posts/nathan-finn-0ab87598_the-world-is-chaotic-chaos-breads-anxiety-activity-6971082228579663873-scRL.

16. Frederica Mathewes-Green, "The Subject Was Noses: What Happens When Academics Discover That We Have Bodies," *Books and Culture*, January/February 1997, 14–16.

17. Allison, *Embodied*, 38.

18. Allison, *Embodied*, 14n2.

19. Albert Mohler, *The Conviction to Lead: 25 Principles for Leadership That Matter* (Minneapolis: Bethany House, 2012), 99.

20. Mohler, *Conviction to Lead*, 141.

21. Mohler, *Conviction to Lead*, 143.

22. Mohler, *Conviction to Lead*, 146.

Chapter 5 The Care and Cultivation of Team Members

1. Chapter 5 is slightly longer than other chapters, both owing to the importance of this dynamic of organizational leadership and owing to the significant attention surveyed leaders gave to the themes covered here.

2. Mark W. McCloskey, *Learning Leadership in a Changing World: Virtue and Effective Leadership in the 21st Century* (New York: Palgrave Macmillan, 2014), 131.

3. Richard Daft, *Leadership: Theory and Practice* (Fort Worth: Dryden, 1999), 351.

4. James Laub, *Leveraging the Power of Servant Leadership: Building High Performing Organizations* (New York: Palgrave Macmillan, 2018), 73–111.

5. Michael E. McNeff and Justin A. Irving, "Job Satisfaction and the Priority of Valuing People: A Case Study of Servant Leadership Practice in a Network of Family-Owned Companies," *SAGE Open* 7, no. 1 (January–March 2017), https://doi.org/10.1177/2158244016686813.

6. Justin A. Irving and Mark L. Strauss, *Leadership in Christian Perspective: Biblical Foundations and Contemporary Practices for Servant Leaders* (Grand Rapids: Baker Academic, 2019), 120.

7. Amy J. C. Cuddy, Matthew Kohut, and John Neffinger, "Connect, Then Lead," *Harvard Business Review*, July–August 2013.

8. David G. Bowers and Stanley E. Seashore, "Predicting Organizational Effectiveness with a Four-Factor Theory of Leadership," *Administrative Science Quarterly* 11 (1966): 238–63; Robert R. Blake and Jane S. Mouton, *The Managerial Grid III* (Houston: Gulf, 1985).

9. See, e.g., Irving and Strauss, *Leadership in Christian Perspective*; Justin A. Irving and Julie Berndt, "Leader Purposefulness within Servant Leadership: Examining the Effect of Servant Leadership, Leader Follower-Focus, Leader Goal-Orientation, and Leader Purposefulness in a Large U.S. Healthcare Organization," *Administrative Sciences* 7, no. 2 (2017), https://doi.org/10.3390/admsci7020010; Valorie C. Nordbye and Justin A. Irving, "Servant Leadership and Organizational Effectiveness: Examining Leadership Culture among Millennials within a US National Campus Ministry," *Servant Leadership: Theory & Practice* 4, no. 1 (2017): 53–74.

10. Irving and Strauss, *Leadership in Christian Perspective*, 11.

11. Danny Akin, "Installation Service for Paul Akin," Southern Baptist Theological Seminary, September 1, 2022.

12. Laub, *Leveraging the Power of Servant Leadership*.

13. Nathan Finn, LinkedIn post, accessed September 14, 2022, https://www.linkedin.com/posts/nathan-finn-0ab87598_when-i-am-looking-for-someone-to-join-my-activity-6951171146796998656-Y8Lg.

14. Francis J. Yammarino, "Indirect Leadership: Transformational Leadership at a Distance," in *Improving Organizational Effectiveness through Transformational Leadership*, ed. Bernard M. Bass and Bruce J. Avolio (Thousand Oaks, CA: Sage, 1994), 28.

15. Irving and Strauss, *Leadership in Christian Perspective*, 72–73.

16. Irving and Strauss, *Leadership in Christian Perspective*, 25.

17. See discussions related to this in chap. 8 of Irving and Strauss, *Leadership in Christian Perspective*.

18. John Coleman, "Feeling Demotivated? Consider How Your Job Helps Others," *On Purpose*, August 25, 2022, https://onpurpose.substack.com/p/feeling-demotivated-consider-how.

19. For readers interested in navigating the needs of the hybrid workplace, I recommend *Close: Leading Well across Distance and Cultures*, by Ken Cochrum.

Chapter 6 Collaboration and Team Alignment

1. Gordon T. Smith, *Institutional Intelligence: How to Build an Effective Organization* (Downers Grove, IL: IVP Academic, 2017), 214 (emphasis added).

2. David Gyertson, "Leadership in Transition," August 9, 2022, episode 25 in *In Trust Center Podcast*, produced by In Trust Center for Theological Schools, 46:44, https://intrust.org/Resources/Podcasts.

3. Daniel Levi, *Group Dynamics for Teams*, 4th ed. (Thousand Oaks, CA: Sage, 2014), 33.

4. Peter Northouse, *Leadership: Theory and Practice*, 7th ed. (Thousand Oaks, CA: Sage, 2016), 364.

5. Glenn M. Parker, *Team Players and Teamwork* (San Francisco: Jossey-Bass, 2008).

6. Justin A. Irving and Mark L. Strauss, *Leadership in Christian Perspective: Biblical Foundations and Contemporary Practices for Servant Leaders* (Grand Rapids: Baker Academic, 2019), 72–73.

7. Ryan Hartwig and Warren Bird, *Teams That Thrive: Five Disciplines of Collaborative Church Leadership* (Downers Grove, IL: IVP Books, 2015), 44.

8. E. Stanley Ott, *Transform Your Church with Ministry Teams* (Grand Rapids: Eerdmans, 2004), 5.

9. Wayne Grudem, *Systematic Theology: An Introduction to Biblical Doctrine* (Grand Rapids: Zondervan, 1994), 257.

10. The kings of Israel and Judah serve to illustrate the negative side of this. The people of God wanted a human king to be placed over them (1) because they had rejected God as their king and (2) so that they might be like all the nations surrounding them (1 Sam. 8). In other words, the kingly examples of individual or singular leadership we see in Israel and Judah originate out of a distorted motivation. Additionally, most of the kings over Israel and Judah serve as examples (or contrasts) that point to what the awaited Messiah and King over Israel would be like. The failures of Israel's leaders to embody what God requires of his leaders (see Ezek. 34) serve to magnify the beauty and majesty of Jesus Christ—the One who fully and finally provides what God's people most need. Even though kings were always part of God's plan (see Gen. 35:11), Jesus Christ is the ultimate king to which such promises point.

11. Grudem, *Systematic Theology*, 933.

12. Alexander Strauch, *Biblical Eldership: An Urgent Call to Restore Biblical Church Leadership* (Littleton, CO: Lewis & Roth, 1995), 36.

13. Hartwig and Bird, *Teams That Thrive*, 50.

14. Hartwig and Bird, *Teams That Thrive*, 48.

15. Thomas R. Schreiner, *Paul, Apostle of God's Glory in Christ: A Pauline Theology* (Downers Grove, IL: InterVarsity, 2020), 335.

16. Hartwig and Bird, *Teams That Thrive*, 45.

17. Grudem, *Systematic Theology*, 257.

18. Irving and Strauss, *Leadership in Christian Perspective*, 188.

19. Patrick Lencioni, *The Ideal Team Player: How to Recognize and Cultivate the Three Essential Virtues* (San Francisco: Jossey-Bass, 2016).

20. Frank M. J. LaFasto and Carl E. Larson, *When Teams Work Best: 6,000 Team Members and Leaders Tell What It Takes to Succeed* (Thousand Oaks, CA: Sage, 2001).

21. See CliftonStrengths website (Gallup), accessed November 9, 2022, https://www.gallup.com/cliftonstrengths/en/strengthsfinder.aspx; Working Genius website (Table Group), accessed November 9, 2022, https://www.workinggenius.com/.

22. Carl E. Larson and Frank M. J. LaFasto, *TeamWork: What Must Go Right, What Can Go Wrong* (Thousand Oaks, CA: Sage, 1989); Timothy M. Franz, *Group Dynamics and Team Interventions: Understanding and Improving Team Performance* (Malden, MA: Wiley-Blackwell, 2012).

23. Gary Yukl, *Leadership in Organizations*, 5th ed. (Upper Saddle River, NJ: Prentice Hall, 2002), 306.

24. Bruce W. Tuckman, "Developmental Sequence in Small Groups," *Psychological Bulletin* 63, no. 6 (1965): 384–99.

25. Greg L. Stewart, Charles C. Manz, and Henry P. Sims Jr., *Team Work and Group Dynamics* (New York: Wiley & Sons, 1999).

26. Larson and LaFasto, *TeamWork, 26.*

27. Patrick Lencioni, *Death by Meeting: A Leadership Fable about Solving the Most Painful Problem in Business* (San Francisco: Jossey-Bass, 1965).

28. LaFasto and Larson, *When Teams Work Best*, 99.

29. Santiago "Jimmy" Mellado (president and CEO, Compassion International), LinkedIn post, September 21, 2022, https://www.linkedin.com/posts/jimmymellado_through-years-of-leadership-ive-learned-activity-6978391844237828097-9Pzq.

30. Ken Sande, *The Peacemaker: A Biblical Guide to Resolving Personal Conflict* (Grand Rapids: Baker Books, 2004), 11.

Chapter 7 Communication, Clarity, and Conviction in the Thriving Organization

1. Justin A. Irving and Mark L. Strauss, *Leadership in Christian Perspective: Biblical Foundations and Contemporary Practices for Servant Leaders* (Grand Rapids: Baker Academic, 2019), 141.

2. Everett M. Rogers and Rekha Agarwala-Rogers, *Communication in Organizations* (New York: Free Press, 1976), 7.

3. Pamela Shockley-Zalabak, *Fundamentals of Organizational Communication: Knowledge, Sensitivity, Skills, Values* (Boston: Allyn & Bacon, 2002), 4–5.

4. Jonathan Edwards, *The Works of Jonathan Edwards Series*, vol. 13, *The Miscellanies*, ed. Thomas A. Schafer (New Haven: Yale University Press, 1994), 410.

5. William Messenger, ed., *Theology of Work Project, Genesis through Revelation*, vol. 1, Theology of Work Bible Commentary (Peabody, MA: Hendrickson, 2014), 6.

6. Thomas R. Schreiner, *Hebrews: Evangelical Biblical Theology Commentary* (Bellingham, WA: Lexham, 2020), 53.

7. Albert Mohler, *The Conviction to Lead: 25 Principles for Leadership That Matter* (Minneapolis: Bethany House, 2012), 91.

8. James Kouzes and Barry Posner, *The Leadership Challenge*, 3rd ed. (San Francisco: Jossey-Bass, 2002), 165.

9. David Horsager, *The Trust Edge: How Top Leaders Gain Faster Results, Deeper Relationships, and a Stronger Bottom Line* (Minneapolis: Summerside, 2010), 48.

10. Gordon T. Smith, *Institutional Intelligence: How to Build an Effective Organization* (Downers Grove, IL: IVP Academic, 2017), 33.

11. Rob Goffee and Gareth Jones, *Why Should Anyone Work Here? What It Takes to Create an Authentic Organization* (Boston: Harvard Business Review Press, 2015), 17 (emphasis added).

12. John Baldoni, *Great Communication Secrets of Great Leaders* (New York: McGraw Hill, 2003), 9.

13. Ken Blanchard, Margie Blanchard, and Pat Zigarmi, "Determining Your Leadership Point of View," in *Leading at a Higher Level: Blanchard on Leadership and Creating High Performing Organizations*, ed. Ken Blanchard (Upper Saddle River, NJ: Prentice Hall, 2007), 278.

14. Patrick Lencioni, *The Advantage: Why Organizational Health Trumps Everything Else in Business* (San Francisco: Jossey-Bass, 2012), 77.

15. Baldoni, *Great Communication Secrets of Great Leaders*, 9.

16. Horsager, *Trust Edge*, 48.

17. Bert Decker, *You've Got to Be Believed to Be Heard*, 2nd ed. (New York: St. Martin's Press, 2008).

18. Mohler, *The Conviction to Lead*, 92.

19. Justin A. Irving and Julie Berndt, "Leader Purposefulness within Servant Leadership: Examining the Effect of Servant Leadership, Leader Follower-Focus, Leader Goal-Orientation, and Leader Purposefulness in a Large U.S. Healthcare Organization," *Administrative Sciences* 7, no. 2 (2017), https://doi.org/10.3390/admsci7020010.

20. Susan A. Wheelan, *Creating Effective Teams: A Guide for Members and Leaders*, 3rd ed. (Thousand Oaks, CA: Sage, 2010), 44.

21. Frank M. J. LaFasto and Carl E. Larson, *When Teams Work Best: 6,000 Team Members and Leaders Tell What It Takes to Succeed* (Thousand Oaks, CA: Sage, 2001), 70.

22. Pat Zigarmi and Judd Hoekstra, "Strategies for Managing a Change," in Blanchard, *Leading at a Higher Level*, 236.

23. Smith, *Institutional Intelligence*, 101.

24. Mark W. McCloskey, *Learning Leadership in a Changing World: Virtue and Effective Leadership in the 21st Century* (New York: Palgrave Macmillan, 2014), 239.

25. Margaret J. Wheatley, *Finding Our Way: Leadership for an Uncertain Time* (San Francisco: Berrett-Koehler, 2005), 120.

26. Wheatley, *Finding Our Way*, 120.

27. R. Robert Creech, *Family Systems and Congregational Life: A Map for Ministry* (Grand Rapids: Baker Academic, 2019), 43.

28. Baldoni, *Great Communication Secrets of Great Leaders*, 11.

29. Wheatley, *Finding Our Way*, 121.

30. Katie Allred, *Church Communications: Methods and Marketing* (Nashville: B&H Academic, 2022), 128.

31. Allred, *Church Communications*, 128.

32. Kouzes and Posner, *Leadership Challenge*, 165.

33. Tod Bolsinger, *Tempered Resilience: How Leaders Are Formed in the Crucible of Change* (Downers Grove, IL: InterVarsity, 2020), 175.

34. Zigarmi and Hoekstra, "Strategies for Managing a Change," 236.

35. Gerald L. Sittser, *Water from a Deep Well: Christian Spirituality from Early Martyrs to Modern Missionaries* (Downers Grove, IL: InterVarsity, 2007), 19.

36. Kouzes and Posner, *Leadership Challenge*, 359.

37. Kouzes and Posner, *Leadership Challenge*, 363.

38. J. Martin and M. E. Power, "Organizational Stories: More Vivid and Persuasive Than Quantitative Data," in *Psychological Foundations of Organizational Behavior*, ed. B. M Staw (Glenview, IL: Scott, Foresman, 1982), 161 68.

39. Stephen Denning, "Telling Tales," in *On Communication: HBR's 10 Must Reads* (Boston: Harvard Business Review Press, 2013), 117.

40. Kouzes and Posner, *Leadership Challenge*, 361.

41. Don Carew et al., "Is Your Organization High Performing?," in Blanchard, *Leading at a Higher Level*, 10.

42. Kouzes and Posner, *Leadership Challenge*, 164.

43. Denning, "Telling Tales," 118 (emphasis added).
44. Kouzes and Posner, *Leadership Challenge*, 191–92.
45. McCloskey, *Learning Leadership in a Changing World*, 187–200.

Chapter 8 Culture and Thriving Organizations

1. Quoted in Jacob M. Engel, "Why Does Culture 'Eat Strategy for Breakfast'?," *Forbes*, November 20, 2018, https://www.forbes.com/sites/forbescoachescouncil/2018/11/20/why-does-culture-eat-strategy-for-breakfast/.
2. Daniel Harkavy, *7 Perspectives of Effective Leaders: A Proven Framework for Improving Decisions and Increasing Your Influence* (Grand Rapids: Baker Books, 2020), 52.
3. Max De Pree, *Leadership Is an Art* (New York: Dell, 1989), 11.
4. Cheryl Bachelder, *Dare to Serve: How to Drive Superior Results by Serving Others* (Oakland: Berrett-Koehler, 2018), 81–82.
5. Terrence E. Deal and Allan A. Kennedy, "*Corporate Cultures: The Rites and Rituals of Corporate Life* (Cambridge, MA: Perseus Publishing, 2000), 4.
6. Edgar Schein, *Organizational Culture and Leadership*, 2nd ed. (San Francisco: Jossey-Bass, 1992), 17.
7. Mark W. McCloskey, *Learning Leadership in a Changing World: Virtue and Effective Leadership in the 21st Century* (New York: Palgrave Macmillan, 2014), 59.
8. Bachelder, *Dare to Serve*, 81.
9. Deal and Kennedy, "Strong Cultures," 283.
10. Francis J. Yammarino, "Indirect Leadership: Transformational Leadership at a Distance," in *Improving Organizational Effectiveness through Transformational Leadership*, ed. Bernard M. Bass and Bruce J. Avolio (Thousand Oaks, CA: Sage, 1994), 44.
11. As quoted in David Horsager, *The Trust Edge: How Top Leaders Gain Faster Results, Deeper Relationships, and a Stronger Bottom Line* (Minneapolis: Summerside, 2010), 56.
12. "Chiropractic Adjustment," Mayo Clinic, accessed October 4, 2022, https://www.mayoclinic.org/tests-procedures/chiropractic-adjustment/about/pac-20393513; "What Exactly Is a Chiropractic Alignment?," Integrated Health & Injury Center, accessed October 4, 2022, https://integratedhealthandinjury.com/what-exactly-is-a-chiropractic-alignment/.
13. Rasmus Hougaard and Jacqueline Carter, *The Mind of the Leader: How to Lead Yourself, Your People, and Your Organization for Extraordinary Results* (Boston: Harvard Business Review Press, 2018), 163–64.
14. Hougaard and Carter, *Mind of the Leader*, 164.
15. Hougaard and Carter, *Mind of the Leader*, 164.
16. Eric Geiger and Kevin Peck, *Designed to Lead: The Church and Leadership Development* (Nashville: B&H, 2016), 102.
17. Michael Wilder and Timothy Paul Jones, *The God Who Goes before You: Pastoral Leadership as Christ-Centered Followership* (Nashville: B&H Academic, 2018), 16.
18. Wikipedia, s.v. "Iceberg," last modified September 21, 2022, https://en.wikipedia.org/wiki/Iceberg.
19. De Pree, *Leadership Is an Art*, 11.
20. Rick Warren, *The Purpose Driven Life: What on Earth Am I Here For?* (Grand Rapids: Zondervan, 2002), 17.
21. Sharlene G. Buszka and Timothy Ewest, *Integrating Christian Faith and Work: Individual, Occupational, and Organizational Influences and Strategies* (New York: Palgrave Macmillan, 2020), 217.
22. David Gergen, *Hearts Touched with Fire: How Great Leaders Are Made* (New York: Simon & Schuster, 2022), 143.
23. Simon Sinek, *Start with Why: How Great Leaders Inspire Everyone to Take Action* (New York: Penguin Group, 2009), 95.

24. Patrick Lencioni, *The Advantage: Why Organizational Health Trumps Everything Else in Business* (San Francisco: Jossey-Bass, 2012), 82; see also James C. Collins and Jerry I. Porras, *Built to Last: Successful Habits of Visionary Companies* (New York: HarperBusiness, 2002).

25. "Get to Know Us," Presbyterian Homes & Services website, October 5, 2022, https://www.preshomes.org/get-to-know-us.

26. Horsager, *Trust Edge*, 57.

27. C. William Pollard, "Mission as an Organizing Principle," in *Beyond Integrity: A Judeo-Christian Approach to Business Ethics*, ed. Scott B. Rae and Kenman L. Wong (Grand Rapids: Zondervan, 2012), 278.

28. Hougaard and Carter, *Mind of the Leader*, 167.

29. Justin A. Irving and Mark L. Strauss, *Leadership in Christian Perspective: Biblical Foundations and Contemporary Practices for Servant Leaders* (Grand Rapids: Baker Academic, 2019), 189.

30. Wilder and Jones, *God Who Goes before You*, 40.

31. Edgar Stoesz and Chester Raber, *Doing Good Better: How to be an Effective Board Member of a Nonprofit Organization* (Intercourse, PA: Good Books, 1997), 22.

32. Warren Bennis, in the foreword for Burt Nanus, *Visionary Leadership* (San Francisco: Jossey-Bass, 1992), xv.

33. McCloskey, *Learning Leadership in a Changing World*, 213–14.

34. "Popeyes Louisiana Kitchen Franchise Cost & Profit Opportunity Review," Franchise KnowHow, March 21, 2019, https://www.franchiseknowhow.com/popeyes-louisiana-kitchen/.

35. Gergen, *Hearts Touched with Fire*, 142.

36. Cherie Harder, "Cherie Harder on Intellectual Hospitality," October 11, 2021, season 1, episode 9 in *Leading Forward Podcast*, produced by Leading Forward: Building Healthy Leaders for Healthy Organizations, 51:59, https://www.leadingforwardpodcast.com/1818872/9087275-cherie-harder-on-intellectual-hospitality.

37. James C. Collins and Jerry I. Porras, "Organizational Vision and Visionary Organizations," in *Leading Organizations: Perspectives for a New Era*, ed. Gill Robinson Hickman (Thousand Oaks, CA: Sage, 1998), 238.

38. Joanne Soliday and Rick Mann, *Surviving to Thriving: A Planned Framework for Leaders of Private Colleges and Universities* (Charleston, SC: Advantage Media Group, 2018), 38.

39. Terrence E. Deal and Allan A. Kennedy, *Corporate Cultures: The Rites and Rituals of Corporate Life* (New York: Perseus Books, 2000), 21, 23.

40. John Carver, *Boards That Make a Difference: A New Design for Leadership in Nonprofit and Public Organizations* (San Francisco: Jossey-Bass, 1997), 22.

41. Bachelder, *Dare to Serve*, 83.

42. Lencioni, *Advantage*, 92.

43. Collins and Porras, "Organizational Vision and Visionary Organizations."

44. Peter Summerlin cites this research and its influence on his award-winning landscape design plan for Magnolia River Ranch, "ASLA 2006 Student Awards," American Society of Landscape Architects, accessed October 5, 2022, https://www.asla.org/awards/2006/studentawards/282.html.

45. Quoted in Steve Cuss, *Managing Leadership Anxiety: Yours and Theirs* (Nashville: Thomas Nelson, 2019), 181 (emphasis added).

46. Max De Pree, *Leading without Power: Finding Hope in Serving Community* (San Francisco: Jossey-Bass, 1997), 117.

47. Horsager, *Trust Edge*, 49.

48. Nanus, *Visionary Leadership*, 8.

49. Irving and Strauss, *Leadership in Christian Perspective*, 156.

50. Irving and Strauss, *Leadership in Christian Perspective*, 156.

51. Marshall Sashkin, "Visionary Leadership," in *The Leader's Companion: Insights on Leadership through the Ages*, ed. J. Thomas Wren (New York: Free Press, 1995), 403.

52. Soliday and Mann, *Surviving to Thriving*, 47.
53. Jerry C. Wofford, *Transforming Christian Leadership: 10 Exemplary Church Leaders* (Grand Rapids: Baker, 1999), 69.

Chapter 9 Crisis Leadership and Facing Organizational Challenges and Threats

1. Ronald Heifetz, Alexander Grashow, and Marty Linsky, "Leadership in (Permanent) Crisis," in "How to Lead in a Time of Crisis," special issue, *Harvard Business Review*, Summer 2020, 13.
2. This quotation is cited in Warren Bennis, *On Becoming a Leader* (New York: Addison Wesley, 1989), 189.
3. Michael Z. Hackman and Craig E. Johnson, *Leadership: A Communication Perspective*, 4th ed. (Long Grove, IL: Waveland, 2004), 234.
4. Daniel McGinn, "Leading, Not Managing, in Crisis," in "How to Lead in a Time of Crisis," special issue, *Harvard Business Review*, Summer 2020, 34.
5. This list is adapted from Hackman and Johnson, *Leadership*, 235. See also I. I. Mitroff, C. M. Pearson, and L. K. Harrington, *The Essential Guide to Managing Corporate Crises: A Step-by-Step Guide for Surviving Major Catastrophes* (New York: Oxford University Press, 1996).
6. Stephen Fink, *Crisis Management: Planning for the Inevitable* (New York: AMACOM, 2000), adapted from Hackman and Johnson, *Leadership*, 236–37.
7. Hackman and Johnson, *Leadership*, 236.
8. Johnson is quoted in McGinn, "Leading, Not Managing, in Crisis," 34.
9. Steve Cuss, *Managing Leadership Anxiety: Yours and Theirs* (Nashville: Thomas Nelson, 2019), 9.
10. McGinn, "Leading, Not Managing, in Crisis," 34–35.
11. William Ury, *Getting Past No: Negotiating in Difficult Situations* (New York: Bantam, 1993).
12. Jim Herrington, Trisha Taylor, and R. Robert Creech, *The Leader's Journey: Accepting the Call to Personal and Congregational Transformation*, 2nd ed. (Grand Rapids: Baker Academic, 2020), 100.
13. Christopher S. Howard and Justin A. Irving, "The Impact of Obstacles Defined by Developmental Antecedents on Resilience in Leadership Formation," *Management Research Review* 37, no. 5 (2014): 466–78, https://doi.org/10.1108/MRR-03-2013-0072; Christopher S. Howard and Justin A. Irving, "A Cross-Cultural Study of the Role of Obstacles on Resilience in Leadership Formation," *Management Research Review* 44, no. 4 (2020): 533–46, https://doi.org/10.1108/MRR-02-2020-0067; additional studies in process.
14. Tod Bolsinger, *Tempered Resilience: How Leaders Are Formed in the Crucible of Change* (Downers Grove, IL: InterVarsity, 2020), 5.
15. McGinn, "Leading, Not Managing, in Crisis," 34.
16. McGinn, "Leading, Not Managing, in Crisis"; Tim Johnson, *Crisis Leadership: How to Lead in Times of Crisis, Threat and Uncertainty* (New York: Bloomsbury Business, 2017).
17. Burke is quoted in Warren Bennis, *On Becoming a Leader*, 153 (emphasis added).
18. Burke is quoted in Warren Bennis, *On Becoming a Leader*, 154.
19. John Baldoni, *Great Communication Secrets of Great Leaders* (New York: McGraw Hill, 2003), 11.
20. Winston Churchill, "Blood, Toil, Tears and Sweat," speech to the House of Commons, May 13, 1940, available at https://winstonchurchill.org/resources/speeches/1940-the-finest-hour/blood-toil-tears-sweat/.
21. Hackman and Johnson, *Leadership*, 241.
22. Daniel Eisenberg, "Firestone's Rough Road," *Time*, September 10, 2000, https://content.time.com/time/magazine/article/0,9171,54426,00.html.

23. J. Peter Scoblic, "Learning from the Future: How to Make Robust Strategy in Times of Deep Uncertainty," *Harvard Business Review*, July–August 2020, 40.

24. Scoblic, "Learning from the Future," 44.

25. McGinn, "Leading, Not Managing, in Crisis," 34.

26. Alaa Elassar, "A Chick-fil-A Manager Saved a Drive-Thru Covid-19 Vaccination Clinic after Traffic Backed Up," *CNN*, January 31, 2021, https://www.cnn.com/2021/01/31/us/chick-fil-a-drive-thru-covid-vaccine-trnd/index.html.

27. Ronald Heifetz, *Leadership without Easy Answers* (Cambridge, MA: Belknap Press, 1994).

28. Northouse, *Leadership*, 261–62.

29. Heifetz, *Leadership without Easy Answers*, 128. See also Northouse, *Leadership*, 261–72.

30. Heifetz, *Leadership without Easy Answers*, 128.

31. Northouse, *Leadership*, 258.

32. Heifetz, *Leadership without Easy Answers*, 128.

33. Heifetz, *The Practice of Adaptive Leadership: Tools and Tactics for Changing Your Organization and the World* (Boston: Harvard Business Review Press, 2009), 14.

34. R. Robert Creech, *Family Systems and Congregational Life: A Map for Ministry* (Grand Rapids: Baker Academic, 2019), 43.

35. McGinn, "Leading, Not Managing, in Crisis," 34–35.

36. Heifetz, *Leadership without Easy Answers*, 274.

37. Lisa Lai, "Managing When the Future Is Unclear," in "How to Lead in a Time of Crisis," special issue, *Harvard Business Review*, Summer 2020, 57.

Chapter 10 Change Leadership and a Thriving Future for the Organization

1. Peter Drucker, *Management Challenges for the 21st Century* (New York: HarperCollins, 1999), 90.

2. K. A. Mathews, *Genesis 11:27–50:26*, The New American Commentary (Nashville: Broadman & Holman, 2005), 104–5.

3. Justin A. Irving, "37 Barriers to Change," *Purpose in Leadership* (blog), October 14, 2014, https://purposeinleadership.com/2014/10/14/37-barriers-to-change/.

4. Peter Northouse, *Leadership: Theory and Practice*, 7th ed. (Thousand Oaks, CA: Sage, 2016), 261–62.

5. Gregg R. Allison, *Embodied: Living as Whole People in a Fractured World* (Grand Rapids: Baker Books, 2021), 16n2.

6. Justin A. Irving, "Right Vision . . . Right Time—Are You Ready for Change?," *Purpose in Leadership* (blog), July 16, 2014, https://purposeinleadership.com/2014/07/16/right-visionright-time-are-you-ready-for-change/.

7. Everett M. Rogers, *Diffusion of Innovations*, 4th ed. (New York: Free Press, 1995), 392.

8. William Bridges, *Managing Transitions: Making the Most of Change* (New York: Perseus Books, 1991); W. Warner Burke, *Organization Change: Theory and Practice*, 4th ed. (Thousand Oaks, CA: Sage, 2014); Jim Herrington, Mike Bonem, and James H. Furr, *Leading Congregational Change: A Practical Guide for the Transformation Journey* (San Francisco: Jossey-Bass, 2000); Alan Nelson and Gene Appel, *How to Change Your Church (without Killing It)* (Nashville: Word, 2000).

9. John P. Kotter, *Leading Change* (Boston: Harvard Business School Press, 1996).

10. For an example of the power of iterative thinking, see Tom Wujec, "Build a Tower, Build a Team," TED, February 2010, 6:35, https://www.ted.com/talks/tom_wujec_build_a_tower_build_a_team.

11. Justin A. Irving, "Macro Change through Micro Improvements," *Purpose in Leadership* (blog), August 14, 2014, https://purposeinleadership.com/2014/08/14/macro-change-micro-improvements/.

12. Stefan Thomke, "Building a Culture of Experimentation," *Harvard Business Review*, March–April 2020, 43.

13. Burt Nanus, *Visionary Leadership* (San Francisco: Jossey-Bass, 1992), 8.

14. Justin A. Irving and Mark L. Strauss, *Leadership in Christian Perspective: Biblical Foundations and Contemporary Practices for Servant Leaders* (Grand Rapids: Baker Academic, 2019), 65.

15. David Horsager, *The Trust Edge: How Top Leaders Gain Faster Results, Deeper Relationships, and a Stronger Bottom Line* (Minneapolis: Summerside, 2010), 49.

16. John P. Kotter, "Leading Change: Why Transformation Efforts Fail," in *On Change Management: HBR's 10 Must Reads* (Boston: Harvard Business Review Press, 2011), 61.

17. Kotter, *Leading Change*, 56.

18. Rogers, *Diffusion of Innovations*, 262.

19. Nelson and Appel, *How to Change Your Church*.

20. See John P. Kotter, "Leading Change."

21. Jeff Iorg, *Leading Major Change in Your Ministry* (Nashville: B&H, 2018), 117–34.

22. Irving and Strauss, *Leadership in Christian Perspective*, 181.

23. Drucker, *Management Challenges for the 21st Century*, 90.

24. Kotter, "Leading Change: Why Transformation Efforts Fail," 2.

25. Rogers, *Diffusion of Innovations*, 392.

26. Nelson and Appel, *How to Change Your Church*, 49.

SCRIPTURE INDEX

Old Testament

Genesis

Exodus

Numbers

Deuteronomy

Joshua

1 Samuel

Ezra

Job

Psalms

Proverbs

Ecclesiastes

Isaiah

Jeremiah

Lamentations

Ezekiel

SUBJECT INDEX